A Maske at Ludlow

A Maske at Ludlow

ESSAYS ON MILTON'S *COMUS*

Edited by
JOHN S. DIEKHOFF

With the Bridgewater Version of Comus

THE PRESS OF
CASE WESTERN RESERVE UNIVERSITY
Cleveland 1968

Printed in the United States of America.

Library of Congress Catalogue Card Number 68–19066.

To
John Schoff Millis,
friend and colleague

Preface

This volume contains eleven essays on Milton's *Comus,* by nine authors. They are essays that I have found illuminating, in the reading of them or in the writing of them. Although no editor seeking to collect the best criticism of *Comus* could exclude many of these, another editor might have chosen a somewhat different group. For there are other illuminating essays on *Comus.* The student who wants more will find plenty of leads in the bibliography.

I like *Comus.* I have been interested in it for a long time. The earliest essay in this volume, printed here as an appendix, I wrote myself in 1937. The latest, also of my writing, is published here for the first time. I wrote it in 1967. The other essays, by eight different authors, range in date from 1941 to 1965. Many people have been interested in *Comus.*

There are five versions of *Comus,* including two in manuscript: the Trinity Manuscript, in Milton's handwriting; the Bridgewater Manuscript, in the handwriting of a professional scribe; the edition of 1637, prepared for publication by Milton's friend Henry Lawes, with Milton's cooperation but without his name; the edition of 1645, in which *Comus* is published by Milton with his other early poems; and the edition of 1673, the last during Milton's lifetime. There are also two manuscript versions of five songs from *Comus* with "Airs" by Lawes. The relationships among the various texts are discussed in the Appendix, "The Text of *Comus,* 1634 to 1645."

I have chosen to reprint the Bridgewater version of *Comus,* for three reasons. The performance of *Comus* at Ludlow Castle in 1634 is the subject of the first essay in this volume, and the Bridgewater Manuscript is the nearest to a stage version that we have. It is not nearly so accessible as other versions. It differs from other versions more than they differ from one another. This is enough, I think, to give it special interest.

In the first essay, quotations are from the Bridgewater version, except for lines which do not appear in that version. Those lines are quoted from the 1645 edition. The authors of the other essays quote from a variety of editions—from 1637, from 1645, or from modern editions. The reader is warned, therefore, that line references in most of the essays do not correspond with those in the poem as it is printed here. A convenient source of the 1645 edition, with which line references will correspond generally, is Brooks and Hardy, *Poems of Mr. John Milton: The 1645 Edition with Essays in Analysis.*

I am grateful to the following for permission to reprint the essays included in this volume: to the University of Toronto Press for the two essays by A. S. P. Woodhouse; to Chatto and Windus Ltd. and to Miss Angela Tillyard for the essay by E. M. W. Tillyard; to the Johns Hopkins Press for the essay by Don Cameron Allen; to the Cornell University Press for the essay by Robert M. Adams; to the English Association and to Mr. A. E. Dyson for his essay; to the Harvard University Press for Rosemond Tuve's; to the Columbia University Press for C. L. Barber's; to the Modern Language Association of America for my essay on "The Text of *Comus,* 1634 to 1645" and for Sears Jayne's on "The Subject of Milton's Ludlow *Mask.*" I am especially grateful to Professor Jayne for letting me have a revised and much expanded version of his essay.

The University of Illinois Press has permitted me to use, as a source of the text, the transcription of the Bridgewater Manuscript in Harris Francis Fletcher's edition, *John Milton's Complete Poetical Works, Reproduced in Photographic Facsimile* (4 vols.; Urbana: University of Illinois Press, 1943–48), Volume I. I have also depended on Professor Fletcher's facsimile for my quotations from the 1645 edition.

I wish to acknowledge also, as the source of the songs from *Comus* by Henry Lawes and the accompanying text by Hubert J. Foss, *The Mask of Comus: The Poem, Originally Called "A Mask Presented at Ludlow Castle, 1634, &c.," Edited by E. H. Visiak. The Airs of the Five Songs Reprinted from the Composer's Autograph Manuscript, Edited by Hubert J. Foss,* with a Foreword by the Earl of Ellesmere, published in 1937 by The Nonesuch Press Ltd.

Mrs. Deborah Hilty and Mrs. Marian Shapiro, graduate students and students of Milton at Case Western Reserve, undertook major responsibility for reading proof when illness prevented me from doing it. I owe them a good deal. My secretary, Miss Carol MacKay, has been patient and expert in preparing the manuscript and in helping it through the press.

John S. Diekhoff
Case Western Reserve University

Contents

A Maske at Ludlow

A Maske at Ludlow

John S. Diekhoff

I. Casting and Staging

Comus, like *Arcades,* was an "entertainment" provided for a social occasion. Milton's friend Henry Lawes provided the music, played a major role, was producer and director. No doubt he solicited the script. Probably he and Milton planned it together.

We can imagine Lawes insisting that there be a part for himself and parts for two boys and a girl. For the rest, we can hear him say, "Keep the list down. There isn't much talent available. And use little machinery. Carriage to Ludlow is too expensive and there isn't room anyway." We can imagine him explaining the setting and the circumstance. The presentation would be in the Great Hall—the council chamber, later known as "Comus Hall" [1]—but there would be a crowd, and there must be a dais for the Earl and Countess, as well as a stage. Since the Great Hall was only thirty feet by sixty feet, the stage would be small.

The masque, to be performed at Ludlow Castle on September 29, 1634, would celebrate the Earl of Bridgewater's appointment (in 1631) to the Lord Presidency of Wales and the Marches and his more recent assumption of residence at Ludlow. The audience would be friends and neighbors of His Lordship and His Lordship's family, the Egertons—"a large concourse of neighbouring nobility and gentry." [2] The usual graceful compliments would be in order. Since the audience would be friends and relatives, they would tend to see the players instead of the parts played—especially the child actors but also Lawes himself, their music master. His own part and those of the Egerton children must be sympathetic. Someone else would play the villain. And Lawes needed a song

[1] David Masson, *The Life of John Milton,* I, 610, n. 3.

[2] William Oldys, quoted in Masson, *Life,* I, 610.

for a young soprano he had in mind. A cast of six, then, including three amateurs aged nine, eleven, and fifteen, though various mob scenes might form part of the action. There should be plenty of dancing. After all, the production was to be a masque.[3]

This reconstruction is not sheer fiction. There is ample evidence that Lawes and Milton consulted, if they did not collaborate, in planning, producing, publishing, and even in writing, certainly in revising, *Comus*.[4]

Surely it was Lawes who insisted that twenty lines from the epilogue be moved to the beginning. The change provides an opening that parallels that of *Coelum Britannicum,* in which he had taken part.[5] It lets him open the performance with a song and close it with a song, songs of his own composition, with himself as singer. It also opens the masque with the line, "ffrom the heavens nowe J flye," to explain the entrance Lawes would make from above if a cloud machine were available.

Although Willa Evans describes the operation of a cloud machine in detail, from accounts of its use in *Coelum Britannicum,* and assumes its use in *Comus,*[6] I doubt whether it was possible to use one at Ludlow. The Bridgewater Manuscript has the initial stage direction, "The first sceane discovers a wild wood, then a guardian spiritt or demon descendes or enters." The Trinity Manuscript says, "A Guardian spirit or Daemon," with "the first scene discovers a wild wood" written in the margin. I am sure Lawes hoped at some time to perform the masque with machinery to provide descent from heaven and a flying exit. But I think "descendes or enters" in the stage direction at the beginning and "J can flye or J can run" in the closing song indicate that Lawes could not count on a cloud machine at Ludlow. The chamber was hardly large enough.

Surely it was Lawes who cut more than a hundred lines from the

[3] Enid Welsford, Eugene Haun, Don Cameron Allen, C. L. Barber, and others have questioned, with differing answers, whether *Comus* is properly called a "masque." For our purposes it is enough that Lawes and Milton thought it was. See Enid Welsford, *The Court Masque,* pp. 315–18; Eugene Haun, "An Inquiry into the Genre of *Comus,*" in *Essays in Honor of Walter Clyde Curry,* pp. 221 ff.; Don Cameron Allen, "The Higher Compromise," pp. 62–64 in this volume; and C. L. Barber, "A Mask Presented at Ludlow Castle," pp. 188–206 herein.

[4] See David Harrison Stevens, "The Bridgewater Manuscript of *Comus,*" in *Milton Papers,* pp. 14 ff., and John S. Diekhoff, "The Text of Comus, 1634 to 1645," pp. 251–75 herein.

[5] Willa McClung Evans outlines the parallels in detail in *Henry Lawes, Musician and Friend of Poets,* p. 96.

[6] *Ibid.,* pp. 86–87.

masque. No doubt with a less stubborn author he would have cut more. Perhaps he did in the performance. Surely it was Lawes who divided among himself and the two brothers the lines toward the end in which Sabrina is invoked. These are all assigned to Thyrsis (Lawes) in the versions other than Bridgewater; but unless they are divided among the three, the brothers have little part to play just before the curtain. Few of Thyrsis' own lines were cut, and none of the compliments. When Lawes cut lines for the child actors, however, he sacrificed a good deal of what Comus calls "meere morrall babble." It was also Lawes, presumably, who provided stage directions not originally in the Trinity Manuscript.

Whether Lawes could arrange an invitation to the festivities for the young author, we do not know.[7] Probably not. The author would have enjoyed being lionized; but I am not sure he would have enjoyed hearing his lines mouthed in the piping sopranos of amateur child actors. We may hope he was not condemned to hold the prompt book while a nine-year-old fought through the vocabulary and cadences of blank-verse philosophizing about his fifteen-year-old sister's virginity. If D. C. Allen finds the masque "totally wanting in humorousness," the performance could hardly have been lacking in absurdity, even in an age of child actors. And surely there is conscious humor in Milton's employment of the masque tradition which allows a participant to be at once a fictitious person and himself. It is in this context that Rosemond Tuve observes, "*Comus* is not so bleakly grave a piece as some read it." [8]

Big parts for the older children and for Lawes were musts, then, and a good part for the nine-year-old. The masque was at least as much an opportunity for the Egerton children to show off (and to be a credit to their music master) as it was a compliment to their noble father.

Evidently they liked to play, as did others of their family. In 1630, their sister Penelope had appeared at Whitehall in Ben Jonson's *Chloridia.*[9] Masson indulges in the reasonable speculation that Lord

[7] Emile Saillens argues that Milton must have taken an active part in rehearsals and goes on from that assumption to argue that he became an unsuccessful suitor of one of the Egerton daughters. He even suggests that it was the girl who played Sabrina. (*John Milton, Man, Poet, Polemist,* pp. 522–55.) It is a pleasant fiction, for which there is no evidence, based on a hint from Harris Fletcher: "How did he first meet them [the Egertons] and why did the connection terminate so suddenly with the writing of *Comus?*" (Harris Francis Fletcher, ed., *The Complete Poetical Works of John Milton,* p. 16.)

[8] Rosemond Tuve, "Image, Form and Themes in *A Mask,*" p. 132 herein, n. 8. For a discussion of the mixture of pretence and reality in masques, see pp. 129–32.

[9] Lady Alix Egerton, ed., *Milton's Comus, being the Bridgewater Manuscript,* p. 31.

Brackley, Mr. Thomas Egerton, Lady Alice (the "chiefe persons" of *Comus*), and other children of the family had taken part in 1632 in a masque in honor of their grandmother: "*Arcades.* Part of an entertainment presented to the Countess Dowager of Darby at Harefield, by som Noble persons of her Family, who appear on the Scene in pastoral habit, moving toward the seat of State, with this Song." [10] Lawes was composer and producer of this entertainment.

Viscount Brackley and Mr. Thomas Egerton were indeed among the young lords and noblemen's sons who had taken juvenile parts in Carew's masque of *Coelum Britannicum* in February, 1633/4—with music by Lawes.[11] Special costumes were ordered for that occasion: two suits for Lord Brackley and one for Mr. Thomas Egerton. An inventory of 1636 lists "a hamper of 'Maskin cloathes'" for the two youngsters—reusable costumes, presumably.[12] Lawes in his double role in *Comus* wore a costume left over, Willa Evans suggests, from *The Triumph of Peace,* and worn again in *Coelum Britannicum*—a "skie-coloured Taffata Robe seeded with starres." [13] He doffs these "skye webs, spun out of Jris wooffe" to "take the weeds and liknesse of a Swayne/ that to the service of this house belongs." Comus, "that damn'd magitian," also in a double role, need not change costumes when he wishes to be taken for "some harmles villager"; instead he hurls his "dazlinge spells" into the air, scattering a "magick dust" that cheats the eye with "bleare illusion" and gives it false presentments. As a result he is seen as "gentle shepheard" only by the Lady.

The parts of Comus and the demon or attendant spirit (Thyrsis) are big ones in the masque. We do not know who played Comus, nor who Sabrina. We know that Lawes played Thyrsis because he says so in dedicating the 1637 edition to Lord Brackley:

> Live sweet Lord to be the honour of your Name, and receive this as your owne, from the hands of him, who hath by many favours beene long oblig'd to your most honour'd Parents, and as in this repraesentation your attendant Thyrsis, so now in all reall expression Your faithfull, and most humble Servant, H. Lawes.

But on the title page of the Bridgewater Manuscript, the scribe who prepared it has written, "The chiefe persons in the representacion were," and the names are added in Lawes's handwriting:

[10] Masson, *Life,* I, p. 598.
[11] *Ibid.,* p. 587.
[12] Egerton, *Comus,* p. 28.
[13] Evans, *Lawes,* p. 83. C. L. Barber herein suggests that the animal heads worn by Comus's rabble were also left over from *Coelum Britannicum.*

The Lord Brackley
The Lady Alice } Egerton
Mr. Thomas }

On the title page also, in the handwriting of the second Earl of Bridgewater (our Lord Brackley) is the notation, "author Jo. Milton." [14]

Masson speculates that some "connexion" of the Bridgewater family may have played Comus and that one of Lady Alice's musical sisters could have done Sabrina; Marjorie Nicolson's favorite for the role is the Lady Penelope.[15] I doubt it. The chief *parts* included Comus and Thyrsis, but obviously the chief *persons* were the Earl's children. If others of the family had played the other parts, they would be listed in the manuscript.

When he wrote his masque, Milton did more than write sympathetic parts for Lawes and the three children. He kept their relationship. He had a precedent for the story of brothers searching for a sister in Peele's *The Old Wives Tale,* to be sure; [16] but the precedent does not alter the facts that real siblings are also siblings in the masque and that Lawes is their mentor.[17] Oldys reports that the central incident is based on fact—that the three children

> had been on a visit at a house of their relations, the Egerton family in Hertfordshire; and in passing through Haywood forest were benighted, and the Lady Alice was even lost for a short time.[18]

The story is probably apochryphal, but if it is not, it gives clearer meaning to the first words of Lawes's dedication to Lord Brackley:

> This Poem, which receiv'd its first occasion of birth from yourselfe, and others of your noble familie, and much honour from your own Person in the performance. . . .

It hardly matters. The point here is that these masquers were unmasqued from the beginning; Milton emphasizes the players, rather

[14] The second Earl recorded his later opinion of Milton on the title page of his copy of *Defensio pro Populo Anglicano:* "Liber igne, Author furca, dignissimi," which Masson translates, "Book most worthy of the fire, Author of the gallows." David Masson, ed., *The Poetical Works of John Milton,* I, p. 182. The Earl did not burn the book, however. It remained in the Bridgewater Library.

[15] Masson, *Works,* I, pp. 160–61. Nicolson, *John Milton: A Reader's Guide to His Poetry,* p. 69.

[16] John Arthos, *On "A Mask Presented at Ludlow Castle,"* pp. 1 ff.

[17] Robert M. Adams reminds us that "daemons . . . were not angels but tutelary spirits." "Reading *Comus,*" p. 93–94 herein.

[18] Henry J. Todd, ed., *The Poetical Works of John Milton,* VI, p. 198. Todd cites Warton, who quotes Oldys.

than the parts played, when he casts them in their real sibling relationship and in something like their real relationship to Henry Lawes. One of the few verbal substitutions made in the Bridgewater Manuscript cancels the word *lady* and substitutes the word *sister* in the only speech in which the Elder Brother addresses the Lady:

> Come sister while heav'n lends vs grace
> let vs fly this cursed place.

In other versions, the speech is assigned to the Demon and reads "lady."

II. The Cuts

For the presentation at Ludlow several significant cuts were made in Milton's masque, totaling at least 121 lines.[19] The Bridgewater Manuscript omits 33 lines from the Lady's first long speech as it appears in other versions, leaving 27, which are followed by the Echo Song. The lines omitted include those in which the Lady sees visibly pure-ey'd Faith, white-handed Hope, and unblemish't Chastity, and expresses the belief that the Supreme good would send a glistering guardian, if need were, to keep her life and honour unassail'd. Masson guesses that some of these lines, and lines 697–700,[20] which are also omitted, are such as the Earl and Countess "would hardly have liked to hear their young daughter . . . speaking aloud" and that they would have preferred other lines (omitted from Comus's speeches) not to be addressed to her.[21] For much of the dialogue with Comus is missing, including the "neglected rose" speech, in which Comus makes his address to a coy mistress:

> List Lady be not coy, and be not cosen'd
> With that same vaunted name Virginity,
> Beauty is natures coyn, must not be hoorded,
> But must be currant, and the good thereof
> Consists in mutual and partak'n bliss.

The second half of the Lady's answer is also missing: ll. 779–99 in 1645. Since these lines appear neither in the Bridgewater nor in the Trinity Manuscript, but are found for the first time in Lawes's 1637

[19] Bridgewater has 908 lines, the 1645 edition has 1,023; but Willa Evans shows (*Lawes*, p. 100) that the performed version was at least six lines shorter.

[20]
> Hast thou betrai'd my credulous innocence
> With visor'd falshood, and base forgery,
> And wouldst thou seek again to trap me here
> With lickerish baits fit to ensnare a brute?

[21] *Works*, III, p. 251.

edition, we must assume them not to have been written in 1634. They are important to the "argument" of the poem, for they include the statement of

> The sublime notion, and high mystery
> That must be utter'd to unfold the sage
> And serious doctrine of Virginity.

Missing with them is Comus's soliloquy (ll. 799–806) which begins, "She fables not."

Masson, observing that the moral of the masque would have been sufficiently clear to the spectators without the missing lines, also observes that Milton took care "to make the expression of the moral more definite" by restoring the omitted lines and adding lines 779–806.[22] We may also suspect that Lawes was less interested than Milton in the moral and in posterity and more interested than Milton in the performance, the occasion, the young actors, and the immediate audience.

III. Glozing Words

No compliments disappeared. When Milton's well-placed words of glozing[23] courtesy are taken from the poem and looked at out of context, as I propose to do, they add up to a large part of the whole—139 lines of a total of not more than 902 in the acted version. We can imagine the attentive ears of the special audience and surmise how much more this audience, too, would be interested in the compliment and in the actors than in the theme of the masque.

At the very beginning, immediately after the opening song, there is the compliment to those served by the Demon, who turn out to be Egertons:

> . . . some there be that with due steppes aspire
> to laye their just hands on that goulden keye
> that opes the pallace of Æternitie:
> To such my errand is, and but for such
> J would not soile theese pure ambrosiall weedes
> wth the ranke vapours of this sin-worne moulde.

The Demon then moves quickly into his task, which requires him to explain Neptune's rule over islands and gives him occasion to praise England and to compliment the Earl of Bridgewater and his children:

[22] *Ibid.* For discussion of the significance of these additions, see E. M. W. Tillyard, "The Action of *Comus,*" pp. 43–47 herein.

[23] Line 161. The Bridgewater copyist wrote "gloweinge." All other versions read "glozing." Cf. *Paradise Lost,* I, 93, and IX, 549.

. . . but this Jsle
the greatest and the best of all the Maine
he quarters to his blew haired dieties,
and all this tract that fronts the fallinge sunn
a noble Peere of mickle trust and power
has in his Chardge, wth tempred awe to guyde
an ould and haughty nacion, proude in armes
where his faire ofspringe nurst in princely lore
are cominge to attend their fathers state
and newe entrusted scepter.

Lawes as the Demon has the grateful task of serving the virtuous, of protecting the "faire ofspringe." But that compliment is made more explicit later. The children have not yet appeared, and we may imagine that the attention of the audience during these lines was focused on the Earl and Countess, seated conspicuously in their chairs of state. We can see their smiling acknowledgments.

The compliment concluded, the exposition proceeds with the account of Comus and his rout until the Demon can again imply the special merit of the Egertons:

. . . when any favour'd of high Jove
chaunces to pass through this advent'rous glade,
swift as the sparcle of a glauncinge starre
J shoote from heaven, to give him salfe convoy
as nowe J doe. . . .

It is here that Milton chooses to underline the identification of the Demon with Lawes, in compliment to Lawes:

. . . but first J must put off
these my skye webs, spun out of Jris wooffe,
and take the weeds and liknesse of a Swayne
that to the service of this house belongs
whoe wth his softe pipe, and smooth dittied songe
well knows to still the wild winds when they roare,
and hush the wavinge woods.

Milton is not content to praise Lawes's musicianship only, for the passage continues:

. . . nor of less faith
and in this office of his mountaine watch
likeliest and neerest to the present ayde,
of this occasion.

The audience here gets the break of a grotesque interlude, which provides some of the spectacle necessary to a masque:

Comus enters wth a charminge rod in one hand & a glass of liquor in the other wth him a route of monsters like men & women but headed like wilde beasts their apperell glist'ringe, they come in makinge a riotous and unruely noise wth torches in their hands.

Then, when Comus has set the time and the tone, he leads his followers in a dance, "a wild, rude, & wanton Antick." Lady Alix Egerton suggests that the "Countrie daunces and sports" that conclude the masque, except for the twelve lines of verse that Lawes retained in the epilogue, "may have been performed by the 'Morrice dancers' of the neighbourhood." [24] Whoever the dancers were, they may have doubled as the rout of Comus. In any event, as the revised masque begins and ends with song, so there is also an early interlude of dance and a final one.

The first "measure" ends by order of Comus, because he feels "the different pace/ of some chast footinge, neere about this ground/ . . . some virgin sure." So, the rout scattered and Comus hiding, the Lady (Alice Egerton) enters, explains her plight, and (incapable, presumably by reason of gentility, of "hollowing" to her brothers) makes such noise as suitably she can: the Echo Song.

The Echo Song, of course, gives opportunity for extravagant compliment to the Lady Alice Egerton, in the speech by Comus that follows the song. The whole speech is in her praise:

> Can any mortall mixture of Earths mould
> breath such divine enchauntinge ravishment [25]
> sure somethinge holye lodges in that brest
> and with these raptures moves the vocall ayre
> to testifie his hidden residence
> how sweetely did they floate vpon the wings
> of silence, through the empty vaulted night,

[24] *Comus,* p. 30.

[25] Apparently the Lady Alice could sing. In 1653 Lawes dedicated his *Airs and Dialogues* . . . to Alice, Countess of Carberry, and Mary, Lady Herbert of Cherbury and Castle-Island—our Lady Alice and her sister. The dedication reads in part as follows (Evans, *Lawes,* p. 196):

> . . . no sooner I thought of making these Publick, than of inscribing them to Your Ladiships, most of them being Composed when I was employed by Your ever Honour'd Parents to attend Your Ladishipp's Education in Musick; who (as in other Accomplishments fit for Persons of your Quality) excell'd most Ladies, especially in Vocall Musick, wherein you were so absolute, that You gave Life and Honour to all I set and taught You. . . .

at every fall smoothinge the raven downe
of darkness till she smil'd, J have oft heard
my mother Circe with the Sirens three
amidst the flowrie-kyrtled Niades
cullinge their potent herbs and balefull druggs
whoe when they sung, would take the prisond soule
and lap it in Elisium, Scilla wept
and chid her barkinge waves into attention
and fell Caribdis murmurd soft applause
yet they in pleasinge slumber lulld the sence
and in sweete madnes rob'd it of it selfe,
but such a sacred and homefelt delight
such sober certentie of wakinge bliss
J never heard till now, Jle speake to her
and she shalbe my Qweene; Haile forreigne wonder
whome certaine these rough shades did never breede
vnless the goddess that in rurall shrine
dwel'st heere with Pan or Silvan, by blest song
forbiddinge every bleake vnkindly fogg
to touch the prosperinge growth of this tall wood.

The Lady having demonstrated notable modesty in her reply, the dialogue moves quickly into praise of Lord Brackley and Mr. Thomas Egerton:

Co[*mus*]: were they of manly prime, or youthfull bloome?
La[*dy*]: as smooth as Hebes their unrazor'd lipps.
Co: Two such J sawe, what tyme the labour'd oxe
in his loose traces from the furrowe came
and the swink't—hedger at his supper sate,
J sawe em under a greene mantlinge vyne
that crawles alonge the side of yon smale hill
pluckinge ripe clusters from the tender shoots,
their porte was more than humane as they stood,
J tooke it for a faerie vision
of some gaye creatures of the Element
that in the cooleness of the raynebow live
and playe i'the plighted clouds; J was awe-strooke
and as J past J worship't: if those you seeke
it were a Jorney like the path to heav'n
[to] helpe you finde them.

This description, which leads to the exit of Comus and the Lady, prepares for the entrance of the brothers, who in their "Maskin cloathes" no doubt do represent

> . . . gaye creatures of the Element
> that in the cooleness of the raynebow live.

Lady Alix Egerton describes their costumes for another masque: "2 gaberdynes of tinsell lynd with Callico," in carnation and white.[26]

The dialogue of the brothers is so much a part of the moral of the masque, so much a part of what is left of its exposition after Lawes's excisions, that we tend to overlook the fact that it is also in praise of the Lady's virtue. If we remember that the Lady is also the Lady Alice Egerton, this emphasis is restored:

> J doe not thinke my sister soe to seeke
> or soe unprincipl'd in vertues booke,
> and the sweete peace that goodness bosoms ever
> as that the single want of light and noise
> (not beinge in danger, as J hope she is not)
> could stirr the constant mood of her calme thoughts
> and put them into misbecomminge plight
> vertue could see to doe what vertue would
> by her owne radiant light, though sun & moone
> were in the flatt sea sunke.

The next speech of the Elder Brother continues this theme:

> my sister is not soe defencelesse left
> as you immagine brother, she has a hidden strength
> wch you remember not, *2 bro.* what hidden strength?
> vnless the strength of heav'n, if you meane that?
> *el:bro* J meane that too: but yet a hidden strength
> wch if heaven gave it, may be tearm'd herowne,
> tis Chastitie, my brother Chastitie.

The succeeding lines in praise of chastity, with their implied comparison of the Lady with Diana and Minerva and the assertion of angelic guards for chastity, are less directly descriptive of the Lady's virtue but also continue the theme.

The dialogue ends with an offstage shout, at which the Elder Brother exclaims,

> That hallowe J should knowe . . .

There must have been a laugh when the voice he recognizes turned out to be that of his music master, Lawes, playing the Demon, pretending to be Thyrsis, habited like a shepherd. But the identification leads immedi-

[26] Egerton, *Comus,* p. 28.

ately to more compliment, of which Lawes is the object. First he is identified, then praised:

> . . . tis my fathers shepheard sure
> *el:b:* Thirsis? whose art full straynes have oft delayed
> the hudlinge brooke to heere his madrigall
> and sweetned every muskerose of the dale.

The Demon's response to the question, "how camst heere good shepheard . . . ?" is in kind. Despite the urgency of the Lady's need in the dramatic situation, there is time for praise of the Elder Brother and the Lady:

> *De*[*mon*]: O my Lov'd masters heire, and his next Joye
> J came not heere on such a triviall toye
> as a strayed Ewe, or to pursue the stealth
> of pilferinge wolfe; not all the fleecie wealth
> that doeth enrich these downes is worth a thought
> to this my errand and the Care it brought.
> but O my virgin lady where is she.

The Demon's account of his somewhat ineffective surveillance of the area gives him another opportunity to describe the Lady's song:

> at last a sweete, and solemne breathinge sound
> rose like the softe steame of distill'd perfumes [27]
> and stole vpon the aire, that even silence
> was tooke ere she was ware, & wisht she might
> denye her nature and be never more
> still to be soe displac't, J was all eare
> and tooke in th streines that might create a sowle
> vnder the ribbs of death. but O ere long
> two well J might perceive, it was the voice
> of my most honor'd lady, your deere sister
> amaz'd I stood, harrow'd with greife, & feare,
> and O poore hapless nightingale thought J
> how sweete thou singst, how neere the deadly snare.

The Second Brother's response to this speech prompts the Elder Brother to repeat his affirmation of the power of (his sister's) virtue and

[27] These two lines are heavily revised in the Trinity Manuscript, apparently after the Bridgewater Manuscript was transcribed. That the reading arrived at is also substantially that of the 1637 and later editions is part of the evidence that Lawes and Milton worked together on the masque after its performance at Ludlow, for Lawes was responsible for the 1637 edition. The reading there is as follows:

> At last a soft, and solemne breathing sound
> Rose like a steame of rich distill'd Perfumes.

to end his remarks with a bombastic statement of his intentions toward Comus, promising to "cleave his scalpe/ downe to the hipps." The Demon is understandably prompted to remark:

> Alas good ventrous youth
> J love the [thy] Courage yet, and bold emprise.

The Moly-Haemony passage follows. Half is omitted, but not Thyrsis's comment on his own music. He speaks of the "shepheard lad/ of smale regard to see to":

> he lov'd me well, and oft would begg me singe,
> wch when J did, he on the tender grasse
> would sit, and hearken even to extasie.

If the audience speculated about the identity of the "shepheard lad," so may we. It is probably Milton. There is no doubt whose music he admired and praised.

The exit of Thyrsis and the brothers ends the scene. The action shifts to Comus's palace, where the Lady exemplifies in dialogue the virtues her brother has attributed to her, while Comus repeats his raptures on her beauty. But we must forget the "neglected rose" lines; as we have noted, they are not there. The "ougley headed Monsters" are there, however. Comus undertakes to persuade the Lady in their presence, despite the example of their animal heads!

Now the story races on as the brothers rush in with swords drawn, break Comus's glass, drive out his rout; and fail to reverse his wand. Thus the rescue is left to Sabrina, whose intercession is sought by Thyrsis and the two brothers. They invoke her in lines assigned to Thyrsis in the Trinity Manuscript and in the printed editions but divided among the three in Bridgewater. Merritt Hughes points out how welcome Sabrina would be to a Ludlow audience, as a significant touch of local color. They would know her as the goddess of the Severn, the local river.[28]

Music and spectacle rise in importance as we near the end of the masque.[29] Sabrina is invoked in song. She "rises attended by the water nimphes and singes," then frees the "brightest lady" and descends.

[28] *John Milton: Complete Poems and Major Prose,* p. 109, note on ll. 826–32.

[29] Eugene Haun argues, "on the basis of the Bridgewater Manuscript, . . . there is every reason to assume that *Comus* was continuous music from the invocation of Sabrina to the end of the masque, with only one interval of speech of nineteen lines." "An Inquiry," p. 236. We should note that no music survives for Sabrina's song, however. It has been suggested that the lady who played the part could not sing after all.

Pretence is dropped. Thyrsis becomes Lawes, the "faithfull guide" conducting not characters in a masque but the masquers, the Lady Alice Egerton, the Lord Brackley, and Mr. Thomas Egerton, to their father's residence,

> where this night are met in state
> many a freind to gratulate
> his wisht presence, and beside
> all the swaynes that neere abide
> with Jiggs, and rurall daunce resorte
> wee shall catch them at this sporte,
> and our suddaine Cominge there
> will double all their mirth, and cheere.

And so they do catch them, the scene changing to Ludlow town and the Lord President's castle, where the country dancers perform until Thyrsis stops them, again with song. In a second song Thyrsis then presents the child actors, now in their real persons, to their real parents in the real hall of the real castle which is represented in the stage setting:

> Noble Lord and Lady bright
> J have brought yee new delight
> heere behould soe goodly growne
> three fayer branches of your owne
> Heav'n hath timely tri'd their youth
> their faith their patience, and their truth
> and sent them heere through hard assaies
> wth a Crowne of death lesse praise
> to triumphe in victorious Daunce
> ore sensuall folly and Jntemperance.

The bows and curtsey that we can imagine are followed by a dance of triumph; and then Thyrsis, ending the masque with the dozen lines left of the epilogue, states the simple moral in the last six of them:

> Mortalls that would follow me
> love vertue, she alone is free
> she can teach you how to clyme
> higher then the sphearie chime
> or if vertue feeble were
> Heaven it selfe would stoope to her.

If the applause for the Earl and Countess and for their three fair branches mingled with that for the masque and its performance and for the speaker of the epilogue, we can imagine that they all acknowledged it with satisfaction as Lawes ascended into the clouds or—more probably and prosaically—ran from the stage.

IV. Epilogue

Whether Comus has been much overread, as R. M. Adams tells us,[30] or whether it justifies the wealth of subtle analysis and interpretation by which it has been illuminated, we find when we imagine ourselves members of its original audience that there is still another way to read it. It was written for a special occasion, for performance by a specified group of actors. A major purpose was to flatter members of the Egerton family. It was performed before an audience primarily interested in the occasion and in their host, well acquainted with the actors, less interested than the author would be in the conventional moral allegory of the masque, certainly less interested in the response of posterity to the poem.

The collaboration between Lawes and Milton resulted in a masque in which "the leading persons" were never dissociated from their real-life roles and relationships and in which at the end the dramatic role was dropped. It is a masque from which in this essay I could excerpt 139 lines of direct compliment to the Earl, the Countess, and their guests; to the Lady Alice Egerton, Lord Brackley, and Mr. Thomas Egerton; to Henry Lawes. About 16 per cent of the lines are devoted to praising these people. It is a masque in which the producer-actor-composer had the opportunity to open and close the performance by singing songs of his own composition. It gave local dancers opportunity for early and late appearances. It contains a reference to the local river, and the final scene is a representation of the town and castle where the audience was gathered. If the poet's somewhat mystic moral message was weakened by Lawes's cuts, and if some of the lyric quality admired by Sir Henry Wootton was lost in the readings of the child actors, there were enough discriminating viewers to spread the fame of the masque, and as Lawes says, to tire his hand with the often copying of it to give his several friends satisfaction. Publication for a more contemplative audience was thus justified. This essay reminds that more contemplative audience, which sometimes forgets, that the poem is a masque, an entertainment, and was written partly to give three children an opportunity to perform for the pride and pleasure of their parents and family friends.

Everyone knows that Milton did not call his masque *Comus,* that he

[30] P. 78 herein.

gave it no title at all. But it had a title. It was called "A Maske Represented before the right ho:^{ble} the Earle of Bridgewater Lord president of Wales and the right ho:^{ble} the Countesse of Bridgewater. At Ludlow Castle the 29th of September 1634." [31] That was its title and that is what it was.

[31] This is how the Bridgewater Manuscript title page reads. In Trinity the work is simply called "A maske." In the 1637 edition it is called "A Maske presented At Ludlow Castle, 1634: On Michaelmasse night, before the Right Honorable, John Earle of Bridgewater, Vicount Brackly, Lord President of Wales, And one of His Majesties most honorable Privie Counsell." In the 1645 edition it is called "A Mask Of the same Author Presented At Ludlow-Castle, 1634. Before The Earl of Bridgewater Then President of Wales." And in 1673 it is called "A Mask presented at Ludlow-Castle, 1634. &c." If Lawes in Bridgewater and in 1637 put more emphasis on the occasion than Milton did in the 1673 edition, Milton did not lose sight of it even there, and he gave it full stress in 1645.

The Argument of Milton's *Comus*

A. S. P. Woodhouse

No complete study of *Comus* exists. Such a study would necessitate four separate steps. The first is an examination of *Comus* in the light of the essential tradition of the masque, the inherited pattern which Milton adopts (having indeed no choice in this instance) and of course adapts to his purposes. The second is an effort to determine more precisely the content of the poem, what it is that Milton is saying or, as I have called it, the argument of *Comus.* The processes of criticism are, or ought to be, self-conscious: it is their only safeguard. So one would avoid the pitfall of attempting an impossible separation of form and content, and merely centre attention first on the one and then on the other, with the object of ultimately bringing them together and restoring a sense of the poem's unity and individuality. The third step is in that direction; for it is an effort to discover the relation for Milton, and in this poem, of experience, thought, and art. The fourth step views the poem once more as an independent unit and applies to its interpretation whatever has been discovered in the first three stages of the examination. If anyone wishes to contend that only the fourth step is literary criticism, and the first three at best preparations for literary criticism, I shall not think the point worth arguing—or the preliminary steps less than necessary. In the present essay I can deal with only one of the questions raised: what it is that Milton is saying, or the argument of *Comus.*[1]

Reprinted by permission of the University of Toronto Press from *The University of Toronto Quarterly,* XI (1941), 46–71.

[1] I have only one substantial debt to record. It is to Professor J. H. Hanford's "The Youth of Milton" (*Studies in Shakespeare, Milton and Donne,* University of Michigan Publications, Language and Literature, I, 87–163, especially 139–43, 152). Since I shall have occasion to disagree with him at some points, I wish to express here not only my deep sense of obligation, but also my

I

I will not pause to establish on theoretic grounds what is so abundantly evident in experience, that intellectual content, wherever it contributes to imaginative and emotional content, becomes an indispensable factor in the total aesthetic effect of the poem. But I must pause to state the conditions which attach to intellectual content when it becomes a subject of investigation. As a vehicle of ideas poetry labours under a disability, but also enjoys a unique advantage. No poem perhaps—certainly not one whose form is as limiting as the masque—can hope to present ideas with complete precision or to make all their implications specific. On the other hand, poetry has powers of suggestion denied to prose and can convey more than is fully stated or proved. The student of thought in poetry will take due cognizance of both these facts: he will seek to draw forth the argument, to render its implications more precise and specific than he finds them, and in so doing he will be guided by the suggestions which the poet has been able to give, here by an image, there by an overtone.

Willing response, however, to the poet's suggestion is not by itself enough. Everybody is familiar with the common criterion for judging the adequacy of a work of popular art: that it should be self-sufficient, should contain within itself whatever is necessary for comprehending it. On the level of ideas, however, this test cannot be very strictly applied. Often one must look outside the poem for what may be called the intellectual frame of reference, common to the poet and his contemporary readers, but lost to a later age: the thing taken for granted in the thought content as the instinctively apprehended capacities and limits of the particular *genre* are taken for granted in the aesthetic effect. The intellectual frame of reference may not be set forth in the poem; but indications of it will be present, and its correct formulation will be a key to unlock the poem's meaning, while its ability to do this will, in turn, test the correctness of the formulation.

There is nothing esoteric about the intellectual frame of reference for *Comus*. It will serve for innumerable works of literature in the seventeenth and earlier centuries and is, indeed, indispensable for understanding their thought—the thought of Spenser, for example, not less than

conviction that his is in general the wisest and most penetrating essay on Milton ever written. In dealing with Spenser I have been helped by the *Variorum Spenser* and by Mr. C. S. Lewis's brilliant *Allegory of Love* (1936). My friend Professor Douglas Bush has made some very valuable criticisms and suggestions.

the thought of Milton. Within this frame of reference there is room for every degree of difference in attitude and emphasis: it is a frame of reference, not a body of doctrine, and is tacitly assumed not by the religious only, but by the secular and even the anti-religious writer, who may deny the reality of what I shall describe as "the order of grace" but rarely has the hardihood to ignore it as a concept. The frame of reference may be formulated with sufficient precision in this way. There are in the life of man, and in the vast array of circumstances which form the setting of the human drama, two levels or, better perhaps, two orders of existence, the natural and the religious, or what we may call the order of nature and the order of grace. To the religious mind, of course, each is dependent on the power and providence of God, but in a manner sufficiently different to warrant the restriction of the term *religious* (which means Christian) to one order only. To the order of nature belongs not only the whole physical world, but also man himself considered simply as a denizen of that world. The rule of its government is expressed not only in the physical laws of nature, but in natural ethics (in what is significantly called the Law of Nature), and even in natural, as opposed to revealed, religion. This order is apprehended in experience and interpreted by reason; and it has its own wisdom, for upon the simple law of nature, by experience and reason, is erected the ethical system of a Plato, an Aristotle, or a Cicero. It has its own institutions, of which the highest is the state; but this is an aspect of the order of nature which need not detain us here. . . . To the order of grace belongs man in his character of supernatural being, with all that concerns his salvation and the two dispensations, the old and the new. The rule of its government is the revealed Law of God, received and interpreted by faith, which includes a special kind of experience, called religious experience. It also has its appropriate institution, the Church, which, like the state, does not concern us here. . . . Now on the precise relation subsisting between the order of nature and the order of grace a great variety of opinion is possible and, especially in the seventeenth century, is met. There are those who insist on the sharp contrast and wide divergence of the two orders; and this class includes individuals and sects of opposite principles. The ascetic and the rigorist (for in this they agree, though not in the action that it entails) insist on the divergence, to depress nature and exalt grace; the naturalist, to exalt nature and depress grace, finding the demands of the higher order "unnatural" and denying their validity. There are those who insist on the clear-cut separation of the two orders with the intention of accepting them both (though perhaps with different degrees of conviction) while avoiding all inference from the one to the other. Such is the fideist, who takes the order of grace on authority, but in the order of nature pursues his experimental and sceptical way; the Baconian scientist, with his two philosophies, natural and divine; the Puritan extremist, reactionary in the realm of grace, progressivist in the realm of nature. All of these—though for different ends—apply what I have elsewhere called the *principle of segregation.*[2] Opposed to them is the large class of thinkers who (with many differing shades of emphasis and inference) agree in responding to the profound human instinct for a unified view of life, and who refuse to divorce the two orders. They insist that the order of grace is the superstructure whose foundations are securely laid in nature; that there is no interval between the two orders, which merge in an area common to both; that grace comes to perfect nature (an idea including discipline), not to destroy it; that man's well-being must be defined in terms of the two orders simultaneously,[3] and that what is for his good as a natural being cannot be for his harm as a supernatural, or *vice versa.* This is the position of the Christian humanist, whose special relevance to *Comus* will in due course appear. What we are concerned with now is simply the intellectual frame of reference afforded by the conception of the two orders of nature and grace; for to one of the two, or to an area common to them both, every idea and every value must pertain. Only in reference to this framework can the argument of *Comus* be fully understood.

The common assumption, correct so far as it goes, is that the argument of *Comus* has for its theme chastity. But more careful examination reveals that coupled with the doctrine of chastity (not identified with it as a careless reader might suppose, but coupled with it) are two others: a doctrine of temperance and continence (the "holy dictates of spare Temperance") and a doctrine of virginity ("the sage And serious doctrine of Virginity"). When these facts are brought into relation with the intellectual frame of reference, we observe that temperance and continence are virtues on the natural level; that chastity, the central virtue of the poem, moves in an area common to nature and grace; and that the

[2] *Puritanism and Liberty* (1938), introd. 39–40, 58–9, 84–5.

[3] Cf. Milton's assertion, in his seventh Prolusion, that "nothing can be recounted justly among the causes of our happiness unless in some way it takes into consideration both that eternal and this temporal life"; and his twofold definition of the end of education (*Prose Works,* Bohn ed., III, 464, 467).

doctrine of virginity belongs exclusively to the order of grace, which in the poem it is used to illustrate and even symbolize. Or, if one may resort to a simple visual formulation, what we have is this:

(1) The *doctrine of temperance,* which, in the circumstances presented in the poem, is necessarily: (2) A *doctrine of continence,* which, to render it secure, and to translate it from a negative to a positive conception, requires to be completed by:	Nature
(3) The *doctrine of chastity,* which is thus grounded in nature. This is, moreover, elaborated, still on the level of nature, in terms of the Platonic philosophy, to the point where it can be taken over by Christianity, which sanctions the natural virtues and, by the addition of grace, carries them on to a new plane. Of this new plane	Nature and Grace
(4) The *doctrine of virginity* becomes in the poem the illustration and symbol (but not the complete synonym).	Grace

We are concerned here with the argument of *Comus,* and not with the relation of that argument to Milton's personal experience. But it happens, most fortunately, that we are able to test our formulation of the intellectual frame of reference as it is applied in *Comus,* by comparing it with the celebrated account in retrospect which Milton gave of his experiences during the period when the poem was written. This account, in the *Apology for Smectymnuus,* was offered in rebuttal of the charge of youthful incontinence made by his adversaries, but it attaches itself to Milton's conception of the ideal poet which he sought to become, one whose life was itself a true poem. Here we find him commencing on the natural level, passing (not without aid from Plato) to the verge of the religious level, and finally moving securely thereon: we find the doctrine of continence bringing the doctrine of chastity, and at last the doctrine of virginity, in its wake, as the poet ascends from the order of nature, through an area where the two orders meet, to the order of grace. As in *Comus,* we may describe the doctrine of chastity as the central theme; and, even if we discard the reservation in the *Apology* in favour of the married state as belonging to a time after the poem was written, we shall still recognize that the doctrine of virginity is not regarded as the whole of Christian teaching on the subject of chastity, though it is regarded as a doctrine specifically Christian and hence one that would be eligible as a symbol of the order of grace. Giving due weight to the direction of his "natural disposition," Milton tells us how he was led onward and upward, first by the writings of the poets, then by the philosophy of Plato, with its "abstracted sublimities" (a phrase we shall have occasion to remember), and to his final goal by Christianity, its plain injunctions and "high mysteries" (another phrase to be remembered)—that Christianity which evidently confirms, while it transcends, the dictates of natural ethics and the highest wisdom of the philosophers. Milton writes in part:

> Thus from the laureat fraternity of the poets, riper years and the ceaseless round of study led me to the shady spaces of philosophy; but chiefly to the divine volumes of Plato and his equal, Xenophon: where if I should tell ye what I learned of chastity and love, I mean that which is truly so, whose charming cup is only virtue, which she bears in her hand to those who are worthy; (the rest are cheated with a thick intoxicating potion, which a certain sorceress, the abuser of love's name, carries about;) and how the first and chiefest office of love begins and ends in the soul, producing those happy twins of her divine generation, knowledge and virtue; with such abstracted sublimities as these, it might be worth your listening. . . .[4]

"Last of all," he continues, "not in time, but as perfection is last, that care was ever had of me not to be negligently trained in the precepts of the Christian religion." And these precepts confirmed and built upon "a certain reservedness of natural disposition, and moral discipline learnt out of the noblest philosophy," which alone would have been sufficient to ensure first a disdain of incontinence, then a love of chastity. But now he was able to receive the doctrine of chastity on the religious level, "unfolding those chaste and high mysteries, . . . that 'the body is for the Lord, and the Lord for the body.' " "Nor did I slumber," he concludes, "over that place expressing such high rewards of ever accompanying the Lamb with those celestial songs to others unapprehensible but not to those who were not defiled with women, which doubtless means fornication; for marriage must not be called a defilement." Continence may be achieved on the basis of natural ethics (and be taught by those good teachers the poets, though not religiously inspired). Chastity, even in its "abstracted sublimities," may be learned from the wise and virtuous pagan philosophers (also poets in their way), who move likewise on the natural level but strain upward to the very verge of the religious. And these teachings Christianity by its precepts confirms. But above the natural level is the religious and there Christian doctrine is the only guide. Such is the scheme of the *Apology;* and, broadly speaking, it is identical with that of *Comus.*

[4] *Prose Works,* III, 119–22.

II

That the doctrine of chastity is the central theme in the argument of the poem is obvious from the emphasis that it receives. The virtues of temperance and continence are treated with brevity, and subordinated to it, while the mysterious merits of the virgin state are but hinted in expounding the doctrine of chastity in its highest reaches. But that doctrine itself is set forth at large by the Elder Brother, and is symbolized by the Lady, who speaks for temperance and continence, it is true, but stands for chastity. We shall do well, however, to consider the virtues in the ascending order in which we have already presented them; and if the space which we give to the lower virtues seems disproportionate, it is because the significance of their presence in the poem has never been observed and because it can be brought out only by detailed exposition and some comparison with a chief moulding influence, Spenser, and with Milton's later thought.

In the temptation scene the attack of Comus is not against chastity in the full meaning of the term, but against continence, which he derides as "the lean and sallow Abstinence." The solicitation that meets the Lady is identical in kind with that which meets Guyon in the Bower of Bliss, an episode immensely impressive to Milton,[5] and the real centre of Spenserian influence on *Comus,* as is quite natural, for Acrasia is Spenser's elaboration of the Circe motif and Comus is Milton's. The special mark of both is the prostitution of natural powers to the purposes of mere sensual pleasure. This is strongly underlined by Spenser and is symbolized by the scenery of the Bower of Bliss, where art counterfeits and even perverts nature and the beauty is as subtly false as that of the contrasted Garden of Adonis is natural and true. In *Comus* there is no such elaboration of this symbol; but the wizard's palace "set out with all manner of deliciousness" is, like the Bower of Bliss, of art, not nature, and (as we shall see) the Garden of Adonis, with its wealth of natural beauty, also finds its place in Milton's poem.

It is in another form, however, that the theme of nature chiefly enters into *Comus.*[6] By an appeal to nature the magician seeks to undermine

[5] *Faery Queen,* 2.12. Cf. *Areopagitica* (*Prose Works,* II, 68).

[6] Lines 706–80. Comus's appeal to nature is no invention of Milton's but a Renaissance Ovidian commonplace, found in Spenser's Phaedria, and in Marlowe, Donne, Randolph, and others; see Douglas Bush, *Mythology and the Renaissance Tradition in English Poetry* (1932), 135, 267, and *Paradise Regained* etc., ed. M. Y. Hughes (1937), xliii–iv.

the virtue of continence, and this in two ways. Overtly his argument is that the natural world by the profusion of its gifts invites men to a life of unrestricted enjoyment: for this the abundance of nature was ordained, and to refuse it "in a pet of temperance" is to manifest ingratitude and thwart nature's plan. But there is a second suggestion: the note of nature is abundance, profusion, and *a wasteful fertility:*

> Wherefore did Nature pour her bounties forth
> With such a full and unwithdrawing hand,
> Covering the earth with odours, fruits and flocks,
> Thronging the seas with spawn innumerable . . . ?

"Nature," said Renan, "knows nothing of chastity." It is the very contention that Comus is seeking to illustrate. And the application to humanity is not left in doubt: one should not be cozened by words, but reflect that

> Beauty is Nature's coin . . .
> and the good thereof
> Consists in mutual and partaken bliss.

(Observe that the magician's argument ends not in the provision of life for its own replenishment, but in mere gratification.) In a double sense, then, temperance (which here means continence) is, he suggests, unnatural. This specious argument, says the Lady, is untrue, it is "false rules pranked in reason's garb":

> Imposter! do not charge most innocent nature
> As if she would her children should be riotous
> With her abundance; she, good cateress,
> Means her provision only for the good,
> *That live according to her sober laws,*
> *And holy dictates of spare Temperance.*

And she continues with the famous attack on "lewdly-pampered Luxury" as opposed to nature's plan.

Now it is interesting and significant to observe that the Lady does not contradict the picture of nature given by Comus: she merely points out its incompleteness and repudiates his inference. Nature is marked not by abundance only, but by order and rationality. To live according to nature in the true sense is not to live riotously, prostituting her gifts to sensual gratification, but temperately and in conformity with her rational character and ends. This is plainly Stoic doctrine, and it is not for nothing that Comus is made to warn the Lady in advance against "those budge doctors of the Stoic fur." In the years after *Comus,* Milton was to elaborate his doctrines of nature ("most innocent nature"), of reason and of temperance. In so doing he altered much, substituting a monistic for a dualistic philosophy and reacting, temporarily at least, against every suggestion of asceticism. I am very far from denying—indeed I insist upon—the wide interval between *Comus* and Milton's later thought. Only one must not exaggerate the differences or fail to recognize similarities where they exist. And for all the change in his metaphysic of nature, and in the tone of his ethic, the twofold aspect of nature remains, and constitutes the groundwork of his no longer ascetic (though still rigoristic) doctrine of temperance; and the role of reason (which is only hinted in *Comus*) is not reversed, but confirmed and emphasized. The nature described by Comus and the Lady is the nature whose production is to be recounted by Milton in the seventh book of *Paradise Lost.* There creation is a twofold process, corresponding to the two complementary aspects of nature. For nature is a living whole, a vital scale, embracing life in all its profusion, and the process of creation in this aspect approximates very closely to gestation and birth. But before nature is a living, it is an ordered whole, a rationally graduated scale. And here creation does not approximate to birth; it is the imposition of form and order on chaos, the endowment of nature with a rational principle, as the other is her endowment with a vital principle. Thus Milton later elaborates the view of nature already implicit in *Comus.* And similarly he elaborates the doctrine of temperance. It means a proper use of the gifts of nature, a proper choice made by reason among them; for "reason is but choosing." It is nature the vital, the abounding, that furnishes the materials of the choice, and nature the ordered, the rational, that furnishes the principle of choice. For not only is reason the prerogative (indeed Milton calls it the essence) of the soul, but it is also imprinted upon the world: as Whichcote said, there is the reason of the mind, and the reason of the thing. Thus Milton elaborates his view of nature, of reason and of temperance. There are important changes, of course: a new metaphysic of nature (but it is, in one sense, just an elaboration of the idea implicit in the phrase about "most innocent nature"), a new emphasis on the role of reason (which is hardly explicit[7] in the original formulation), and a more liberal specific content for the term *temperance,* no longer qualified by the epithet "spare." But it is an elaboration (and modification), not a simple

[7] That it is implicit is confirmed not only by such allusions to reason as that in line 529, but by the fact that (as Professor Bush remarks) Milton evidently follows Sandys's interpretation of the Circe myth.

reversal: some at least of the primary intuitions on which it is grounded are already present in *Comus.*

As in Spenser, temperance (we have shown) is treated primarily as a virtue on the natural level, not on the religious. Of course Milton cannot afford Spenser's wealth of detail, and indeed there is little evidence of direct Spenserian influence on Milton's theory; no hint, for example, of Spenser's exposition of the virtue in terms of the Aristotelian mean, which was perhaps always foreign to Milton's mind, or in terms of the Platonic control of the rational over the irrational (whether the irascible or the appetitive), which should have been more congenial to him. But there are important similarities to Spenser in emphasis and tone, not all of which we have yet mentioned. Though treated on the natural level, Spenser's reading of the virtue of temperance in Book 2 of the *Faery Queen* impresses us as distinctly rigoristic, culminating, as it does, in the destruction of the Bower of Bliss. This is partly accounted for by the fact that, with increasing definiteness as the book proceeds, Spenser couples with temperance the Aristotelian continence: the story of Guyon is the legend of temperance *and continence.* And in *Comus* a like impression springs from a similar coupling of virtues—Spenserian virtues, though not directly Aristotelian. But these virtues are not sufficient in Spenser's experience: they must be rendered secure and translated from negative to positive terms by the addition of chastity, which means not mere abstention from evil but an active pursuit of the good. To the virtue of chastity the next book of the *Faery Queen* is devoted. And so is the next stage in the argument of *Comus.*

Having spoken for temperance, inevitably interpreted in the circumstances as continence, the Lady proceeds:

> Shall I go on?
> Or have I said enow? To him that dares
> Arm his profane tongue with contemptuous words
> Against the sun-clad power of Chastity,
> Fain would I something say;—yet to what end?
> Thou hast nor ear, nor soul, to apprehend
> The sublime notion and high mystery
> That must be uttered to unfold the sage
> And serious doctrine of Virginity.[8]

Here we are brought face to face with a difficulty. It is not that the Lady fails to expound the doctrine of chastity; for that has already been done by the Elder Brother, whose exposition the reader is invited to re-

[8] Lines 779–87 (not in Bridgewater MS).

call—an invitation of which we shall avail ourselves. The difficulty is that here, and in the speech of the Elder Brother, there is no such clear-cut distinction between the doctrine of chastity and that of virginity as there is between the doctrine of chastity and that of temperance and continence. The two seem to merge; so that Mr Tillyard can ask whether in *Comus* Milton is primarily concerned with premarital chastity or rather with the special virtue attached to the state of virginity considered in itself, and can declare, with M. Saurat, for the second alternative. But the intellectual frame of reference, supported as it is by the autobiographical passage in the *Apology,* enables us to answer the question: Milton is concerned with both as interdependent parts in a system that includes nature and grace; but the central theme is the doctrine of chastity, which is illustrated on the purely religious level by the Christian doctrine of virginity. And that this is the correct answer is proved by the fact that it clears the sense of the whole poem. There is a second, but less formidable difficulty connected with the transition from the order of nature to the order of grace. It is the fact that in *Comus,* in contrast with (for example) the *Nativity Ode,* Milton is reticent in the introduction of specifically religious terminology. A moment's reflection shows that this is attributable to the *genre* and occasion of the poem; but, confessedly, it slightly obscures the scheme of the argument, and forces us to read between the lines.

That argument as it deals with chastity moves in the area common to nature and grace. The speeches of the Elder Brother,[9] though not highly dramatic, develop naturally enough as part of a dialogue on the fate of the lost Lady. But the points made, and the order in which they are made, have a special interest.

(1) First the poet emphasizes the power and security of virtue in general, and in itself, without particular reference either to chastity or to anything above the natural level. "The mind is its own place," as Milton already knows. And virtue arms the mind, first with inward peace ("the sweet peace that goodness bosoms ever"), and then with inward illumination

> (He that has light within his own clear breast
> May sit i' the centre and enjoy bright day).

We are to remember this when we hear the Lady's defiance of Comus: "Thou canst not touch the freedom of my mind"; and once more (as we shall see) before the poem closes.

[9] Lines 359–475, 584–99.

(2) Then he suggests that chastity is in very special degree a strength and protection to the person that possesses it: a strength and protection referable (like all good gifts) to Heaven, but still the mind's own

> (a hidden strength,
> Which if Heaven gave it, may be termed her own).

We are still on the natural level,[10] but the idea of virtue's—and specifically of chastity's—ultimate (though perhaps unrecognized) dependence on God's gift is suggested. This is a point of juncture between the two orders, which permits grace to build upon nature in a way to be described in points 4 and 5; but first,

(3) the grounding of chastity, and its power, in the order of nature is emphasized by a deliberate reference to non-Christian wisdom:

> Do ye believe me yet, or shall I call
> Antiquity from the old schools of Greece,
> To testify the arms of chastity?
> Hence had the huntress Dian her dread bow,
> Fair silver-shafted queen for ever chaste. . . .
> What was that snaky-headed Gorgon shield
> That wise Minerva wore, unconquered virgin, . . .
> But rigid looks of chaste austerity
> And noble grace that dashed brute violence . . . ?

(4) And only now do we come to the passage to which the Lady's speech to Comus is designed to send us back:

> So dear to Heaven is saintly chastity,
> That when a soul is found sincerely so,
> A thousand liveried angels lackey her,
> Driving far off each thing of sin and guilt,
> And in clear dream and solemn vision
> Tell her of things that no gross ear can hear;
> Till oft converse with heavenly habitants
> Begin to cast a beam on the outward shape,
> The unpolluted temple of the mind,
> And turns it by degrees to the soul's essence,
> Till all become immortal.

[10] Professor Bush remarks that in their Miltonic meaning Wisdom and Contemplation (lines 375, 377) suggest something above natural reason. I agree that in another context they would do so. I do not think that they have here a specifically religious content, but that they will take on a religious meaning only when submitted to, and reviewed in the light of, grace. The same thing applies to the image of lines 375–80, which (as he points out) seems to be an allusion to the ascent of the soul in the *Phaedrus* of Plato.

Here one recognizes Platonic doctrine, the doctrine taught by Spenser:

> For of the soule the bodie forme doth take,
> For soule is forme, and doth the bodie make;

the doctrine, also, accepted by Milton, of "chastity and love . . . : how the first and chiefest office of love begins and ends in the soul, producing those happy twins of her divine generation, knowledge and virtue." For to peace and freedom and illumination of mind on the level already stated, is here added illumination of a higher order, whose note is not self-sufficiency, but self-surrender, and whose communication is rapture. And as in the passage from the *Apology,* the "abstracted sublimities" (what the Lady calls "the sublime notion") of Platonism lead on directly to "those chaste and high mysteries" (the Lady's phrase is identical, "the high mystery") of Christian teaching; for to Milton, at this stage of his development, Platonism marks the highest reach of thought on the natural level and its point of juncture with the divine. But here in contrast to the *Apology,* Platonic and Christian doctrine merge, though it may well be (as we shall observe) that there is ascent within the order of grace and that more is meant by the Lady's allusion to the "high mystery" than is contained in the Elder Brother's exposition.

(5) Finally, the recurring idea of chastity's self-protective power receives, on the religious level, its confirmation and its explanation, in the doctrine of Eternal Providence. It is for the Christian preeminently that "all things work together for good." The ideas here uttered are repeated in a larger context in *Paradise Lost* and are a ground of the optimism which is one of its notes. Not malice, and not

> that power
> Which erring men call Chance,

but the power and providence of God reign supreme. On this the Christian stakes everything; for

> if this fail,
> The pillared firmament is rottenness,
> And earth's base built on stubble.

The emphasis on Providence is reinforced by the presence of the Attendant Spirit, who is its minister and almost its symbol.

We have said that, like Spenser, Milton realizes the necessity of ascending from a doctrine of temperance and continence to a doctrine of chastity. Professor Hanford goes much further, emphasizing the extent to which "Milton has been influenced by his master's romantic allegory of chastity in the third book of the *Faerie Queene*,"[11] and finding in that book, not in book 2 (as we have done), the main contact of *Comus* with Spenser. What impresses us in the doctrine of chastity is not the similarity of *Comus* to the *Faery Queen*, but its significant dissimilarity. In book 3 Spenser's main emphasis is so different from Milton's in *Comus* that the two poets might almost seem to be writing on different subjects; for Milton's doctrine of chastity culminates in—though even on the religious level it is not co-extensive with—a doctrine of virginity, whereas Spenser's doctrine of chastity is elaborated in connection with an ideal of wedded love. Spenser's legend of chastity is also his legend of love; not the intellectual love of Platonism, as set forth by Milton in the *Apology*, and in *Comus* merged with Christian doctrine, and assuredly not the "high mystery" of Christian heavenly love, also set forth in the *Apology*, and presented in *Comus* as the highest reach of Christian thought, but love as it manifests itself in human marriage. Spenser's knight of chastity, the warrior maiden Britomart, is virginal, but by no means vowed to virginity: on the contrary, she is vowed to the love of one good man, and in her single devotion passes unscathed through every danger, unassailed by any temptation. The security with which Spenser's idealism is here rooted in the realities of ordinary human nature is evidenced by a wealth of psychological insight, nowhere more impressive than in Britomart's dream in the temple of Isis. I am far from denying the influence of Christianity on Spenser's treatment of chastity: what he presents is in one aspect a Christian ideal of marriage (the history of the subject is far too complicated to talk about *the* Christian ideal of marriage), but it is an ideal of marriage, or of chastity culminating in marriage, and it is idle to try to approximate it to an ideal of chastity culminating in virginity.[12] In *Comus* chastity is never, even by implication, viewed in connection with the wedded love which Milton was later to hail. It is here that *Comus* stands at its greatest distance from *Paradise Lost*, and at a distance almost as great from book 3 of the *Faery Queen*.[13]

[11] *Op. cit.*, 140–1.

[12] I would not be thought to reduce *F.Q.* 3. to a sermon in dull domestic virtue. Spenser, the Platonist, views chastity and love as incentives to high idealism and heroic action. But in Britomart these incentives are expressed in relation to marriage, and not to any cult of virginity: that is the only point with which I am concerned.

[13] Nor have the minor characters in which Spenser deals with other aspects of chastity more relation than Britomart to Milton's masque, with one possible

It will not have escaped the reader, that in drawing out the argument of *Comus* I have been contending against the common view that it is simple, unrelievedly austere, and negative in conception. There can be no doubt, however, that its doctrine of chastity culminates in what Milton calls the sage and serious doctrine of virginity. This allusion is to be partly understood in relation to the mingled Platonic and Christian teaching of the Elder Brother's speech, but also as carrying a specifically Christian content, as symbolizing chastity, indeed, not merely in the order of grace, but there in its utmost reach. It may be granted that this last fact is not directly stated and that one can deduce it only by a consideration of the poem as a whole, and by cross-reference to other passages (in the *Apology* and at the conclusion of *Lycidas* and the *Epitaphium Damonis*) alluding to the Christian doctrine of heavenly love as set forth in Revelation 14. 4, which Milton evidently reads as the transcendent Christian version of Plato's doctrine of "chastity and love." That Milton, at the time of the writing of *Comus,* set a marked value on the Christian conception of virginity seems certain: so marked a value that he was willing to regard it as the highest culmination of chastity and to use it as the symbol of chastity in the order of grace—as the highest culmination and the symbol, but, as the *Apology* (even if we omit the reservation in favour of marriage) makes clear, not as co-extensive with the Christian teaching on chastity. Whether or not Milton's doctrine of virginity appears unrelievedly austere, and negative in conception, will presumably depend on the reader's beliefs. But the impression will certainly be modified when it is viewed in its proper context, that is to say, as the ideal culmination of an ethical scheme whose foundations are laid in the order of nature, and which ascends through the whole range of human experience.

---

exception, Belphoebe, Spenser's version of the classical Diana. To Britomart Professor Hanford would trace "the martial conception [that] underlies such passages as *Comus* 440 ff." (*op. cit.,* 141). But the conception, though militant, is not martial; and to me the lines with their allusions to Diana and Minerva recall the spirit of Spenser's portrait not of Britomart, but of Belphoebe. More plausible is Professor Hanford's contention that the Lady's rescue, which can be completed only by the reversal of the enchanter's charm, owes something to the rescue of Amoret (*F.Q.* 3. 12. 36), though there is a possible common source in Ovid, *Metamorphoses* 14. 301–2 (Hughes). But least plausible of all is the assumption that Milton's emphasis on providential intervention to guard chastity requires a source and finds it in the rescue of Florimel by Proteus (*F.Q.* 3. 8. 29 ff.). And anyway these would be mere surface borrowings: the characters and situations of Amoret and Florimel have nothing in common with the Lady's. In one instance Professor Hanford exaggerates Milton's divergence from Spenser: it is the one certain and significant borrowing from book 3, the allusion to the Garden of Adonis (see below, p. 65 [pp. 37–38 herein]).

Such an effort of comprehension is just as important as what is said on any particular level. And that the effort of comprehension is real and fundamental is put beyond all doubt by the Epilogue. But before turning to it we must briefly notice some further effects of the effort of comprehension.

III

It is not contended—and I think it quite impossible to contend—that the effort of comprehension is completely successful, that Milton avoids all occasion of conflict between nature and grace. I mean, of course, *unnecessary* occasion of conflict; for wherever one has an ascending scale of values, whether it extends to the religious level or pauses on the humanistic, there will be subordination of the lower to the higher: there will be necessary renunciation within a scheme whose note is not renunciation, but *comprehension and ascent.* It is sufficient to recognize that in *Comus* the effort after such a scheme is being made.

Despite the seeming austerity of its doctrine, *Comus* is a very different poem from *Paradise Regained,* the later work with which it presents the most obvious points for comparison. In *Paradise Regained* Milton comes nearer than anywhere else in his writings to asserting an absolute division between the goods of the order of nature and those of the order of grace, comes nearer to applying what I have called the principle of segregation. One must, of course, be on one's guard against too easily supposing that what Christ rejects, he necessarily rejects as in itself evil, and not as evil merely by occasion because unfitting to present circumstances and because offered by Satan with evil intent. But as one observes the careful exclusion from the things offered of all the gross outward signs of evil so evident in the temptation of Comus, and scans the terms in which Christ's rejection is made, it is hard to avoid the conclusion that Milton has come to regard with deep suspicion beauty (to which he has been so constantly devoted), knowledge (with which he has so laboured to enrich himself for God's service), and—though here no comparison with *Comus* is possible—the exercise of power even for good ends. In conformity with his new attitude we find that *Paradise Regained,* as compared with *Paradise Lost,* and also with *Comus,* is relatively bare of Milton's rich additions of poetic beauty and quite bare of philosophic thought; and that this does not depend wholly on the subject is indicated by a like quality in *Samson Agonistes.* Milton's repudiation of wisdom on the natural level, of ancient Greece and its philosophers, who have formed his mind, is notorious and inescapable:

> he who receives
> Light from above, from the fountain of light,
> No other doctrine needs, though granted true;
> *But these are false or little else but dreams,*
> *Conjectures, fancies, built on nothing firm.*[14]

In *Comus,* on the contrary, beauty and the appreciation of beauty are everywhere: even the wizard claims kindred with the Attendant Spirit and the other good characters in his response to it. And for wisdom on the natural level, for philosophy ("How charming is divine philosophy!"), Aristotle (through the medium of Spenser) and the Stoics together give the rule for temperance and continence, and the doctrine of Plato inculcates chastity and points on to, almost merges in, the teaching of Christianity. And Christianity, far from repudiating the findings of natural wisdom, confirms before it transcends them. There is no conscious divorce between nature and grace, and no interval between the two orders. So much our exposition of the argument of *Comus* has been designed to make clear. But the question of beauty, both for its intrinsic importance and because it is so intimately bound up with the meaning of the Epilogue, demands a word or two more.

The beauty of *Comus* is natural beauty in the sense of belonging to the order of nature, but aesthetically speaking it cannot be described as simple natural beauty. It has a certain Arcadian quality which readily merges with the pastoral and, beyond that, with a more generalized idyllic note, and this in turn permits the inclusion of an element of myth, classical and native. These facts belong rather to a consideration of *Comus,* the masque; but they must be taken into account if one is to gauge aright the extent of beauty on the natural level to which response is indicated. It has been made a matter of wonder that Comus shares with the Attendant Spirit (and we may add, though in lesser degree, the Brothers and the Lady) an immediate response to this beauty.[15] But there is no mystery here. The response of the good characters means that for Milton beauty is to the good a good, and one to be received with joy. Like other goods on the natural level it depends on good use, and is susceptible of perversion. Almost it seems that beauty, like nature, "means her provision only for the good." We have seen how, when beauty is perverted to evil ends, Spenser presents it as art imitating and falsifying nature, and we have caught one hint of this in Milton also. But in general Milton is quite ready to admit that the beauty which is to

[14] *Paradise Regained* 4. 288–92.
[15] Enid Welsford, *The Court Masque* (1923), 321.

the good a good is the same beauty which the evil pervert to evil ends. This indeed is characteristic of his whole attitude to the natural order. So with daring, and a subtlety quite wasted on his modern critics, he shows us Comus responding to beauty in words that might be mistaken for those of the Attendant Spirit, but perverting it to evil—to what Milton takes to be evil—in the very act of response. To quote the lines in question [16] is to prove the point, but lest it should still be missed we will call italics to our aid:

> The star that bids the shepherd fold
> Now the top of heaven doth hold;
> And the gilded car of day
> His glowing axle doth allay
> In the steep Atlantic stream. . . .[17]
> Meanwhile, welcome joy and feast,
> *Midnight shout and revelry,*
> *Tipsy dance and jollity.*
> *Braid your locks with rosy twine,*
> *Dropping odours, dropping wine.*
> *Rigour now is gone to bed. . . .*
> *We that are of purer fire*
> *Imitate the starry quire,*[18]
> Who, in their nightly watchful spheres,
> Lead in swift rounds the months and years.
> The sounds and seas with all their finny drove,
> Now to the moon in wavering morrice move;
> And on the tawny sands and shelves
> Trip the pert faeries and the dapper elves.
> By dimpled brook and fountain-brim
> The wood-nymphs, decked with daisies trim,
> Their merry wakes and pastimes keep:
> *What has night to do with sleep?*
> *Night has better sweets to prove:*
> *Venus now wakes and wakens Love.*[19]

[16] Lines 93–144.

[17] Originally, it would seem, this allusion was intended to recall the opening speech of the Attendant Spirit, where there was a reference to "the wide Atlantique" (cancelled passage, preserved in Cambridge MS).

[18] This couplet is italicized because, for all its beauty and seeming innocence, it is untrue. The spheres with their "ninefold harmony," audible only to the pure in heart, have for Milton a special significance: they represent the highest degree of perfection in the natural order, the point of contact with the supernatural. See below, p. 71 [pp. 41–42 herein].

[19] The Venus and Cupid here alluded to represent, of course, wanton love; see below, p. 67 [pp 40–41 herein].

Come, let us our rites begin;
'Tis only daylight that makes sin,
Which these dun shades will ne'er report.
Hail, goddess of nocturnal sport,
Dark-veiled Cotytto,[20] *to whom the secret flame*
Of midnight torches burns! mysterious dame,
That ne'er art called but when the dragon womb
Of Stygian darkness spets her thickest gloom,
And makes one blot of all the air!
Stay thy cloudy ebon chair
Wherein thou ridest with Hecate, and befriend
Us thy vowed priests, till utmost end
Of all thy dues be done. . . .
Come, knit hands, and beat the ground
In a light fantastic round.[21]

It is the more necessary to be clear about Milton's meaning in this speech because in the aesthetic and in the intellectual pattern it is evidently intended to stand in a relation of contrast with the Epilogue.

IV

The Epilogue is not easy to interpret. On the surface it presents a description of the Attendant Spirit's abode, though even of this some doubt might be entertained were it not for the cancelled lines of the Spirit's opening speech, preserved in the Cambridge MS, with their allusions to the stream Ocean (and also to the Atlantic, a link with the speech of Comus quoted above), to the Hesperian garden and to hyacinth and roses. But evidently "more is meant than meets the ear," and the method employed is less that of allegory than of symbol. The question is, precisely what is symbolized? "In the Spirit's Epilogue," says Professor Hanford,

Milton sings of Paradise. The language is highly esoteric . . . and Milton expressly calls attention in the parenthesis, "List mortals, if your ears be

[20] The non-classical reader will not appreciate the full extent of licentiousness conveyed by the name, though he will recognize the association with evil implied by Hecate and the blotting out of light. See C. G. Osgood, *The Classical Mythology of Milton's English Poems,* 24–5.

[21] Another seemingly innocent couplet, which instantly reminds us indeed of a genuinely innocent one,

Come and trip it as ye go
On the light fantastic toe,

a type of the "unreproved pleasures free" of L'Allegro (lines 33–4, 40). But, as Osgood makes clear, Comus is still alluding to the obscene rites of Cotytto.

true," to the hidden spiritual meaning. The bliss proposed is that of Heavenly love as the ineffable compensation for a life devoted to the ideal of chastity. . . . In adopting Spenser's image of the Garden of Adonis Milton entirely changes its application. . . . The pagan image of the love of a mortal youth for a goddess draws insensibly nearer to the truth in the reversed symbol of the union of the God of love himself with Psyche, the human soul, and if Milton's classic taste prevents him from concluding with an allusion to the Lamb and his eternal bride it is because there is no need.[22]

This interpretation has been very generally accepted, but I do not think that Milton's allusion is to Paradise, or (at least in Professor Hanford's sense) to the rewards and compensations of the chaste soul hereafter. The whole deeper significance of the Epilogue lies in its symbolical character; and I should be disposed to look for some larger symbolism, which might include the reward of the chaste soul hereafter but would not be restricted to it. I believe that nothing less is symbolized in the Epilogue than life itself, as the Christian mind, grounded in nature but illuminated by grace, alone can apprehend it. I do not think that in adopting Spenser's image of Venus and Adonis Milton entirely changes its application, or indeed changes it at all: I believe that he relies upon a brief—perhaps too brief—allusion to recall what Spenser had implied. On the relation of Milton's image of Cupid and Psyche to Spenser's, Professor Hanford is silent: I believe that Milton's meaning is very similar to the interpretation commonly given to Spenser's lines, but not to Spenser's true intention. (I realize that my argument would be simpler and perhaps more convincing if I could say that Milton followed Spenser throughout. Unfortunately, I do not find that Spenser's lines will bear the interpretation commonly put upon them, though it is possible that Milton may have given them that interpretation and thus have supposed himself to be following Spenser throughout.) I think that, in the progression which Milton adopts, the specifically and exclusively religious level is not reached even in the allusion to Cupid and Psyche, much less in the allusion to Venus and Adonis, but only in the concluding lines of the Epilogue. And in the light of those lines, of course, the whole is to be read. So I interpret the Epilogue up to this point as symbolizing the transfigured view of life which the practice of virtue and the experience of grace induce. On no other hypothesis can I explain the ascent through the order of nature to the order of grace which the lines evidently embody, beginning on the plane of natural beauty, expressed in and with classic mythology and idyllicism, and culminating at last in Christianity.

[22] *Op. cit.*, 152.

The journey commences in the *idea* of whatever is fresh and beautiful in the natural world: ocean, air, and the flowering earth, and the reader lingers

> amidst the gardens fair
> Of Hesperus and his daughters three
> That sing about the golden tree.
> Along the crisped shades and bowers
> Revels the spruce and jocund Spring;
> The Graces and the rosy-bosomed Hours
> Thither all their bounties bring. . . .
> Iris there with humid bow
> Waters the odorous banks that blow . . .
> And drenches with celestial dew
> (List, mortals, if your ears be true)
> Beds of hyacinth and roses,
> Where young Adonis oft reposes,
> Waxing well of his deep wound
> In slumber soft, and on the ground
> Sadly sits the Assyrian queen:
> But far above in spangled sheen
> Celestial Cupid, her famed son advanced,
> Holds his dear Psyche sweet entranced,
> After all her labours long,
> Till free consent the gods among
> Make her his eternal bride,
> And from her fair unspotted side,
> Two blissful twins are to be born,
> Youth and Joy. . . .

The joyous acceptance of natural beauty by the good is unmistakably indicated, and the mind of the reader is carried back to Comus, who accepts but perverts to evil in the act of accepting. The first problem arises with the allusion to Venus and Adonis.

On the details of Spenser's allegory of the Garden of Adonis [23] critics have not always agreed. It will be enough here to state very briefly what appears to be its main intention. In classic myth and its elaborations one recognizes three different roles assigned to Venus: she is the goddess of wanton love (as in the speech of Comus already quoted); she is the great mother, a principle of generation in all things; and she is the celestial Venus, the symbol of intellectual or spiritual love. In the passage in question Spenser clearly has in mind the second of these roles,

[23] *Faery Queen* 3. 6.

with no suggestion of the third. It is an allegory of form and substance [24]—of material forms, represented by Adonis, the masculine principle, and material substance, represented by Venus, the feminine principle—and it sets forth the processes of decay and replenishment throughout the natural world. Further, there is (as we have remarked) a contrast between the Garden of Adonis and Acrasia's Bower of Bliss, where natural powers are prostituted (as they are by Comus) to purposes of mere pleasure, a contrast pointed in Spenser by the opposing Geniuses who guard the two portals and by the types of beauty found beyond them.[25] This allegory of Spenser's, Milton recalls in his allusion to the Garden of Adonis. It symbolizes life on the natural level: the life processes of "most innocent nature." And its appropriateness, once more, is found in the contrast to all that Comus stands for. There is no need to assume with Professor Hanford that Milton alludes to the third role of Venus, the celestial Venus,[26] or that he translates Spenser's image to a higher (even the highest) level; for (as we have shown) the natural also has its place in Milton's scheme. This is the world of nature as the chaste and religious are able to apprehend it, and only they. That is the significance of the admonition uttered just before the image of Venus and Adonis is introduced: "List, mortals, *if your ears be true.*"

The myth of Cupid and Psyche, which goes back to the charming fairy-story told by Apuleius, had long been allegorized when Spenser added to his picture of the Garden of Adonis his account of how Cupid

> Thither resorts, and laying his sad darts
> Aside, with faire Adonis playes his wanton parts.
>
> And his true love faire Psyche with him playes,
> Faire Psyche to him lately reconcyld
> After long troubles and unmeet upbrayes
> With which his mother Venus her revyld,
> And eke himselfe her cruelly exyld:
> But now in stedfast love and happy state

[24] Brents Stirling in *Variorum Spenser,* III, 347–52.

[25] See C. S. Lewis, *op. cit.,* 324 ff., 361 ff.

[26] One should record Hughes' note on *Assyrian Queen,* line 1002, that "according to Pausanias I. 14. 6, 'the Assyrians were the first men to revere the Celestial Aphrodite.'" But surely the phrase *Assyrian Queen* is sufficiently accounted for by the myth of Venus and Adonis itself, which, as Milton well knew (cf. *Nativity Ode* 204) is of Eastern origin. Thammuz was adopted as Adonis. Astoreth or Astarte, the original of the Venus of this myth, was herself identical with the Assyrian goddess Istar. *Assyrian Queen* is thus one of Milton's learned devices of poetical adornment. Cf. Verity's notes on *Comus* 1002, and *P.L.* I. 438–41.

> She with him lives and hath him borne a chyld,
> Pleasure, that doth both gods and men aggrate,
> Pleasure, the daughter of Cupid and Psyche late.

That Spenser adopted an allegorical meaning already attached to the myth, is the usual assumption:

> The allegorical meaning . . . is clearly developed by Boccaccio and fits Spenser's intention. Boccaccio says, "Psyche is the soul . . . and there is joined with her that which preserves the rational element, that is pure Love," Psyche passes through trials and purgations. "At length . . . she attains to the consummation of divine joy and contemplation, and is joined to her lover forever, and with mortal things sloughed off is born into eternal glory; and from this love is born Pleasure, which is eternal joy and gladness." Pleasure so interpreted is very similar to Plato's *Eudaimonia*. . . .[27]

It seems far from certain that this is the meaning of Spenser's lines when taken in their context. There is no indication that it is the celestial Cupid that is intended. The allegory appears to move on the same level as that of Venus and Adonis, to which Spenser attaches it so closely. For him the story of Venus and Adonis represents the spirit of love and the principle of generation operating throughout the natural order; and the story of Cupid and Psyche should somehow represent the same spirit and principle in their specifically human application, which is marriage with its productiveness and legitimate pleasure, opposed once more to the illegitimate pleasures of Acrasia, at war with productiveness.[28] Considering Spenser's free adaptation of myth to the purposes of allegory elsewhere in the *Faery Queen,* it does not seem an insuperable difficulty that this reading of the myth, the only one wholly consonant with text and context, should fall short of other allegorical interpretations current when he wrote.

Be this as it may, Milton's meaning is something quite different from that which I have been bold enough to attribute to Spenser, and resembles the interpretation of the myth given by Boccaccio. Unlike Spenser, Milton indicates clearly that he is not treating the story on the same level as that of Venus and Adonis: on the contrary, this is the *celestial* Cupid, and he is seen *far above* the figures in the Garden. There is no allusion, as in Spenser, to marriage, but to a Platonic doctrine of intellectual or spiritual love, the love "whose charming cup is only

[27] Lotspeich in *Variorum Spenser,* III, 261.

[28] It is for marriage that Amoret is educated by Psyche with her own daughter, Pleasure. Actually the education turns out to be insufficient. It has to be completed by Britomart.

virtue," and whose "chiefest office begins and ends in the soul, producing those happy twins of her divine generation, Knowledge and Virtue." And yet there is a difference. For if Milton does not name the offspring of Cupid and Psyche *Voluptas* or Pleasure, like Apuleius and Spenser, neither does he call them simply Knowledge and Virtue, as in his other account of Platonic love, but Youth and Joy. In bestowing on Cupid and Psyche *twin* offspring he means to parallel them with that other pair of the soul's "divine generation," Knowledge and Virtue. These indeed Milton has implied in every line of the poem; so now he can afford to shift the emphasis. Like Knowledge and Virtue the offspring of Cupid and Psyche are not primarily the symbol of a reward to be expected in heaven, but something that the chaste soul rises to here and now. And if this is so, their names are significant indeed. For the conclusion mitigates the austerity, though not the strictness of Milton's doctrine. He repudiates false pleasures, but not joy; wantonness, but not the spirit of youth. The quest is arduous, he would seem to say, and demands renunciation, but among its rewards may be reckoned not only virtue and knowledge, illumination of mind, peace of mind, but the very things that the adversary would declare to be taken away: life and youth and joy. And to these the final lines of the Epilogue will add one further note: freedom.

First, the beauty of nature, with all its gracious associations, which Comus perverts; secondly, in the image of Venus and Adonis, the powers and processes of nature, which Comus (like Acrasia) would prostitute and thwart; thirdly, in the image of Cupid and Psyche, ascent to the highest virtue and wisdom accessible on the natural level, or rather ascent to an area common to nature and grace: thus far the summary has proceeded. But there is one more step to take:

> Mortals that would follow me,
> Love Virtue: she alone is free;
> She can teach ye how to climb
> Higher than the sphery chime;
> Or if Virtue feeble were,
> Heaven itself would stoop to her.

The terminology is not overtly religious (it seldom is, as we have said, in *Comus*), but here at last we are on the level of grace alone. For the first allusion—and it is literally the first in Milton's writings—is to a doctrine which is to be enormously important in his thinking, the doctrine of Christian liberty.[29] It is to receive much elaboration and many different applications which are without significance here. But it never ceases to be for Milton a cardinal principle of specifically Christian ethics; for his interpretation of this doctrine, as of religion in general, is always (as *Comus* illustrates) predominantly ethical: "Know that to be free is the same as to be pious, to be wise, to be temperate and just, to be frugal and abstinent, and lastly, to be magnanimous and brave. . . ."[30] One recognizes (as no doubt Milton did) the kinship with Stoic doctrine; but for him freedom through virtue, through *voluntary* obedience to the will of God, is the special mark of Christianity: it is *Christian* liberty, which gathers up into the light of revelation the experience of the freedom of mind and will already alluded to in the poem. And the pointing on to a level "higher than the sphery chime" confirms this interpretation of the lines. To hear the music of the spheres indeed is given only to the pure in heart. To ascend above it is to enter the Christian heaven and "hear the unexpressive nuptial song."[31] And the final note of all is unmistakably Christian. We have been told in the body of the poem how Providence intervenes for the protection of virtue. Now this idea, too, is gathered up into the full light of Christian revelation. Here is a note not very often heard in Milton. And it might almost be called the essential note of Christianity; for it speaks to us not of God's power merely, or even of his providence, but of the Divine condescension and mercy to men who would do the will of God but are weak.

In *Comus* Milton does not repudiate the order of nature; he does not deny an area common to nature and grace, or the ascent through it from natural wisdom to divine; he does not seek to divorce the two orders. But he believes that experience on the level of grace will cast a light back upon nature and enable one to realize its true significance.[32] The

[29] See my "Milton, Puritanism and Liberty" (UNIVERSITY OF TORONTO QUARTERLY, IV, 1935, 483–513).

[30] *Second Defence* (*Prose Works,* I, 298).

[31] E. M. W. Tillyard (*Milton,* 1934, 376 ff.) seems to hold that in *At a Solemn Music* Milton identifies the two, and to wish to read *Comus* in the light of this supposed identification. What the text says is that the two strains *answer* each other. Milton does not divorce the different orders of existence, but neither does he confuse them. There is something *higher than the sphery chime.* It is the unexpressive nuptial song.

[32] There are hints of this earlier in the poem. It is in the light of the religious experience that the dictates of temperance become "holy" and that chastity can be described not as "sun-clad" merely, but as "saintly."

idea—or rather the experience—is not unique: Cowper expresses it in simple evangelical terms in *The Task,* and Carlyle, in more philosophical terms, in *Sartor Resartus.* To record this experience is the function of the Epilogue, which thus becomes a key to the whole poem, or at least to Milton's intention in the poem. That intention is not, I think, successfully executed at all points: there are notes that jar, especially upon the modern (and uninstructed) ear. But the Epilogue itself is triumphantly successful. And it too casts a light back upon the long road travelled, which it is folly to ignore.

The Action of *Comus*

E. M. W. Tillyard

I. Introductory

The centre of *Comus* is the scene where the Lady, imprisoned in the magic chair, conducts an argument with the Enchanter on the subject of chastity. It is disputed who had the best of it. Professedly the Lady, and Comus is made to admit it; but Comus speaks so well that Milton has been accused of being here (as elsewhere) on the Devil's side without knowing it. Beneath every opinion is the assumption that one or other of the disputants is right, Milton being singled out from the great poets as the one to whom the privilege of being on both or on neither side at the same time must be denied. The assumption is false. Comus and the Lady are both wrong, or, if right, in ways they did not perceive. And if Milton is on the Devil's side at any point, he knew very well what he was doing. Not till the final words of the Attendant Spirit is the truth revealed.

If these contentions could be proved they change the action of the masque. *Comus,* instead of being an academic dispute ending in stalemate or at best in an unexciting victory with a final dose of lyricism to anaesthetize the reader's critical fastidiousness, will have a plot that answers all the previous questions. What follows is my case for this hypothesis.

II. The Texts of 1634 and 1637

The crucial passage is the Attendant Spirit's epilogue (line 976, 'To the ocean now I fly', to the end); and unfortunately this is one of the few places in the whole poem where there are serious textual variations. These must first be pointed out.

Reprinted from *Studies in Milton* (London: Chatto & Windus, 1951), pp. 82–99, by permission of the publishers and of Miss Angela Tillyard.

Comus was performed at Michaelmas 1634, but it was not printed till 1637. The earliest printed edition agrees substantially with the later editions and thus represents Milton's final recension.[1] There are two manuscript versions, one preserved, with other writings of Milton, in the Trinity Manuscript, the other once in the possession of the family in whose honour *Comus* was written and known as the Bridgewater or Egerton Manuscript. The latter, containing a slightly altered and abbreviated version for stage production, need not concern us. The various changes within the Trinity Manuscript have no decisive importance; and the significant changes are those between the completed first draft as contained in the Trinity Manuscript (which I call the first or 1634 version) and the first printed text (which I call the 1637 version). These changes consist of additions to the Lady's refutation of Comus and to the Spirit's epilogue; and it is just in these added lines that I find the clue to the way Milton meant us to interpret the debate between Comus and the Lady. I must therefore go on to discuss them.

In the Trinity Manuscript the Lady begins her last speech to Comus in answer to his grand tirade on the bounties of nature and the unnaturalness of virginity, in the words we know, 'I had not thought to have unlockt my lips in this unhallow'd air', and goes on to defend temperance against luxury. But when she reaches her climax on this theme,

for swinish gluttony
Ne're looks to Heav'n amidst his gorgeous feast,
But with besotted base ingratitude
Cramms, and blasphemes his feeder,

she ends and Comus replies, as at the end of line 806 in the version we know,

Com, no more,
This is meer moral babble, and direct
Against the canon laws of our foundation.

The Lady's defence of the sun-clad power of chastity and of the sage and serious doctrine of virginity, with Comus's admission (spoken aside) that she fables not and that he is frightened, are not there, being added in the 1637 edition. The epilogue begins in the Trinity Manuscript in the familiar way, 'To the ocean now I fly', and goes on to talk of the

[1] For convenient summaries of the textual variants of *Comus*, referring to previous discussions, see John S. Diekhoff in *Publications of the Modern Language Associations of America*, 1937, pp. 705, 725 ff. My remarks here on the texts are abbreviated from my original version in *Essays and Studies*.

Hesperian gardens. Four lines (984–7) from the description of them are not in the manuscript but were added in 1637. These are ornamental, not important for the general meaning. But a little after, in describing Iris, the manuscript begins to differ from the familiar version, reading as follows:

> Iris there with humid bow
> Waters the odorous banks that blow
> Flowers of more mingled hew
> Than her purfl'd scarfe can shew,
> Yellow, watchet, greene, and blew,
> And drenches oft with manna dew
> Beds of Hyacinth, and roses,
> Where many a cherub soft reposes.

And omitting all reference to the Garden of Adonis, Venus, Cupid and Psyche, the manuscript goes on to the last lines of all, 'Now my message well is done'. The 1637 edition added the lines on the Garden of Adonis, and in the passage just quoted altered *many a cherub* to *young Adonis;* and for *Yellow, watchet, greene, and blew* substituted *List mortals, if your ears be true,* to draw attention to the special allegorical significance of the Adonis passage.

III. The Reason for the 1637 Additions

Why did Milton add these two passages between 1634 and 1637? If the first passage stood alone, we might answer very simply: to give sufficient weight to the Lady's reply to Comus. In the early version she had answered only his arguments for profusion and luxury, not his cheapening of 'that same vaunted name Virginity', and something on the latter subject too would give better balance. But the second addition admits of no such explanation. First, the deliberate exhortation 'List mortals, if your ears be true' shows that Milton thought the meaning important and wanted it heeded. And secondly, the passage itself points to high and solemn themes. It was Thomas Warton who noticed that the passage referred to Spenser's account of the Garden of Adonis in the sixth canto of the third book of the *Faerie Queene,* and his contention has not been disputed; but I doubt if people have realized how much this reference amounts to. But first for the truth of the reference: we must have no doubts of that if we are to give much weight to the passage. Iris, wrote Milton, in the paradisiac region where the Attendant Spirit will return,

drenches with *Elysian* dew
(List mortals, if your ears be true)
Beds of *Hyacinth,* and roses
Where young *Adonis* oft reposes
Waxing well of his deep wound
In slumber soft, and on the ground
Sadly sits th' *Assyrian* Queen.
But far above in spangled sheen
Celestial *Cupid* her fam'd son advanc't,
Holds his dear *Psyche* sweet intranc't,
After her wandring labours long,
Till free consent the gods among
Make her his eternal Bride,
And from her fair unspotted side
Two blissful twins are to be born,
Youth and Joy; so *Jove* hath sworn.

Spenser's Garden of Adonis consists of an outer realm, the seminary of all created things, and of an inner sanctuary, overgrown with hyacinth and other plants, where Venus, mistress of the garden, enjoys the love of Adonis, the boar which wounded him now being bound in a 'strong rocky cave' hewn beneath the mountain on which the bower is situated. It is to this inner sanctuary, described in stanzas 45 to 50, that Milton refers, but he varies his version by imagining an earlier moment before Adonis is quite healed of his wound. Cupid, too, inhabits Spenser's Garden of Adonis with his Psyche, who has already borne him a child, Pleasure. Milton again varies by putting the marriage in the future and foretelling a second child, Youth, as the offspring of it. The component parts of the two passages are mythological commonplaces, accessible to any poet, but the identity of the parts themselves, the above variations excepted, and the order they are arranged in are so close that I can see no alternative to Milton's intending a reference to Spenser.

To perceive what such a reference meant, we must consider Milton's readers. In the year 1637 Spenser was still the great modern poet. It was no longer the fashion to imitate his style, but he was the unchallenged poetic classic of modern English literature, and everyone read him. Now the episode of the births of Belphoebe and Amoret and of the Garden of Adonis was one of the most famous in the whole of the *Faerie Queene.* When Milton wrote *Comus* the *Faerie Queene* had been published upward of forty years, and its familiarity would be roughly that of one of the best-known episodes from the *Pickwick Papers,* say the case of Bardell *v.* Pickwick, in the year 1880; while the more restricted passage to which Milton refers would be as familiar as Sam Weller's evidence in that same trial. Further we must remember that Milton's readers were nearer to the Middle Ages than to ourselves in their readiness to allegorize classical myth. For all his modernity Bacon could write the *Wisdom of the Ancients,* which to a modern is a tissue of dreary and unprofitable fantasy. Here is a typical passage:

> Pan's crook also contains a fine representation of the ways of nature, which are partly straight and partly crooked; thus the staff, having an extraordinary bend towards the top, denotes that the works of divine providence are generally brought about by remote means or in a circuit, as if somewhat else were intended than the effect produced, as in the sending of Joseph into Egypt etc. So likewise in human government they who sit at the helm manage and wind the people more successfully by pretext and oblique courses than by such as are direct and straight; so that in effect all sceptres are crooked at the top.

Bacon did not mean this to be funny, nor would Milton's contemporaries have taken him otherwise than seriously. Bred to such ways of thinking about allegory, contemporary readers of *Comus* would have been eager to get the hidden meaning of the passage to which the Attendant Spirit calls special notice.

For the above reasons Milton's second important addition to *Comus* would have stood out as a most significant passage, the very reverse of lyrical sedative and able to give a decisive turn to the meaning of the whole poem.

IV. The First Version of *Comus*

Up to the time of *Comus,* Milton's longest poetical exercise had been *L'Allegro* and *Il Penseroso.* These, I have argued, are modelled on the form of the university prolusion or disputation, *L'Allegro* being in praise of day and *Il Penseroso* of night. There is no third section attempting to reconcile the two pleas. It was quite natural that Milton should use the same technique for constructing the first version of *Comus.* There are of course complications, but the centre of the masque is an academic disputation for and against chastity, with the Lady and Comus as disputants. Milton was doing nothing new in treating the topic in this argumentative way; Marlowe, for instance, is much more academic when he makes Leander argue thus with Hero:

> This idol which you term virginity
> Is neither essence subject to the eye,
> No, nor to any one exterior sense,

> Nor hath it any place of residence,
> Nor is't of earth or mould celestial,
> Or capable of any form at all.
> Of that which hath no being, do not boast:
> Things that are not at all, are never lost.

Now the disputant might be called on to support either side of a debated question: he was not expected to say what he happened to think himself. Thus Milton is impartial in his treatment of day and night in *L'Allegro* and *Il Penseroso.* It may be that this habit of impartiality helped him to make his Comus put his case so well. Milton of course takes sides, and the Lady is made to win. But her victory is not at all emphatic; half Comus's plea is unanswered. And the rest of the masque does nothing to answer his declaration that beauty such as the Lady's could be better employed than in spinning or embroidery. It is in structure no more than the coda to a piece of action already concluded.

But though structurally the 1634 *Comus* was an elaborated university disputation, it is in some ways more serious than *L'Allegro* and *Il Penseroso.* Milton has emerged from the relatively personal and local to the public and the traditional. The allegorizing of Circe's herd into human beings subdued by one or other form of sensuality must have begun in Greek times. It was a commonplace of the Christian classicizers; it was a medieval possession through Boethius; and it was popular in the Renaissance. Milton in using a variant of the theme competes with all western literature, just as in choosing the masque form he adopted a standard that had been exalted by the genius of Ben Jonson. He is using public material too in expressing the perplexities and perils of life through the allegory of a dark and tangled forest. In particular he is beginning to compete with Spenser.

Even more important, Milton in *Comus* resembles the greatest Elizabethans in giving us man in his cosmic setting, in his middle position on the great chain of being between the beasts and the angels and attuned in his own microcosm to all the great happenings of the enveloping universe. It is somewhat ironic that of all the characters Comus should do most to help this process. But we must remember that Comus was a god, that the classical gods were orthodox devils in disguise, and that the Devil himself is the chief ape of the Almighty. Comus indeed succeeds wonderfully in expressing the great cosmic commonplaces worthily while giving himself away as an impostor.

> We that are of purer fire
> Imitate the Starry Quire,

Who in their nightly watchfull Sphears,
Lead in swift round the Months and Years.
The Sounds, and Seas with all their finny drove
Now to the Moon in wavering Morrice move,
And on the Tawny Sands and Shelves,
Trip the pert Fairies and the dapper Elves;
By dimpled Brook, and Fountain brim,
The Wood-Nymphs deckt with Daisies trim,
Their merry wakes and pastimes keep.

Comus here speaks of the traditional picture of the whole universe as one great dance, from the highest angel dancing round God's throne to the humble vine wreathing the elm in its own rhythm or the wind blowing the dust in eddies: the picture given with such compelling charm by Sir John Davies in his *Orchestra* or hinted at in Daedalus's first song in Jonson's masque of *Pleasure Reconciled to Virtue.* But what impudence in Comus to claim that his own disorderly revels are tuned to the music of the spheres and keep the measure of the planets and the tides! The imposture is patent. Again, when Comus makes his great speech to the Lady (line 706, 'O foolishnes of men') and praises the bounty of nature, he is in the tradition of the Fathers of the Church praising the wonders of God's creation in their commentaries on *Genesis* or of the medieval theologians advising their disciples to repair the error of their first parents by seeking God in his works, *per speculum creaturarum.* He is also competing with Spenser, who, himself in this same tradition, described the plenitude of God's creation in the canto of the *Faerie Queene* already referred to, with a rapture equalled only by Milton himself when he came to describe the 'enormous bliss' of Eden in *Paradise Lost.* But here again Comus overdoes it, ending his description with a riot of hyperboles that suggest he has been drinking:

Th'earth cumber'd and the wing'd air dark't with plumes;
The herds would over-multitude their Lords,
The Sea o'refraught would swell, and th'unsought diamonds
Would so emblaze the forhead of the Deep,
And so bestudd with Stars, that they below
Would grow inur'd to light, and com at last
To gaze upon the Sun with shameless brows.

Comus then is more serious in substance than *L'Allegro* and *Il Penseroso* and as such demanded a more emphatic conclusion than the 1634 version provided.

V. The Final Version of *Comus*

The changes Milton made in the 1637 version mainly concern the central theme of chastity. And I must comment on the doctrine of chastity as he conceived it. We must remember that chastity had a wider meaning in Milton's day than in ours. It meant monogamy as well as virginity. The matter is made particularly clear in a poem well known to Milton, Phineas Fletcher's *Purple Island*.[2] Among the various mental qualities personified and described allegorically in this poem are twin ladies: Agnia and Parthenia.[3] Agnia, who is Chastity in the married, is mild and modest, and she wears no armour.

> Upon her arched brow unarmed Love
> Triumphing sat in peaceful victory.

Her emblem is a pair of turtle doves. She receives four stanzas of description. Parthenia, who gets much more attention, is Virginity, or Chastity in the single; and she is militant.

> With her, her sister went, a warlike maid,
> Parthenia, all in steel and gilded arms;
> In needle's stead a mighty spear she sway'd,
> With which in bloody fields and fierce alarms
> The boldest champion she down would bear,
> And like a thunderbolt wide passage tear,
> Flinging all to the earth with her enchanted spear.

She is dazzlingly fair, hotly pursued, but chooses a heavenly not an earthly lover.

> A thousand knights woo'd her with busy pain,
> To thousand she her virgin grant deni'd,
> Although her dear-sought love to entertain
> They all their wit and all their strength appli'd:
> Yet in her heart love close his sceptre sway'd,
> That to an heavenly spouse her thoughts betray'd,
> Where she a maiden wife might live and wifely maid.

It is Parthenia that Milton celebrates in his first version of *Comus* through the Elder Brother's speech. Chastity there is like the huntress

[2] Published in 1633 but written earlier. Giles and Phineas Fletcher were closely connected with Cambridge. Milton would certainly have read the *Purple Island* in manuscript years before he wrote *Comus*.

[3] Canto X, stanzas 24–40.

Diana, like Minerva with her Gorgon-shield, both militant goddesses, and in the end she gives her votaries peculiar powers.

In the revised poem the lines added to the Lady's speech are a fierce defence of chastity. And beyond doubt she is Parthenia. It is the sage and serious doctrine of *virginity* that she defends. And she is extremely fierce, speaking of her rapt spirits being kindled to a flame of sacred vehemence. She is indeed Diana or Minerva in action. Chastity too is a mystery, able to give her votaries supernatural powers. It is all the more surprising therefore that the addition to the epilogue, concerning the Garden of Adonis, should be, as it is, opposed to the strict doctrine of virginity.

In expounding its sense I shall have to consider the whole epilogue; for the added lines put a different interpretation on the existing ones they followed. The Attendant Spirit begins by saying that he will return to a realm where among other denizens are Hesperus and his three daughters; and by so doing he invites his contemporary audience to exercise their allegorical tact, for the Gardens of Hesperus were rich in mythological allegory. Research could probably unearth a wide variety of meaning put on the Gardens of Hesperus with their golden-fruited tree, which a dragon guarded and round which Hesperus's three daughters sang their songs. But there were two prevailing meanings: the paradisiac and the erotic. It was thought that the myth was a pagan reminiscence of the Garden of Eden. In Raleigh's words:

> So also was the fiction of those golden apples kept by the dragon taken from the serpent which tempted Eva. So was Paradise itself transported out of Asia into Africa and the Garden of the Hesperides.[4]

Alternatively the golden apples were symbols of fertility and love. Milton shows a knowledge of both interpretations in *Comus.* In the lines excised from the Trinity Manuscript after the fourth line of the poem the Hesperian Gardens are purely paradisiac. Here is the passage in its setting:

> Before the starrie threshold of Joves Court
> My mansion is, where those immortal shapes
> Of bright aereall spirits live insphear'd
> In regions mild of calme and serene aire,
> Amidst th'Hesperian gardens, on whose bancks
> Bedew'd with nectar and celestiall songs,
> Aeternall roses grow, and hyacinth,

[4] *History of the World,* i, 6, 4.

> And fruits of golden rind, on whose faire tree
> The scalie-harnest dragon ever keeps
> His uninchanted eye.

But in the Second Brother's speech (lines 393–7) the erotic symbolism is obvious:

> But beauty like the fair Hesperian Tree
> Laden with blooming gold, had need the guard
> Of dragon watch with uninchanted eye,
> To save her blossoms, and defend her fruit
> From the rash hand of bold Incontinence.

When, therefore, Milton's readers met the Hesperian Gardens in the epilogue of *Comus* they would be on the alert for allegory and, though ready for pretty well anything, would be especially ready for a paradisiac or an erotic significance or for both at once. Now in the earlier version they would have found only the paradisiac significance to the point: their expectation of the other would just be allowed to drop. But not so in the revised version: there the plain fertility symbolism of the Garden of Adonis would realize the expectation of an erotic significance in the other mythical garden. In fact the whole of the revised epilogue would be concerned with love, as well as with some form of Paradise.

We are at last in a position to examine the meaning which Milton, through Spenser, put on the Garden of Adonis.

The Spenserian episode of the Garden of Adonis occurs in that great unit of the *Faerie Queene,* the third and fourth books, that deals with every form of love from bestiality to the most refined spiritual affection. Its immediate context is the story of Belphoebe and Amoret. These two were twins, daughters of Crysogone, who conceived them miraculously from sunbeams and bore them miraculously in a sleep without pain. Girls from the train of Venus found them while their mother still slept and took them away. Diana adopted Belphoebe and brought her up in perfect maidenhead till she developed into a bright fierce virgin (the plain prototype of Phineas Fletcher's Parthenia). Venus adopted Amoret and brought her up in the inner sanctuary of the Garden of Adonis.

> Hither great Venus brought this infant fair,
> The younger daughter of Crysogone,
> And unto Psyche with great trust and care
> Committed her, yfostered to be
> And trained up in true feminity;
> Who no less carefully her tendered

> Than her own daughter Pleasure, to whom she
> Made her companion and her lessoned
> In all the lore of love and goodly womanhead.

After this education she became the

> loadstar of all chast affection
> To all fair ladies that do live on ground.

She was in fact the pattern of perfect married affection, and appears again as Fletcher's Agnia. In the end she marries Scudamour, and, bred as she was in the very origin and seminary of all earthly life, she was plainly destined to carry out God's command of 'increase and multiply' with a thoroughness calculated to satisfy the exacting procreative standards of Elizabethan England. But that is one side of the Garden of Adonis only. It was in days of Eden that God pronounced his command and in some sort this garden is heaven too. It is Psyche herself, the immortal soul, that teaches Amoret her lore; even though that lore is in part earthly. Like the soul the Garden of Adonis is the great meeting-place of the temporal and the eternal, of the shifting phenomena of nature and the eternal law under which these phenomena operate.

VI. The Meaning of the Additions

What then did Milton mean by referring to this familiar but complicated tissue of erotic lore? May he not have meant to give the whole poem a new turn and in particular to settle the debate between Comus and the Lady?

Comus had spoken magnificently but perversely of the bounty of God. The Lady in reply had countered the perversity by a plea of moderation and of equal distribution, yet in so doing had shown less sense of that bounty than her adversary. The Attendant Spirit by mentioning the Garden of Adonis, the very workshop of nature, gives the solution. This garden has all the bounty described by Comus and all the comeliness and order insisted on by the Lady. Both disputants are shown partly right and partly wrong.

Then for the second topic, chastity. The Lady thinks herself cast for the part of Belphoebe or Parthenia; Comus would like to turn her into a Hellenore, a wanton. That is what he means when he says to her after praising her beauty,

> There was another meaning in these gifts,

and that is what she understands him to mean, and what Milton in his first version meant him to mean and her to understand him to mean. But later Milton saw that both the Lady and Comus were wrong: that there *was* another meaning in these gifts, but that it was not Comus's. The meaning was marriage. The Lady was not really cast for Belphoebe but for Amoret, not for Parthenia but for Agnia. And he conveys his correction—too obliquely for some tastes—by the Attendant Spirit's references to the Garden of Adonis where Belphoebe and Parthenia were out of place.

The gain is great. The ignorance of Comus and the Lady, explained above, becomes dramatic irony, and the whole play instead of being an unresolved debate is given a shape and a solution. The play concerns chastity and the Lady is the heroine. Comus advocates incontinence, Acrasia; the Lady advocates abstinence. The Attendant Spirit gives the solution, advocating the Aristotelian middle course, which for the Lady is the right one; and it is marriage. This perhaps is putting the matter too baldly. The Lady's resistance to Comus is not meant to be bad, as Comus's seductions are. It is good; it may even be an act of a probation: but it is not final. The setting is aristocratic; the Lady, though but young, will one day be a great lady. She must take her place in society and do what is expected of her. And by having triumphed as Belphoebe she is free to proceed to her true part of Amoret.

This interpretation is the more probable when we remember the whole aristocratic setting of the masque-form and the specimen of it to which Milton owed most, Jonson's *Pleasure Reconciled to Virtue.* This figures Hercules routing Comus, 'the god of cheer or the belly', after having killed Antaeus, and crowned for his pains by Hermes. After such labours of virtue, pleasure is no longer inept, but Virtue and Pleasure may be reconciled. A troup of twelve masquers (one of them the Prince, son of Hesperus, King of the West, *alias* James I) issue from their home in Mount Atlas, where they are being educated in austere virtue by Daedalus the wise. They are permitted to dance an allegorical measure with twelve noble ladies, Virtue and Pleasure again being reconciled. But they must return to their hill of superior and difficult education. Finally Virtue is praised in words which Milton remembered when he wrote *Comus:*

> She, she it is in darkness shines,
> 'Tis she that still herself refines
> By her own light to every eye;
> More seen, more known, when Vice stands by;

> And though a stranger here on earth,
> In heaven she hath her right of birth.

Milton's possible debt to certain details of Jonson's masque is well known, but he may have got a more general aid from it. The theme itself, the clear firm outline of the structure, the sense of social responsibility, may well have stimulated him to mend the simplicity of the first prolusional draft. In a way by his alterations Milton approximates his theme to Jonson's; only the title of *Virtue Reconciled to Pleasure* would be more appropriate. In Jonson the emphasis is on the pleasure with the warning note that the conjunction, however legitimate in its proper seasons, can be but temporary. In Milton the emphasis is on the trial and the struggle, through the winning of which Virtue may legitimately be reconciled with Pleasure, the reconciliation being just hinted at the end.

Then there is Fletcher's *Faithful Shepherdess,* of which there are various echoes in *Comus* and which, republished in 1629 and acted at Court on January 6, 1634, with Inigo Jones's setting, must have been known to Milton's audience as well as to himself. This pastoral deals with virginity, wantonness, and especially marriage; for though Clorin, the maid whose virginity gives her special powers, keeps her state for good, the action ends generally with marriage. If Milton, in writing or rewriting *Comus,* had the *Faithful Shepherdess* in mind, he would be ready to include married as well as unmarried chastity in his subject and to assume a readiness for such inclusion in his readers. He could thus afford, if it suited him, to refer to the married state in an indirect, allusive manner.

VII. Epilogue

Aubrey records that Milton was 'extreme pleasant in conversation but Satyricall'. If Milton watched the performance of his own masque (slightly garbled to suit the music and cut to suit the actors) he may have felt some ironical amusement at witnessing an ordinary little girl sustaining the tremendous part of Belphoebe. If so, he may have felt even then the possible irony in the line

> There was another meaning in these gifts,

and have had suggested to him the changes he ultimately made. Moreover, the Earl and Countess of Bridgewater, for whom he wrote the masque, were themselves the parents of an immense family of four sons and eleven daughters. The Garden of Adonis was their spiritual home.

Was it not the spiritual home of their daughter Alice, too, who took the part of the Lady? All this is pure romancing, but if it happened to be true, Milton was not the only ironist. For all his added hints about wedlock, fate contrived that the Lady Alice Egerton, though she married, deceased without issue.

POSTSCRIPT

When I wrote on the action of *Comus* I had not read A. S. P. Woodhouse's profound and interesting article, *The Argument of Milton's 'Comus'* (*University of Toronto Quarterly,* vol. xi, pp. 46–71). Much of this article concerns other matters than have concerned me, but Woodhouse agrees with me on the importance of the Spenser allusion in the epilogue while differing on the use he thinks Milton made of it.

On the interpretation of Spenser's Garden of Adonis and of what both pairs in it (Venus and Adonis, Cupid and Psyche) mean we are agreed. He wrote (pp. 68–9) [p. 39 herein]:

> For Spenser the story of Venus and Adonis represents the spirit of love and the principle of generation operating throughout the natural order; and the story of Cupid and Psyche should somehow represent the same spirit and principle in their specifically human application, which is marriage with its productiveness and legitimate pleasure, opposed . . . to the illegitimate pleasures of Acrasia, at war with productiveness.

Woodhouse thinks that Milton accepts Spenser's presentation of the Garden of Adonis as far as nature is concerned. That garden refutes Comus's bogus plea for the virtue of nature's bounty, as it confutes Acrasia. And here again we agree. But he thinks Milton's Cupid and Psyche different from Spenser's and that unlike Spenser Milton does not refer in the epilogue to marriage. In support he points to Milton's Cupid being *celestial.* Cupid is not the marriage-god but the Love-god of Plato. The trouble here is that his and Psyche's children are the very un-Platonic pair, Youth and Joy. For this trouble Woodhouse has an ingenious explanation. Now Milton's *Joy* is so plain an equivalent of Spenser's *Pleasure,* and Spenser's Pleasure so patently represents the marriage-bed, that I find any other explanation than an erotic one very hard to accept. On the other hand it is not easy to give a predominantly human significance to Milton's *celestial* Cupid who sits far above his mother. But one *can* say that Venus and Adonis represent life below the human and the reproduction of such life, while Cupid, representing human love, is thus above Venus and is celestial because the human soul is a piece of divinity. There are difficulties in any explanation, but the whole trend of the Spenserian original in its proper context is so eminently concerned with marriage that I find it hard to believe that Milton in recalling it could have gone so flatly against that prime concern.

With Woodhouse's contention that Milton in *Comus* was distinguishing between the realm of nature and the realm of grace I incline to agree. But I cannot agree that the last three couplets of the masque ('Mortals that would follow me', etc.) refer to the realm of grace specifically. They do not crown thought; they dismiss the audience. And the tone of such a dismissal simply dictates that the sentiment expressed should be general. The freedom that virtue brings in these lines is neither the freedom from the blows of fate achieved by the virtue of the stoic nor the specifically Christian freedom, but just freedom. Woodhouse's argument rests considerably on these last lines; deprived of this support, I think it is still valid but in a less precise way than he makes out. In that less precise form I do not think his notion either militates against or confirms the notion I have put forward in my essay.

J. C. Maxwell in *The Pseudo-Problem of 'Comus'* (*Cambridge Journal,* i, pp. 376–80) thinks that I complicate unnecessarily, that there is no reference to marriage, and that too much is made of the doctrine of virginity in the poem. Of course it is impossible to *prove* a reference to marriage. All one can do is to repeat that Milton introduced into the 1637 version in a very emphatic place, and in that place called special attention to ('List, mortals, if your ears be true'), an unmistakable allusion to a famous canto of Spenser in which the two dominant themes are the virtuous bounty of nature and the congruence with it of human marriage. Further, Milton knew and admired Spenser and considered himself Spenser's successor. It is unlikely that Milton should have ignored one of the two prime significances of the passage to which he alludes.

As to the doctrine of virginity Maxwell thinks that the prime subject is the test not of virginity but of virtue. It is quite true that when the Attendant Spirit presents the young people to their parents he praises their general steadfastness and that the last lines of all praise virtue. But there has been no question of the brothers' virginity, and to mention virginity when they and their sister are presented would be inept, while to generalize a narrower theme at the end is a matter of politeness to the audience, of making the special theme apply to them all. The central theme is the test of virginity. When Comus praises the Lady's beauty and suggests that it has a meaning, and then presses her to drink, are we to conclude that she looked, in his opinion, as if her destiny was merely to get drunk? It is a virgin, Sabrina (and her virginity is stressed), who has to release the Lady. And behind Sabrina there is Fletcher's *Faithful Shepherdess,* where the theme of virginity and its potency is prominent—even to a distressing degree. In one passage Maxwell advances to show that *virtue* is the main theme (the Elder Brother's 'Vertue may be assail'd, but never hurt', line 589), the word, in the context, bears its possible restricted sense of chastity as well as its more general sense. And why, after all, should Milton not have used the trial of virginity for his central theme? Quite apart from the *Faithful Shepherdess,* its ancestry goes back to the legends of the Saints, while for its dramatic exploitation there are the plays of Roswitha.

Maxwell is of course right in bringing forward the danger of reading too much into a poem, one of the besetting vices of contemporary criticism. But scepticism too may have its own peculiar dangers.

Kenneth Muir touched on the subject of this essay in *Penguin New Writing,* 24, pp. 141–3. He wrote: 'Milton chose neither side in the debate; the licence of Comus is contrasted with the limitations of the Lady'.

D. C. Allen's noteworthy article on *Comus* in *English Literary History,* xvi, 104–19 [reprinted in a revised version, from *The Harmonious Vision,* pp. 58–71 herein], did not reach me till this book was in proof. Since it concerns the success or failure of the total poem and not the more restricted theme of the poem's action, it is really outside the scope of my paper.

The Higher Compromise: "On the Morning of Christ's Nativity" and a Mask

Don Cameron Allen

I know few better seventeenth century illustrations of an attempted reconciliation of opposites that failed than Milton's *Comus*. Beyond this, it is a superior example of poetic synthesis as it was understood at this time, and because of this, it has been only partially understood ever since. Yet, if we read the poem with an ear sensitive to catch the manifold nuances of the young Milton's already mature recollections, if we attempt to feel the poem with our sensibilities sharpened as much as they can be by the more central myths of that century, if we do all this and at the same time avoid the common inclination to regard the poem as a didactic allegory written by a precocious moralist, we shall see *Comus* as something quite different from what we thought it to be and we shall begin to understand Milton's ill success.

Unblinded by traditional preconceptions, we shall notice that this poem is an attempt to establish a *concors discors* on an elaborate scale, that it is essentially an attempted reconciliation of disparate parts, but since it is a frustrated reconciliation—one of those twisted intellectual-emotional experiences indigenous in this generation—it eventuates in confusion rather than in harmony. Unlike the eighteenth century, the age of Milton had not yet learned the fascination that the unharmonized juxtaposition of contraries has for the reasonable man. In its all too cursory pursuit of truth by the paradox, it did much to establish the

Reprinted by permission of the publisher from *The Harmonious Vision: Studies in Milton's Poetry* (Baltimore, Md.: The Johns Hopkins Press, 1954), pp. 24–40.

rational methodology and even the aesthetic comportment of the Enlightenment, but I do not think that the men of this time employed the paradox with a conscious sense of system. For them the paradox was at one and the same time a form of youthful sophistry that could be catalogued as juvenalia and a keen implement of expository understatement; seldom was it a process, as it certainly was in the next century, of convicting oneself of orthodoxy. It was "a signe of admiration," [1] as Puttenham called it, rather than a test, as Cicero thought, "of whether a matter of worth to the learned has any common sense value." [2] But we shall be helped in unriddling the problem of *Comus* if, before we come to a close examination of the masque, we observe Milton's poetic procedure in his most perfect early work.

The conflict between the aesthetic and the intellectual daemons that fought for superior utterance in much of Milton's poetry may be first seen in the moving shadows of the "Nativity Ode." The theme is not original, nor is the poem, in spite of the epodic arrangement of the strophes, exactly an ode. Nevertheless, it is by far the most luxurious of English verses on the Incarnation in its erudition and the most sensitively felt. Before it, the prior offerings of Jonson, Drummond, and Beaumont fade into the commonplaceness of theological cliché. The more original poem of Southwell, which compresses its emotion within the narrow channels of gnomic expression, is companionable mainly in terms of a temperamental emblem. However, the power of this poem does not spring from a true reconciliation of its intellectual and emotional disunities, but rather from the fact that they are not reconciled at all, or, better still, that they are erased in a unity of a higher order. When we observe the conflict in its separateness, it seems like a tug-of-war between teams of gigantic stallions—the thesis and the antithesis pull oppositely, the synonym and antonym stretch each other, the myth dashes itself into divergent metaphors. That we accept the amazing procedure as artistically valid even to the extent that we overlook or apologize for such technical flaws as "When such musicke sweet," or the prolix roll call of the gods, or the badly rendered metaphysical excesses, demonstrates the immediate and isolateral reaction of our own discordant organs of perception to this conflict. It is, to use a favorite Renaissance figure, as a struck lyre that sets all others in vibration. But a discord will do this as well as a harmony.

The "Ode" begins with an induction in which time is negated so that

[1] *The Arte of English Poesie* (Cambridge, 1936), 226.
[2] *Paradoxa Stoicorum,* 4.

the discord between the past and the present, which we plainly understand, may be altered into a concord of eternity, or into an essence of time, which is timelessness. To this end the poem is carefully dated. The title and the induction inform us that it was written in the small hours of December 25, 1620. So that we shall be certain of this fact Milton reinforms us in the sixth elegy: "Illa sub auroram lux mihi prima tulit." This is a matter that Milton does not want the reader to miss because he is about to invent the fable that this fact is untrue, that the real time is the last hour of the pre-Christian era and that he is himself present in a land of palms and snow, a seventeenth century interloper between the events of the Nativity and the Epiphany. This is the temporal conflict, but what Milton does is to reconcile it by pressing towards the eternal consequences of the Incarnation. By annulling the chronology of this event, he extracts the everlasting from the conflict between the past and the present. This is the first higher compromise.

In the "Hymn" there are two central contentions: the minor dissonance between the two aspects of Nature, and the major dissonance between the two kinds of harmony. These contentions are emphasized by the fact that the "Hymn" falls naturally into three sections: stanzas I–VII, VIII–XVIII, and XIX–XXVIII. The symbolic narrative of the sun (embodying the pun familiar to Donne and Herbert) controls the movement of the first section and binds it to the time theme of the induction. As the paramour of pagan Nature, the sun introduces the theme of the first section, and as the discarded and abashed lover, staying in its road to re-emphasize the time motif of the induction, it makes a limitary conclusion. The contrast between the flagrancy of pagan Nature prior to the Incarnation and the subsequent shamefastness of the same personification is implied in the first two stanzas. The reconciliation here takes the form of Redemption. Nature, whose biography is that of the Magdalene—an intrinsically baroque identification—is redeemed by the greater Sun. Hence the redemption that arises from this conflict looks forward to the redemption of man in the latter stanzas, just as Peace, the instrument of the redemption, the *Concordia Christi,* looks ahead to the basic conflict between the *ἁρμονία Christianis* and the *consonantia pagana.* The rescue of Nature by the Peace of the greater Sun from the wanton embraces of the lesser sun is memorialized in the fifteenth stanza, for we know that she is to be registered among the daughters of God just as the woman taken in adultery was placed in the company of saints.

The conflict between Christian and pagan harmony that governs the second and third sections makes the "Hymn" an artistic wonder. Man enters at the beginning of the second section, but he enters to provide an audience for the sacred music which has not been heard since Eve succumbed to the blandishments of Satan. Man seems, in fact, to be almost out of place in this *dramatis personae* which is evenly divided between personified symbols and beings of a supernatural yet mythological order. But the interesting thing is not that man is attentive to the heavenly choir, but that Milton succeeds in effecting an artistic harmony while describing a spiritual disharmony. When he contemplates the difference between the pagan and the Christian world, he finds, like Plato's friend Archytas, a musical explanation. This is totally fitting, for Milton, as a good Graecist, certainly knew that the definition of *ποιητής* expunges the difference between poetry and music. Likewise he is not unaware that the *concordia* that he will now explicate poetically is the linguistic equivalent of the *pax* of the first section.

It is not surprising to discover that Milton's description of Christian harmony begins with a heraldic blending of clearly recognizable emblems: the circle, the globe, light. By the trick of the oxymoron they all become music, not a music of annotation but the essence of music. To this is joined the intermediate music of the spheres and the lower chant that the poet is composing. For Milton realized, as did the authors of the Psalms, that the music of the creatures was a required melody for the bass of Heaven's organ; and he knew, too, that at the moment of the Incarnation, the harmony was without flaw for the first time since the springtime of Creation. Distemperature comes again with the death of God and then the full music cannot be heard until after the Day of Wrath. This is the meaning of this section.

While the integral metaphor of Christian harmony as Milton conceived it has strong elements of pagan Pythagoreanism and while he must have known how often *concordia, consensus,* and *consonantia* appear as moral doublets in classical letters, yet he was unable, even while admiring, to perceive a premier harmony in the ancient philosophy that was the intellectual extension of pagan theology. Throughout his poetry, and especially in *Paradise Regained,* a discrimination is carefully made between Christian and pagan philosophy. Plato and Seneca are great thinkers and noble men when they stand against a non-Christian façade, but they dissolve into nothingness before the Christian revelation. We have, as a result, in the third section of the

"Hymn," a pageant of gods drawn from the Old Testament and costumed by Selden.[3] They have their music, too, but it is a music best described by the "horrid clang" of the Last Judgment. The "Cymbals ring" and call "the grisly king"; and the "dismal dance," which is an awkward contrast to that of the angels, makes their ceremony more dreary.[4] These phrases, together with the cacophonous "Timbrel'd Anthems dark" of the devotees of Osiris, are inserted by Milton to suggest the nature of pagan music now "dumm" before the majesty of the Incarnate song. Hence from this conflict between the limited music of the Church Militant and the discordant melodies of pagan theology, Milton anticipates the multitoned yet perfectly matched harmony of the Church Triumphant. This is the third and greatest compromise.

The "Ode" has, then, three series of poetically expressed contrasts, and from each of them Milton draws a compromise that is far more splendid than the parts conflicting. From the variance between the past and the present, he extracts the solution of timelessness; from that between Nature abandoned and Nature redeemed, he creates a Nature as immutable and untarnished as Faith, Hope, and Peace; from the disagreement between pagan and Christian harmony, he derives the harmony of God. Underlying all of this is the conventional modulation of the universal and the particular which is signified by the movement from the abstract character of Peace to her concrete manifestations, a modulation that is also orchestrated by the epodic contraction and expansion of the metrical line. The result of this artistic procedure is a magnificent unity that greatly affects us.

This method of displaying the opposed unrealities and of drawing from the opposition a high poetic reality is a basic Miltonic technique. It is one of the more obvious methods of the greater poems, and the first two books of *Paradise Lost* afford us an important instance of its use. But Milton is not always successful in this process of bridging the chaos between opposed elements, and it is my contention that his failure to effect a compromise that is both poetically and intellectually greater

[3] The limiting descriptions of the gods probably comes from the *De dis Syris syntagmata II,* published a dozen years before this poem was written.

[4] The pertinent passage on the dance is *PL,* V. 618–27: That day, as other solemn days, they spent / In song and dance about the sacred Hill, / Mystical dance, which yonder starry Sphere / Of Planets and of fixt in all her Wheels / Resembles nearest, mazes intricate, / Eccentric, intervolv'd, yet regular / Then most, when most irregular they seem: / And in thir motions harmony Divine / So smooths her charming tones, that God's own ear / Listens delighted.

than the warring opposites is what causes us so much trouble in the elucidation of *Comus.*

The conflicts in *Comus* are both extrinsic and intrinsic—in structure, in pre-texts, in theme, and in orchestration. They are conflicts that for many reasons Milton could not pacify by a higher compromise. For this reason the poem fails and we are baffled. To begin with, we should notice that the poem is not a masque at all. The bright critical eye of Samuel Johnson took this in at once. The poem, he said, is "deficient" as a drama. It is not a masque because it is not "given up to all the freaks of the imagination." The action, though human, is improbable and unreasonable. The dialogue is not composed of speeches but "declamations deliberately composed and formally repeated, on a moral question." The audience views the work, as a consequence, "without passion, without anxiety." "It is a drama in the epic style, inelegantly splendid and tediously instructive." [5]

All attempts to explain the exterior structure of *Comus* since 1780 have been answers to Dr. Johnson. Warton replied in a note prefixed to his edition of the *Poems:*

> We must not read Comus with an eye to the stage, or with the expectation of dramatic propriety. . . . Comus is a suite of Speeches, not interesting by discrimination of character; not conveying a variety of incidents, not gradually exciting curiosity; but perpetually attracting attention by sublime sentiment, by fanciful imagery of the richest vein, by an exuberance of picturesque description, poetical allusion, and ornamental expression. While it widely departs from the grotesque anomalies of the Mask now in fashion, it does not nearly approach to the natural constitution of a regular play, . . . This is the first time the old English Mask was in some degree reduced to the principles and form of rational composition. . . . On the whole, whether Comus be or be not deficient as a drama, whether it is considered as an Epic drama, a series of lines, a Mask, or a poem, I am of opinion, that our author is here only inferiour to his own Paradise Lost.[6]

Warton, as we see, is as obfuscated as Johnson. *Comus* is not a masque; it is not a play. It may be a drama in the epic style, a rational masque, a suite of verses, or a poem. It is in the last category that the nineteenth century placed the work and so avoided the issue about its structure. Macaulay thought of it as a series of "Majestic soliloquies" and lyrics that are spoiled by the dramatic passages. "It is when Milton escapes

[5] *Lives of the English Poets* (Oxford, 1905), I, 168–69.

[6] Thomas Warton, ed., *Poems upon Several Occasions* (London, 1785), 262–63.

from the shackles of the dialogue, when he is discharged from the labour of uniting two incongruous styles, when he is at liberty to indulge his choral raptures without reserve, that he rises even above himself." Macaulay is truly running for a safe wicket and Walter Bagehot is hard on his heels.

> *Comus* has no longer the peculiar exceptional popularity which it used to have. We can talk without general odium of its defects. Its characters are nothing, its sentiments are tedious, its story is not interesting. But it is only when we have realized the magnitude of its deficiencies that we comprehend the peculiarity of its greatness. Its power is in its style.[7]

The observations of Macaulay and Bagehot are, I think, born of an attempt to side-step the real problem of the external structure of *Comus;* yet in modern times we have gone still further and listed the poem among the moralities, contending that it is a sort of belated *Hickscorner* or *Lusty Juventus.* We have failed to notice the apologetic testimony of the Latin motto, or of the variants between the printed poem and the manuscripts which reflect Milton's own dissatisfaction with the work. Granted that we do not know a great deal about the masque and that those which we possess are essentially royal entertainments, still we must confess that *Comus* is so different from these as to be almost another thing. It is much longer than the masque as written by Jonson or Daniel; its cast of speaking characters is much smaller; its locale of action is much less fantastic; its plot, though not exactly more elaborate, is more tense; its theme is more serious; it is totally wanting in humorousness; and its emphasis is more on dramatic crisis than on spectacle, dance, costume, and even singing. We must also notice that it was given in a narrower hall than the great Jacobean masques, and that it concludes with a mock water pageant that is more properly part of an outdoor entertainment. The want of all these qualities disestablishes *Comus* as a true masque, although it does not make it into a drama. Nonetheless, I think we can say that Johnson was right and Warton wrong when the former criticized *Comus* as a drama and the latter denied the validity of this criticism.

To criticize *Comus* as a drama would be to do no more than extend Johnson's remarks, and Tillyard, who has as fine a sense of style as any academic critic of our time, has already made some telling observations about this problem. In addition, Tillyard has also very perceptively pointed out that the poetic texture of the masque is mixed in a fashion

[7] *Literary Studies* (London, 1879), I, 219.

that suggests confusion rather than the more desirable quality of variety. *Comus,* as he sees it, is a sequence of poetical experiments. The subsurface technique is Arcadian, but there are also lapses into the manner of Elizabethan dramatists, into pastoral expression, into pure poetry, into Jacobean phrasing, and, in one of the excised manuscript passages, into Restoration realism.[8]

But the patchwork of styles does not, it seems to me, end here because the pallium of classical tragedy covers the whole poem. The masque opens with a prologuizer like Polydore's ghost of the *Hecuba;* and though we should expect the Lady and the Brothers—if the theme is what the commentators say it is—to enter next, we have instead the antistrophic choral of Comus which is a modified form of an antimasque. We then have the declamation of the Lady which ends with a lyric followed by the stichomythic section between her and Comus. Other remembrances of an antique nature assail us as we follow the unfolding of the masque, which concludes, we must admit, with as fine an example of the *deus ex machina* as any Athenian could devise. So in its external structure *Comus* is a mélange of various tendencies and styles that never merge into anything intensely organic.

Even if we admit that Milton was handicapped by the occasional requirements of the Bridgewater family and by the physical limitations of the hall in Ludlow Castle, I still cannot see that these restrictions necessarily resulted in attempts that fell short of compromise. Having previously written the *Arcades,* a true masque, Milton was not inexpert in the formal technique. Here he intended to transcend current practice by attempting to create a more dramatic form of short entertainment; and though *Comus* has held the stage better than any other masque, it is, nonetheless, an error in artistic judgment, for a conflict between exterior form and style seldom results in a valid compromise. From a compromise between a masque and a short musical drama, one gets either an unstylized masque or an undramatic play. We miss the formality and the ritual of the masque, and we have a play totally wanting in suspense and character alteration. This is the first attempted reconciliation in *Comus* and it fails; but the unsuccessful pursuit of artistic compromise is further verified by the two pre-texts upon which the theme is founded: the Circe story annotated by Peele's version of the Child Roland legend and modified by Spenser's account of Acrasia and Busyrane, and Geoffrey of Monmouth's eponymic history of Sabrina.

[8] *Milton* (London, 1934), 66–75.

The Circe legend is introduced by the Spirit, who is really the Hermes of Homer in seventeenth century dress. The two brothers are composites of the Wandering Knight, of Ulysses, of Guyon, and of Britomart. Comus is, of course, the son and heir of Circe and the brother of Ariosto's Alcina, Trissino's Acratia, Tasso's Armida, and Spenser's mistress of the Bower of Bliss. The Circe story was authoritatively interpreted during the Renaissance as an allegory of the contention between Reason and Nature.[9] Spenser uses it in the Guyon story as an allegory of the conflict between Temperance and its opposite; whereas the story of the enchantment in the tale of Britomart is an allegory of chastity. The *Old Wives Tale,* which Milton follows so closely, has no special purpose beyond that of the satirically horrific. By attempting to unite all of these motifs with their diverse interpretations, Milton obtains a macaronic translation. We notice, too, that the Miltonic solution does not follow the traditional working-out of the pre-text. Ulysses subdues Circe; Guyon brings down the Bower of Bliss and traps the enchantress; Britomart breaks the power of Busyrane and rescues Amoret. Even the Wandering Knight, assisted by the ghost of Jack, procures the defeat and death of Sacrapant. The brothers, though they have the Heaven-sent advice of the Spirit and the Homeric moly, do not succeed so well as their literary precursors. Comus escapes with his crew of men-beasts; the Lady remains frozen to her chair. The fact that Milton again is trying to combine the masque and the drama makes in the case of this pre-text an unsolved conflict between well-established dramatic and allegorical traditions. Something not unlike this happens to the pre-text of Sabrina.

I have a notion that when the masque was first commissioned Milton intended to write a true masque based on the Sabrina story. The Bridgewater estate was washed by a tributary of the Severn, and everyone living in the district must have known how the river came by its name. Some years before the masque was written, Drayton had elaborated the myth poetically in the *Poly-Olbion* and added a touch of pathos, suggested perhaps by the account in the *Mirror for Magistrates,* to the death of Locrine's natural daughter.[10] But the Sabrina of *Comus* is not the Sabrina of Geoffrey of Monmouth or of Milton's later *History of Britain.* The story as Geoffrey and as, subsequently, Milton recounts it is that Gwendolen, having defeated Locrine and captured his mistress Estreldis and her daughter Sabrina, caused the daughter, offspring of adultery, to be cast in the river and ordered that thereafter the river be

[9] N. Comes, *Mythologiae libri* (Patavia, 1616), 309.
[10] *Works* (Oxford, 1933), IV, 114–15.

called by the name of the unfortunate child.[11] Caught once again by the requirements of the allegory and by the need for a compliment, Milton is forced to change the first pre-text so that he can bring in the Sabrina myth and then he is forced to alter the myth to fit the revised first pre-text. In all previous accounts except "The sad virgin innocent of all" of the second book of the *Faerie Queene,* the emphasis is placed on the betrayal of Gwendolen and this is Milton's emphasis in the *History of Britain.* Here it is changed. Sabrina becomes "a virgin pure" and a "guiltless dame" who, flying the "mad pursuit of her enraged stepdam," commends "her fair innocence" to the river. Milton converts what was thought to be history into saint's legend and governs it in part with the accounts of Circe's anointing of Ulysses and of Florimel in the sea caverns of Proteus. This modification, though suggestive, can only bother those who have the original history in their heads. It is the intellectual texture of the masque that baffles readers on all levels, and it is Milton's failure to bring about a higher compromise again that makes for this difficulty.

Although a number of essays have been written about *Comus,* Woodhouse[12] alone has made an intelligent attempt to untangle its meaning. In his cogently written study he describes the several floors of meaning that we should see in the masque. The central conflict, according to Woodhouse, is between Nature and Grace; Temperance and Continence are the virtues rallied under the first, Virginity under the second. Sharing in both and connecting them in this pagan-Christian duel is the essential doctrine of Chastity. There is, I think, little doubt about the correctness of most of Woodhouse's analyses, but again no effective compromises are made and it does not seem to me that Milton's artistic emphasis coincides with his intended moral emphasis. A close examination of the broad structure of the dramatic movement is likely to support this contention.

After the opening chorals, the two brothers enter. The Second Brother is in a fret for fear that his sister has fallen victim to either the hunger of an animal or the lust of a wild man. "Within the direful grasp / Of savage hunger, or of savage heat?" The First Brother hypothesizes on the nature of her virtue and recommends the wilderness as a place for moral contemplation. The Second Brother admits that all of this may be

[11] See Geoffrey of Monmouth, II, 2–5; *History of Britain, Works* (New York, 1932), X, 15.

[12] "The Argument of Milton's *Comus,*" *University of Toronto Quarterly* (1941–42), XI, 46–71.

true for the lonely anchorite, but he reminds his elder that the Lady is beautiful and, consequently, a desirable prey for the incontinent. The First Brother says that she has hidden strength, and the Second Brother asks whether this is the strength of Heaven. The First Brother then lectures on chastity and virginity, virtues defended by both classical allusions and angelic guardians. His homily is belied almost at once by the Spirit, who—in spite of his announcement in the prologue that he is sent as the "defence and guard" of wanderers in Comus's territory—is forced to report that the Lady has fallen into the hands of Circe's son before he could prevent it. The brothers are now told how to overcome Comus, but it is shortly made obvious that the Second Brother's original fears are sound. Comus escapes unpunished with all his creatures, and the Lady is finally released not because of her virginity or through the offices of just one of "the thousand liveried angels" but through the magic powers of a pagan water spirit, whose myth was renovated and carpentered for this purpose.

The failure of this part of *Comus* to come off according to promise is further complicated by Milton's unsuccessful attempt to establish a true intellectual conflict in the debate between Comus and the Lady. This is, without question, the most dramatic part of the poem and I am quite ready to agree with Johnson that "it wants nothing but a brisker reciprocation of objections and replies to invite attention and detain it." Its effectiveness as a dramatic episode is destroyed by a double flaw. Though it starts out with a certain amount of dramatic excitement, the scene quickly degenerates into a philosophic dialogue as eclectic as one of the dialogues of Cicero, and the initial excitement is immediately quieted by the fact that we know almost at once that there is not the remotest danger of the Lady's accepting the offer of Comus. The ethical premises of the debate are, in the second place, so mixed that the intellectual colors run together and are never well marked. Comus adopts a modified Neo-Epicurean argument that is reminiscent of all humanistic debates on this matter. For this we are hardly prepared since he had earlier been charmed by the Lady's song of "all Heaven's harmonies," "a sober certainty of waking bliss," and had talked of making her his queen. This is as fine a prospect of irrational miscegenation as one is likely to find in the history of marriage. The Lady, in her turn, meets the first half of Comus's proposition with statements that he properly labels as "stoic," and she repels the second half with the quasi-Christian concept of virginity. She is a curious mixture, half-rational, half-intuitive; human she is, indeed, but hardly the banner-bearer of her creed. Her character, like that of Comus, also undergoes a forest-change, for the innocent young maiden of the early poem becomes a *mulier doctissima* with the stern frigidity of an adolescent Isabella. And all of this occurs within the space of a gasp.

We feel that if Comus had preserved his character, he could neatly have countered the Lady's objections with the realistic premise of a Valla: "Nullum in rebus humanis intolerabilius virginitate tormentum est." [13] He does, in fact, almost get to this, but his former crystal-like lucidity breaks down and he becomes almost as dogmatically objectionable as the Lady herself.

> Come, no more,
> This is mere moral babble, and direct
> Against the canon laws of our foundation;
> I must not suffer this, yet 'tis but the lees
> And settlings of a melancholy blood;
> But this will cure all straight, one sip of this
> Will bathe the drooping spirits in delight
> Beyond the bliss of dreams (806–13).

The spinsterish tone of Comus jars us, so we are not surprised in the end when he falls back on the formula of the official Christian tempter and says, "Be wise and taste." Nonetheless, if dramatic logic had been allowed to control this scene, Comus would have made his point. The Lady's victory seems as much a tour de force as the final half-Christian, half-Platonic admonition of the departing Spirit.

Denis Saurat put his finger on the central difficulty when he wrote: "There is little that is Christian about *Comus*." [14] That is a reasonably accurate observation, and yet in recent times the masque has been too often read as a treatise on Christian morals. The virtues celebrated in the poem, as Milton and any other seventeenth century man knew, are Christian only by adoption. Both the sixteenth and seventeenth centuries were aware that Virtue existed before Grace. They frequently noticed that among the pagans there were temperate nations like Sparta, temperate classes like the Magi, and many temperate individuals like Plato and Seneca. Any Englishman of this intemperate English era could also recount the virtuous lives of the chaste Penelope, Lucretia, Sophronia, Zenobia, and Timoclea, or the virginal Biblia, Daria, Spurina, and Euphrosyna. So the core of the theme is Christian only in terms of a special modern prejudice.

[13] D. C. Allen, "The Rehabilitation of Epicurus," *SP,* XLI (1944), 7.
[14] *Milton: Man and Thinker* (New York, 1925), 16.

If the theme is not unspottedly Christian, the time of the action is not necessarily fixed in the calendar limits of Christianity. The temporal circumstances are set by the myths of Sabrina and Comus. Sabrina was the granddaughter of Brute; she lived a generation after the fall of Troy and a great time before the birth of Christ. Though the dramatic time is nowhere stated, there is every reason to believe that Milton thought of the action as taking place in pre-Christian Albion. The Spirit, for example, is not a guardian angel but a daemon (as he is called in the Trinity MS) from the *Timaeus*. He comes from "the starry threshold of Jove's court," talks constantly of the pagan pantheon, of nymphs of wood and stream, and, when he finally leaves the stage, goes off to a pagan paradise. Comus is no refugee from Pandæmonium but a true son of Circe and Bacchus—notice how contemporaneous he is with Sabrina—who is well-acquainted with the upperclass members of the pagan underworld. The Lady and her brothers spend most of their time in a pre-Christian ambient and their conversation is studded with classical mythology. When the First Brother wishes to illustrate his lecture on chastity, he calls "Antiquity from the old schools of Greece" and tells us about Minerva and Diana and not about the martyrs of the Primitive Church. So the dial of the dramatic clock tells pagan time.

But Milton refuses to maintain the obvious chronology. He tries for a temporal compromise by scattering Christian metaphors through the masque in order to accent the utilitarian fiction—as indicated by the first speech of the Spirit and the second or presentation song—that all of this actually happened to the Bridgewater children on their way to join their parents. This is a conflict similar to that of the "Ode," but it cannot be compromised by means of unassimilated Christian metaphors. The two chronological divisions simply cannot be poured together and their metaphors confuse the careful reader. Though the characters in general speak like pagans, they momently become Christian. The Spirit uses expressions like "sainted seats" and "sin-worn"; Comus mentions "the path to Heaven"; the First Brother capitalizes "Heaven" and refers to armored "angels"; and the Second Brother comes out with a Roman turn of phrase: "For who would rob a hermit of his weeds, / His few books, or his beads, or maple dish." The Lady has most of the metaphors: "soft votarist in palmer's weeds," "Conscience," "Faith," "Hope," "hovering Angel," "He, the Supreme Good," who "would send a glistering guardian, if need were, / To keep my life and honour unassailed." Instead of effecting a higher compromise, this method leads us to believe that the characters are uncertain about their theology and their chronology. But, perhaps, I have missed the real point of the masque.

In the printed and manuscript versions the title is "A Mask Presented at Ludlow Castle." This may come as a surprise to some readers because the earliest critics refer to it as *Comus* and few modern Miltonists think of it under any other title. The reason for this is clear; the character of Comus dominates the masque whether Milton intended it or not. One cannot imagine *Macbeth* if it were untitled getting the popular title of *MacDuff*, or *Hamlet* becoming *Claudius*. Likewise if Milton's theme of chastity had been firmly brought home, this masque might be known as *The Mask of Chastity* or *The Mask of the Virgin*. There is, I believe, a reason for this.

Though chastity or temperance triumphs in the masque, the motif that is really dramatically interesting is the process of temptation. This is a theme dear to Milton's heart and one which he elaborated in all of his later works. If we can assume that the time is pre-Christian, *Comus* takes its place as part of a great poetic tetralogy. In *Paradise Lost* we witness temptation at the beginning of things in heaven, in hell (the temptation of Sin), and on earth. In *Samson Agonistes* we see the temptation of a foreshadower of Christ under the Old Law and how it was withstood. In *Paradise Regained* we watch the temptation of "the exalted man" and the ordination of the New Dispensation. In *Comus* we are spectators at a pagan temptation. From all of these vicarious experiences we can draw lessons for our own guidance. The masque seems to me to be an experimental piece in this respect, a prolegomenon to the three great poems. But the conflict between the dramatic theme and the moral theme is never made quite clear and it is certainly never, in my estimation, artistically compromised.

Because the conflicts of the "Ode" eventuate in higher compromises, whereas in the masque the conflicts in external structure, in pre-text, and in thematic substance continue to struggle for an equation that cannot be written, the "Ode" satisfies us aesthetically and the masque does not. The history of *Comus* among the critics suggests that Milton was unable to convey his meaning through a dramatic form; hence it is probably a good thing that "Adam Unparadiz'd" became *Paradise Lost*. Perhaps Milton learned something from his experience with *Comus*.

Comus Once More

A. S. P. Woodhouse

Since my "Argument of Milton's *Comus*"[1] appeared in these pages almost a decade ago, critics have been busy with the poem; and it seems not inappropriate to indicate for the reader where the principal contributions are to be found,[2] and then to go on to add a brief appendix to my former article.

The contentions of that article were: (i) that the argument of *Comus* presupposed an intellectual frame of reference commonly assumed in Milton's day, the assignment of all existence and experience to the level of nature or to the level of grace, which constituted for Milton two adjoining and even interpenetrating orders; (ii) that the argument ascended from nature (while dealing, like Book II of the *Faerie Queene,* with temperance and continence) through an area where nature and grace met (in what was for the poem the central virtue of chastity) up to the level of grace alone (where the highest virtue was symbolized by,

Reprinted by permission of the University of Toronto Press from *The University of Toronto Quarterly,* XIX (1950), pp. 218–23.

[1] *University of Toronto Quarterly,* XI, 1941, 46–71.

[2] E. M. W. Tillyard, "The Action of *Comus*" (*Essays and Studies of the English Association,* XXVIII, 1942, 22–37); William Haller, "Hail Wedded Love" (*English Literary History,* XIII, 1946, 87–90); J. C. Maxwell, "The Pseudo-Problem of *Comus*" (*Cambridge Journal,* I, 1948, 376–80); D. C. Allen, "Milton's *Comus* as a Failure in Artistic Compromise" (*ELH,* XVI, 1949, 104–19); C. Clarke, "A Neglected Episode in *Comus*" (*The Wind and the Rain,* VI, 1949, 103–7); M. K. Macklem, "Love, Nature and Grace in Milton" (*Queen's Quarterly,* LVI, 1949–50, 534–47). The earlier work of D. Saurat, referred to, is his *Milton, Man and Thinker* (New York, 1925), with no change in the second edition of 1944; that of J. H. Hanford, his "Youth of Milton," included in *Studies in Shakespeare, Milton and Donne,* University of Michigan Publications, Language and Literature, I (1925), with no substantial change in his *John Milton, Englishman* (New York, 1949).

but was not coterminous with, virginity); (iii) that if it were properly understood, and a correct meaning assigned to its allusion to the Garden of Adonis, the Epilogue became a key to the meaning of the poem (viewing the ascent from the vantage point of grace, whence the whole natural order appeared in its true light, and the dictates of "most innocent nature" were seen to be ratified before being transcended), and that this the Epilogue effected by retracing the ascent, rapidly and by means of symbols; and finally (iv) that, so understood, the argument of *Comus* was less austere, less purely negative, and less alien to the spirit of the masque, than had been commonly supposed.

A year or two later Mr. Tillyard, working independently, arrived at the conclusion that the Epilogue held an important key to the poem's meaning and that the allusion to the Garden of Adonis was central to the Epilogue. Thereafter, however, we diverged sharply. Mr. Tillyard maintained that when Milton added the allusion (some time before the edition of 1637) he altered the whole tendency of his argument, and that he did this because, in effect, he had bethought him that young ladies have a habit of getting married and that the Lady might well run true to type! To me, I confess, the reason assigned for Milton's second and better thoughts seems insufficient, and quite unnecessary. My concern was with the completed text, but my view was and is that the additions merely clarified and emphasized ideas and a direction present from the earliest version. Later, in a lively article, called "The Pseudo-Problem of *Comus*," Mr. Maxwell took us both to task: Mr. Tillyard and I had, it seemed, invented the problem and then racked our brains for a solution. That he appeared somewhat to prefer mine did not alter the fact that it was all shadow boxing! So easy and agreeable does Mr. Maxwell make everything seem, that one almost wishes he were right. Meanwhile Professor Haller, pursuing his invaluable studies in the Puritan art of love, deplored the too curious questionings of Professors Saurat and Hanford and myself, without at all differentiating between us, and committed himself to two propositions which, if true, would strongly support Mr. Maxwell: that Milton "wrote *Comus* simply to oblige his friend Henry Lawes" (which is surely to confuse the content of the poem with its occasion) and that he "could hardly . . . , in the circumstances, have ventured to bring in the theme of marriage" (which, of course, is exactly what, in the Epilogue, he does). Now Professor Allen, accepting the general soundness of my analysis, has reasserted what I had not indeed denied (though I thought it had been, like the news of Mark Twain's death, a good deal exaggerated), that

Comus was an artistic failure; and Mr. Macklem has carried my thesis farther—and indeed a good deal farther than the evidence warrants—in an effort to show that Milton's position on love and marriage, as formulated in *Paradise Lost,* was already reached in *Comus.* Finally, Mr. Clarke pointed out that my article (and also Mr. Tillyard's) ignored the intervention of Sabrina, and that no interpretation which did so could be regarded as complete. In this he was perfectly correct, but in the intervention of Sabrina, and that no interpretation which did so could be think, completely wrong.

Let me ingenuously confess that I omitted to comment on the intervention of Sabrina because I did not then understand it, as I have long since come to do, and let me devote the limited space at my disposal to explaining the episode and placing it in its context.

As we look at *Comus,* in the light of the frame of reference and the movement of ascent, explained in my earlier article, it seems evident that the action of the piece constitutes a sort of pilgrimage, and that each of its three settings has a clear symbolic value. The Wild Wood through which the journey lies represents this world, the order of nature, where good and evil grow up together and must be discriminated by reason, and where the good, when recognized, must be adhered to by the will; for though nature itself is good, its dictates may be misconceived and its benefits perverted to evil ends, as they are by Comus, and the world thus becomes a place of danger and of "hard assays." The Palace of Comus, situated in the wood, and "set forth with all manner of deliciousness," represents one of those crystallizations of evil, those crises of temptation, which abound in the world, good though it be, and into which through ignorance even the good may enter. Ludlow Town and the Castle, situated without the wood, and at the end of the journey, represent what another poet has called "the kindred points of heaven and home," the goal of the pilgrimage and the reward of virtue; for Ludlow, if it is the parents' dwelling, is also a symbol of the Heavenly City.

In the first setting (the wild wood), the Attendant Spirit appears, fresh from the ideal world that is his dwelling, the world where all "natures" exist in their pure and uncorrupted state; and the Spirit is the agent and symbol, not of grace in its full extent, but of divine protection and a measure of guidance. But in this setting also appear Comus and his rout, symbols of the perversion of natural goods to evil ends. There the Lady is separated from the Brothers, and, deceived by Comus, follows him, while the Brothers stay to discourse of natural virtue, of its self-protective power, of the protection which Providence affords to it (whose recognition is reinforced by the entrance of the Attendant Spirit), and of the ascent of natural virtue to the very verge of heaven. Thus the disquisition of the Brothers and the Spirit lays the necessary foundations in doctrine for the Lady's encounter with Comus and the subsequent action.

In the second setting (the palace of Comus) the Lady defends herself, and the virtues of temperance and continence, by the use of that reason of which the enchanter's "False words prankt in Reason's garb" are a mockery, and by an appeal to that nature whose dictates he wilfully misconceives. For the higher doctrine of chastity, as the Elder Brother has already expounded it, how profitless (she reflects) to utter it to Comus, who has ears but hears not! It is enough to afford to the reader a hint that will recall to him the earlier exposition. And for the highest reaches of the argument, where chastity is gathered up into the order of grace, and finds itself symbolized, but not exhausted, by

> the sage
> And serious doctrine of Virginity.

while the Lady refers to it, one may doubt whether it has yet entered fully into her experience. Else why should she be immobilized by Comus and require (as we shall see she does) a new infusion of grace to effect her release?

It is clear that in *Comus* Milton, unlike Spenser in the third book of the *Faerie Queene,* seeks the dynamic that is to transform chastity into a positive virtue, a principle of action, not in nature, but in grace. It is symbolized, almost indeed stated, in the episode of Sabrina (ll. 814–958). In the preceding lines (659–813) the Lady has successfully resisted the attack of Comus: she has met his argument on the natural level; she has in effect invoked the Elder Brother's account of chastity, but her rescuers find her "In stony fetters fixed and motionless," bound by a spell which she is powerless to break for herself, however firmly principled in virtue, and which requires to be reversed before she can be freed. There is, however, another way, as the Attendant Spirit (who is himself unable to break the spell) knows. It is possible to summon the aid of Sabrina. She comes, performs her task, and explains her role (908–19):

> Shepherd, 'tis my office best
> To help ensnared chastity.
> Brightest Lady, look on me:
> Thus I sprinkle on thy breast

Drops that from my fountain pure
I have kept of precious cure:
Thrice upon thy finger's tip,
Thrice upon thy rubied lip:
Next this marble venomed seat,
Smeared with gums of glutinous heat,
I touch with chaste palms moist and cold.
Now the charm hath lost his hold. . . .

The symbolism is unmistakable. When during the fight with the Dragon (*Faerie Queene,* I, xi, xxix–xxx) Spenser has the Redcross Knight stagger back into a stream of living water and come forth restored, the informed reader immediately recognizes, not a reference to baptism (as critics have too bluntly supposed and said), but the symbol for a renewed infusion of divine grace, whose imagery belongs to the same category of Christian symbolism as finds its most familiar example in the sacrament of baptism. So with the episode of Sabrina: the sprinkling of pure water, those drops of "precious cure," symbolizes an infusion of divine grace, and what is implied is the secure raising of the problem to the religious level where alone it is soluble and where alone the dynamic of true virtue must be sought.

Through the words of the Attendant Spirit, Milton introduces the legend of Sabrina by an allusion to Spenser:

now I bethink me,
Some other means I have which may be used,
Which once of Meliboeus old I learnt,
The soothest shepherd that e'er piped on plains.

The lines have been taken to acknowledge Milton's source for the story of Sabrina, in the *Faerie Queene* (II, x, xvii–xix); [3] and this perhaps is their surface meaning. But of the use to which Milton puts the legend, of the symbolic value which he gives to his elaboration of it, there is no hint in Spenser's story of Sabrina. For that Milton could only turn to the book of the poem which moves throughout on the level of grace, and to such an episode as we have cited above.

Nor, perhaps, does the debt to Spenser stop here. The power of grace to destroy evil is part of its function in freeing the good. In the slaying of Maleger (II, xi, xlv–xlvi) [4] by casting him into the standing lake,

[3] See, for example, Merritt Hughes's note on 1. 822 of *Comus,* in *Paradise Regained, the Minor Poems, and Samson Agonistes* (New York, 1937), 260.

[4] For the interpretation of this incident see my "Nature and Grace in the *Faerie Queene*" (*ELH,* XVI, 1949, 221–2).

Prince Arthur invokes the power of grace, symbolized by water, to destroy evil, just as Sabrina sprinkles the precious drops, not only upon the Lady, freeing her by an infusion of grace, but upon Comus's throne, destroying its evil effect. That the Attendant Spirit, the agent of Providence, should have been unable immediately to effect the Lady's release is also significant: his mission is to protect innocence and virtue in the natural order (like Arthur in the *Faerie Queene,* II, VIII), and to afford a measure of guidance (like Una in Book I); but the operation of grace must be differentiated from protection and even guidance, as it consistently is by Spenser, and must be given its own clearly marked symbols. In this likewise Milton follows his master.

The episode of Sabrina should bring home to us the nature and extent of Spenser's influence on *Comus,* and the fact that, whatever else the poem may be, it is in the fullest sense Spenserian allegory, with different levels of meaning. No doubt it was the local association of the Sabrina legend that prompted its introduction, and set Milton upon his essay in Spenserian myth-making in order to adapt it first to the action, then to the deeper meaning of the poem. And lest we should fail to realize the significance of Sabrina's intervention, and the limitation of his own role, the Attendant Spirit is made to exclaim (938–47):

> Come, Lady, while Heaven lends us grace,
> Let us fly this cursed place . . .
> Not a waste or needless sound
> Till we come to holier ground.
> I shall be your faithful guide
> Through this gloomy covert wide;
> And not many furlongs thence
> Is your Father's residence. . . .

The spell is broken. Mobility is restored. The Lady is freed, by the operation of grace, to resume her journey and to make her way through the wild wood, which is the world, to the "holier ground," the Heavenly City, whose earthly image is Ludlow.

Like Spenser, Milton does not leave us without clues to his deeper meaning if we will read him with sufficient care. The episode of Sabrina, properly understood, is not only consonant with my interpretation of *Comus;* it is essential to that interpretation. For the episode signalizes the secure achievement of the level of grace, and it is from the vantage point of grace that the Epilogue takes its retrospective view, and every good falls into its appointed place in a pattern, a vision of existence, which only the Christian can fully apprehend.

Reading *Comus*

Robert M. Adams

Once upon a time *Paradise Lost, Paradise Regained,* and *Samson Agonistes* were the major works of John Milton; recent criticism has gone a long way toward replacing them with "Lycidas," *Comus,* and the poem "On the Morning of Christ's Nativity." It seems to me that this tendency has involved, as cause or as effect, a major overreading of the three early works, and of *Comus* in particular. By "overreading" I mean overloading the allegory, probing too deeply into the background of the imagery, and enlarging upon the incidental implications of secondary concepts at the expense of the work's total structure.

Overreading a literary work is best accomplished through line-by-line analysis, according to the familiar approach of *explication de texte.* The announced aim of this technique is to reveal the true dramatic form of the work of art; and with this aim none can quarrel. But unfolding the text line by line does not necessarily serve this end any more than methodically inspecting the bricks of a house gives one a notion of its architecture. We may therefore begin our consideration of *Comus,* not with line 1, but by asking what sort of literary work it is and then, in the broadest sense, what it is "about"—what themes it chiefly handles and what sort of impression it seems designed to make.

Though it is often described loosely as a play and sometimes as a poem, *Comus* is so much a masque that this was its original, and for a long time its only, title. Mr. Don C. Allen has argued recently that *Comus* is not a masque because

> it is much longer than the masque as written by Jonson or Daniel; its cast of speaking characters is much smaller; its locale of action is much less fantastic; its plot, though not exactly more elaborate, is more tense; its

Reprinted by permission of the publisher from *Ikon: John Milton and the Modern Critics* (Ithaca, N. Y.: Cornell University Press, 1955), pp. 1–34.

> theme is more serious; it is totally wanting in humorousness; and its emphasis is more on dramatic crisis than on spectacle, dance, costume, and even singing [*The Harmonious Vision* (Baltimore, 1954), p. 31].

But Mr. Allen himself does not use these criteria seriously, or at least consistently; for example, he holds that *Arcades* is a true masque, though it has even fewer speaking characters than *Comus,* lacks humorousness entirely, and is only 109 lines long—far shorter than the masque as written by Jonson and Daniel. Besides, a work of art does not forfeit its position within a genre by differences of this sort; otherwise one might prove, by comparing *Macbeth* with *Everyman,* that Shakespeare had not written a play. In short, if we are not so strict as to correct the author in his very declaration of intentions, "masque" may continue to describe Milton's effort.

Now the masque is a form of literature designed primarily for public recitation and performance. Its major functions are triple: to voice a compliment, to present a moral allegory, and to provide occasion for a spectacle. Each of these requirements lays one more demand on a verse statement which is unalterably public in character; consequently, the "Dorique delicacy" which Sir Henry Wotton remarked in *Comus* was widely recognized as a notably successful style for masques. Simplicity wedded to elegance—this was the style at which the most successful writers of masques generally, and the author of *Comus* in particular, aimed. It is a matter of history that masques were not written in the metaphysical manner; even masques by poets like Carew and Townshend, who were occasionally given to conceited verses, never stray far from the strict Jonsonian style. Consequently a preliminary doubt may be felt, simply on the score of *Comus'* form, that techniques appropriate to reading a metaphysical poem will quite apply here. The unity of a metaphysical poem often lies in a progression of ideas and feelings which must be explicated out of the imagery; as a masque, *Comus* would be expected to possess a much more obvious unity.

This is not to say that wit- and word-play were under a ban or that secondary meanings and patterns could not be included anywhere within the main outlines of the masque; Milton, like Shakespeare, might well be expected to enrich a traditional form with such secondary elements. But one cannot lightly suppose that the writer of a masque would deliberately violate any of the major purposes of the genre to include secondary elements; still less that he would purposely conceal any major part of his statement where it was not easily available to a single hearing by an informed, attentive listener. The history of the writing of *Comus,* so far as it is available from manuscripts, supports this assumption. Whatever Milton had to say in *Comus,* he did not alter it radically in the course of composition; whatever main shape the masque had, it evidently had from the beginning. The textual alterations which are preserved aim at a greater clarity, a less pedestrian statement, a more exact propriety; not one of them is aimed at deepening or elaborating the allegory or symbolism, at adding new overtones to the imagery or harmonizing old ones.[1]

A formalist argument of this sort is, of course, inevitably general and abstract; the fact that Milton was writing a masque is no evidence that *Comus* is like all other masques or that it contains nothing but what is common to all masques. But so long as *Comus* can be read consistently and satisfyingly on the level of a masque for public performance, I think readings which depend entirely on a close analysis of the metaphorical overtones must be held suspect and kept subordinate. They may reinforce and enrich the more accessible meanings when they can do so without strain; they may be called on to mediate conflicts or to fill explicit gaps; but when they are not congruent with those more accessible meanings, the suspicion must persist that they are not significant. Milton at the time when he wrote *Comus* could not foresee that it would be "explicated" or even that it would be published; publication of a masque was unusual, and "explication," so far as it was practiced at all, was called "parsing" or "construing" and reserved for classic authors. We do Milton no more discredit in urging that he did not write a masque for the Earl of Bridgewater to "explicate"—unlovely word!—than we do to Ovid in suggesting that he did not conceive the *Ars amatoria* as a devotional handbook for nuns. One can explicate Milton's masque and allegorize Ovid's treatise, but only at a sizable risk to one's understanding of the "true dramatic form."

The risk of overreading *Comus* may be great; to assess the actual

[1] One set of alterations in l. 995 is devoted to removing an explicitly Judaeo-Christian symbol; the only other changes which seem even indirectly significant on the latent level have to do with ll. 356–58, where Milton removed a Proserpina-Lady comparison from the Younger Brother's speech, probably because it was too blackly diabolic in tone, perhaps also because the Proserpina-fertility connection did not fit well with the Lady's chastity. The fourteen lines which Milton removed from the prologue and rewrote for the epilogue were dramatically inappropriate in their original spot, a fact for which they made explicit and doubly awkward apology. Mr. C. S. Lewis has summarized the direction of Milton's revisions as rejection of the colloquial, the dramatic, and the technical in favor of poetic chastity, smoothness, singleness, and didacticism [*RES,* VIII, 170–76].

damage we must consider the poem's specific content and the violence which has, in fact, been done it by overreading. Since the publication of Mr. A. S. P. Woodhouse's classic account of its "argument," *Comus* has been generally supposed to concern the relations between "virtue" and "grace" [*UTQ,* XI, 46–71]. The virtue with which it deals is variously defined as continence, temperance, chastity, or virginity; whatever its character, Milton may be taken as saying of this virtue either that it co-operates with and leads toward grace or that it is distinctly inferior to grace and insufficient without it. How one reads the masque depends on how one makes these definitions, and vice versa. But on one point there is general agreement; the masque is built around a single central and important incident. Like Milton's tragedy and both his epics, *Comus* has a temptation at the center of it. The Lady, lost in a dark wood and separated from her brothers, is tempted by Comus, who is a magician and a sensualist; if she succumbs by drinking of his cup, her head will be turned to that of a beast. But she is rescued by her brothers, who (guided by an Attendant Spirit and protected by a certain herb which he has given them) drive off Comus, invoke the water nymph Sabrina to release their sister from enchantment, and escort her to their father's court.

The central episode of this story is clearly the temptation; the sort of allurements which are dangled before the Lady and the sort of energies which enable her to withstand those allurements must determine in very large measure the allegorical meaning of the masque. Secondary emphases may be altered by secondary elements—by the destination which the young people are supposed to be seeking, by the debate which the two brothers carry on while they are looking for their sister, by the prologue or the epilogue. But we shall not go far wrong if we look first at the central dramatic conflict of the masque as a means of approaching its intellectual and emotional content.

The relation of Comus to Circe determines a good deal of the significance which attaches to the seducer. In his prologue the Attendant Spirit describes Comus as the son of Circe by Bacchus [ll. 46 ff.]; and, while Bacchus remains largely in the background, the maternal side of Comus' genealogy is several times emphasized throughout the masque. When he hears the Lady singing, Comus is reminded of his mother and the sirens [ll. 251 ff.]; when the Attendant Spirit provides the brothers with a countercharm for Comus' enchantments, he compares it to

that *Moly*
That *Hermes* once to wise *Ulysses* gave [ll. 635–36].

The fate of Comus' victims is akin to that of Circe's; he is armed, like Circe, with a cup and wand; like Circe, he offers his victims food, revelry, and (latently but climactically) sexual enjoyment; the virtues which are invoked against him are the virtues of temperance, which Comus calls "lean Abstinence." It may be worth emphasizing that Milton has inverted the sex relationships of the original Circe story—perhaps to conform to the acting personnel at his disposal, perhaps to avoid too close a retelling of the old story, perhaps for more elaborate psychological reasons. In any event, the part of the fatal temptress, the deadly damsel, is here assumed by a male, the part of the shipwrecked mariners by a wandering lady; and from this fact derive some of the tonalities, and some of the incongruities, of the story.

For Comus is a seducer who makes remarkably few and feeble efforts to seduce; though he possesses the traditional enchanting devices of his mother, a glass and a wand, he never brings them explicitly into play. Instead of offering the Lady his magic brew while she is wandering alone, unsuspecting, and thirsty in the forest, he brings her into a palace, lets her see his troop of "oughly-headed Monsters," and only then, when she is thoroughly aroused and suspicious, tries to argue her into drinking of the cup. His wand is said to have power to "chain up [the Lady's] nerves in Alablaster" [l. 659], but so far as he enchants her at all, it is with a certain magic dust which blears her vision and with an anointed chair which holds her motionless. The wand and the cup, though much in evidence, never exert an active compulsion; and the seduction of the Lady, though unmistakably threatened, never develops into a real possibility. All this means, I suppose, is that the decorums of female innocence had to be very cautiously manipulated in the immediate proximity of symbols which folklore had rendered instinct with sexuality and which were controlled by the lascivious son of one (Circe) who was widely taken as a type of the strumpet.[2]

If the allegorical character of Comus is clear enough (he is Sensual Indulgence with some overtones of priapic fertility, black wizardry, and pagan sophistry), the forces which the Lady opposes to him are by no means simple. Some of her strength is her own, some is her brothers', some is the Attendant Spirit's. Her own strength is itself a complex element; when alarmed, she invokes

[2] But Renaissance mythographers were not all orthodox Freudians, and Alexander Ross in his *Mel Heliconium* (London, 1642), pp. 96–97, interprets the rod of Circe as an instrument of punishment with which one who drinks of the cup is whipped. See also George Sandys, *Ovids Metamorphosis Englished* (Oxford, 1632), p. 481, where the rod reversed is said to symbolize discipline.

> The vertuous mind, that ever walks attended
> By a strong siding champion Conscience [ll. 210–11],

and, in addition, implies that if need were, a special guardian would be forthcoming from heaven. The Elder Brother adds a third element to these two; aside from her natural virtue and the "strength of Heaven," the Lady possesses

> a hidden strength
> Which if Heav'n gave it, may be term'd her own:
> 'Tis chastity, my brother, chastity [ll. 417–19].

The special power of chastity to defend itself against witches, ghosts, fairies, goblins, and wizards is not only the subject of set speeches by the Elder Brother, it is verified in the central action of the masque. Comus is able to surprise the Lady and assail her; he cannot enthrall or hurt her. And without the visible help of heaven she rebukes him until he acknowledges

> that I do fear
> Her words set off by som superior power;
> And though not mortal, yet a cold shuddring dew
> Dips me all o're, as when the wrath of *Jove*
> Speaks thunder, and the chains of *Erebus*
> To som of *Saturns* crew [ll. 799–804].

This "sage and serious doctrine of virginity," which the Lady says she will not reveal to Comus but which suffices to dazzle him anyhow, is said by Mr. Woodhouse to represent a religious aspect of the doctrine of mere earthly chastity enunciated earlier by the Elder Brother. But there is little evidence for this in the text: the Lady uses the "Sun-clad power of Chastity" as a synonym for the "doctrine of Virginity" [ll. 781, 786]; and the Elder Brother not only describes chastity as "Saintly" and "sacred" but uses "true Virginity" as a synonym [ll. 452, 424, 436]. The point has been elaborated in a different context by J. C. Maxwell [*CJ,* I, 376–80]. Thus Mr. Woodhouse, recognizing a possible confusion, is forced to appeal "to the intellectual frame of reference, supported as it is by the autobiographical passage in the *Apology*" [*UTQ,* XI, 56]. Here, it seems to me, the text is in danger of slipping away from us entirely. Valid support for ideas which are only adumbrated in a text may always be sought by appeals to related material; but here we are asked to import bodily, without any textual authority at all, ideas expressed by Milton in another context eight years later and ideas expressed by people other than Milton. This procedure seems unwarranted. Deliberately or otherwise, the text makes no distinction between chastity and virginity; when she rebukes Comus, the Lady does not describe chastity as a lesser virtue than virginity or make explicit reference to any specifically Christian sanctions for either virtue; and one reason for this reticence, aside from possible uneasy feelings on Milton's part about devotional celibacy, may be sought in the social implications of the particular masque he was writing.

For the fact is that in *Comus* Milton faced a rather delicate problem of tact. To make the Lady fully self-sufficient would be to eliminate the Attendant Spirit altogether as a functioning element in the story; but to make her virtue wholly dependent on heaven's assistance would scarcely be an overwhelming compliment to pay her. One simply does not tell an earl's daughter that she is chaste only by the grace of God. Thus Milton rather carefully, as it seems to me, manipulates his story to show that female virtue, while possessing defensive powers of its own and not by any means to be supposed vulnerable, much less defective in its own nature, does enjoy a special protection from heaven against such special menaces as Comus. And for this reason it is only after she has given a convincing demonstration of her own moral self-sufficiency that the Lady receives, even indirectly, the help of heaven.

What is the nature of that help? In attacking Comus with drawn swords and dispersing his "rout," the two brothers rely largely on their own powers; perhaps for this reason they are not fully effective in releasing their sister and must invoke the further interesting help of Sabrina. But the brothers are protected against Comus' magic by an herb named "Haemony" which the Attendant Spirit has provided for them; and the argument has been developed by Mr. Edward LeComte from a hint in Coleridge, and avidly accepted by Messrs. Brooks and Hardy, that haemony is a symbol of heavenly grace.[3] This identification rests partly on the name which Milton invented for the herb and partly on some of the things he says about it. The word "haemony" seems to derive primarily from the name for Thessaly (Haemonia), a land particularly rich in magical associations. It may also bear, through its close association with moly, an affinity to the Greek adjective αἵμων, "bloody." For one myth regarding the origins of moly relates it to the fate of the giant Pikolous, who, after the fateful war with Zeus, fled to Circe's isle, attacked her, and was himself attacked and slain by her

[3] LeComte, "New Light on the 'Haemony' Passage in *Comus*," *PQ,* XXI, 283–98; Cleanth Brooks and J. E. Hardy, eds., *Poems of Mr. John Milton* (New York, 1951).

father, Helios. From the drops of blood which Pikolous shed in the struggle with Helios, moly is said to have sprung, hence one possible origin of the name "haemony" and one possible argument, based on its origin in the blood of a god, for its character as a symbol of grace.[4]

The other reasons why haemony may be considered a symbol of grace derive from the things Milton causes Thyrsis (or the Attendant Spirit) to say about it. Haemony, he says, was shown him by a certain shepherd lad, "of small regard to see to" but skilled in herbs:

> Amongst the rest a small unsightly root,
> But of divine effect, he cull'd me out;
> The leaf was darkish, and had prickles on it,
> But in another Countrey, as he said,
> Bore a bright golden flowre, but not in this soyl:
> Unknown, and like esteem'd, and the dull swain
> Treads on it daily with his clouted shoon,
> And yet more med'cinal is it then that *Moly*
> That *Hermes* once to wise *Ulysses* gave [ll. 628–36].

The contrast between "another Countrey" where haemony flowers, and "this soyl," where it does not, is said to represent the contrast between heaven and earth; virtue thus reaches its final perfection in heaven, and indeed the total dependence of virtue on grace is said to be figured in the fact that "the flower is not only the final perfection of the plant, but the source of the seed" [Brooks and Hardy, p. 213]. Furthermore, Mr. LeComte declares that Milton's description of haemony is not unlike that of an herb named "rhamnus," which is mentioned in John Fletcher's *Faithful Shepherdess* (a recognized source of *Comus*) and further described in Gerard's *Herbal* under the popular name of "Christ's Thorn."

There are several difficulties with this interpretation. That the plant grows "in this soyl" but flowers "in another Countrey" is no great invention for Milton to have made on his own. Homer gives to moly (upon which haemony is obviously modeled) a white flower and says simply that it is hard for men to dig; but Pliny gives it a "florum luteum," a bright yellow flower, and reports that it grows in the districts of Pheneus and Cyllene in Arcady. Milton, who wanted to make use of

[4] Two more elements which scholars have, perhaps, been too dignified to throw into the etymological pot of "haemony" are possible puns on the hymen, guardian of virginity, and on harmony, the unruptured state of nature. Milton could have learned of Pikolous from Eustathius' *Commentaries,* a book known to have been in his library.

it in Wales, may well have accounted for its being unknown there by saying that it grows there but flowers elsewhere. The notion that he gave it the name "haemony" as a way of referring not only to Pikolous' blood but to Christ's seems ingeniously esoteric; could Milton really have expected the Earl of Bridgewater and his guests to make on their own the not-even-suggested connection with Eustathius' *Commentaries,* and, supposing they made it, could he have doubted that the equating of Christ with a monster caught in the act of rape would have caused them anything but disquiet? Scarcely less extravagant is the assumption that they would all have read Fletcher's masque and Gerard's *Herbal* and would remember that the rhamnus misprinted in Fletcher was the same as the Christ's Thorn described in Gerard and that Christ's Thorn bore a vague resemblance to haemony.

Difficulties of this sort spring up on all sides as soon as one relaxes one's determination to ignore them. For instance, the simple shepherd lad of small regard to see to is a distinctly casual receptacle for divine grace. Perhaps his pastoral, swainish humility makes him an appropriate figure, but the early and persistent assumption that he is Milton himself or Milton's boyhood friend Diodati militates against his being the agent of grace. To open the door for immodest comparisons of this sort is a Shelleyan, not a Miltonic failing. If haemony is grace, there is another gross, immediate breach of tact in Thyrsis' declaration that in this country it is

> Unknown, and like esteem'd, and the dull swain
> Treads on it daily with his clouted shoon [ll. 633–34].

An audience of country gentlefolk would scarcely have been edified by this thought, particularly the clerical members of it; nor does it conform in the least with Milton's convictions as expressed elsewhere. One does not offhandedly tell the members of a Christian commonwealth that grace is unknown to them, that they trample it underfoot; at least, if one is the sort of immodest fanatic who thinks such thoughts, one does not conceal them in an incidental phrase describing a mythical root. But a magic symbol of temperance, having its origin and power in earthly elements and implying a contrast between Arcadian virtue and modern grossness, would suffer no such disabilities.

Besides, the effect of haemony is not the appropriate effect of divine grace. Maybe it blossoms in heaven, but its virtuous effect occurs on earth and is earthly in nature. All Thyrsis has of the plant is the root (the root traditionally contains the potent element of moly); so that apparently virtue (the root and stalk) is good medicine even without grace (the flower). And haemony is not used in the story to bring anyone to heaven or even to Ludlow Castle, but to avoid the ill effects of lust. It does not release the Lady; it protects the brothers against the enchantments of Comus, who is, allegorically, sensuality. Only in the vague sense that God is responsible for all things and the source of all energies (including the diabolic) did Milton suppose one needed divine grace to avoid drunkenness, riot, and lust. But as for the notion that grace in the Christian sense was necessary to lead a chaste life, the pagan world teemed with evidence to the contrary.

In addition, Milton could not have expected an herb closely associated with and resembling moly to carry for any conceivable audience the allegorical significance of divine grace. This is not a matter of Miltonic origins and derivations but of general, accepted significance. The only evidence that Milton did not derive haemony from some cat's cradle of gods, blood drops, and vegetables involving Pikolous, Osiris, Mithra, Cerberus, Cadmus, Coelus, mandragora, rue, thamnus, dittany, bryony, and garlic is the known quality of his mind and the principle of economy of assumption. But if he associated haemony with moly and did not explicitly indicate a new interpretation, it seems likely that he must have expected the conventional allegorical meaning of moly to be felt. Allegories of the Circe-Ulysses fable might involve physical, moral, or mystical principles in great profusion; but, while the literal existence of moly was still being asserted, allegorical interpretations of the plant were more restrained. The one most easily available to a cultivated, unprofessional audience equated moly with temperance, and it was expressed in explicit detail prior to 1673 (when Milton last published *Comus*) by such men as Andrea dall'Anguillara, Pierre Gautruche, George Sabinus, D. Giphanius, Arthur Golding, Alexander Ross, and George Sandys. The same view is directly implied by Roger Ascham, Fulgentius, Apuleius, Heraclitus, Eustathius, and Boccaccio. For all these representatives of a larger company, moly is temperance or prudence, period.[5]

[5] Anguillara, *Le Metamorfosi di Ovidio* (Venice, 1572), p. 198; Gautruche, *Nouvelle histoire poëtique* (Paris, 1738), p. 316 (first English ed., 1671); Sabinus, ed., *P. Ovidii Metamorphosis* (Frankfort, 1593), p. 491; Giphanius, ed., *Homeri Odyssea* (Strasbourg, 1579), p. 279; Golding, *The XV Bookes of P. Ovidius Naso* (London, 1567), "The Epistle," ll. 276–79; *Ross, Mystagogus Poeticus* (London, 1647), p. 67; Sandys, *The Relation of a Journey* (London, 1632), p. 308; also *Ovids Metamorphosis Englished* (Oxford, 1632), pp. 475, 479–81; Ascham, *The Scholemaster,* ed. D. C. Whimster (London, 1934), p.

There is, to be sure, another allegorical view of the herb, which equates it with divine favor. This view might be found explicitly in Natale Conti, who speaks of the "divina clementia . . . quod per munus Ulyssi a Mercurio datum intelligitur," or in J. Spondanus, who gives a choice of two readings, in which moly may stand either for ethnic magnanimity or for Christian faith.[6] But the religious interpretation is a minority one, easily available to scholars, indeed, but by no means popularly diffused. To the degree that Milton could count on the members of his audience being familiar with any allegorical significance for moly or a molylike vegetable, it was likely to include, if not consist of, the notion of temperance. If he intended a more exalted or particular significance—above all, if he intended that meaning to be exclusively received—he would be unlikely to leave his hearers without a pretty broad hint as to what it was. There is no such hint in the text.

Finally, certain sanctions for the interpretation of moly as temperance may be drawn from Milton's writing before and after *Comus.* Elegy I to Diodati expresses the hope that Milton, with the aid of divine moly, will be able to avoid the fleshpots of London. Are we to suppose the poet so deeply sunk in cant and self-importance that, as early as the age of eighteen, he would consider himself in a state of grace? Temperance is a virtue which turns up with particular frequency throughout the Miltonic canon; it is the subject of Michael's lecture in Book XI of *Paradise Lost* and a major theme of *Paradise Regained,* Book II. "How great a virtue is temperance," cries the *Areopagitica,* "how much of moment through the whole life of man?" Milton here makes none of those reservations which Messrs. Brooks and Hardy would make for him—that virtue is wholly dependent on grace, that it is radically defective in its own nature, that it achieves full flower only in the contemplation of grace. Miltonic temperance is no such passive, contemplative virtue. As Milton's whole life indicates, as well as the history of the causes which he supported, virtue was for him an active, wayfaring, warfaring quality.

68; Fulgentius, *Mythologicon,* ii, 12; Apuleius, *De deo Socratis,* cap. xxiv; Heraclitus, *De incredibilibus,* cap. xvi; Heraclitus (Ponticus), *Allegoriae Homericae,* cap. lxx; Boccaccio, *Genealogiae deorum,* IV, xiv; Eustathius, *Commentarii in Odysseam* (Leipzig, 1825), I, 381, calls moly an allegory of παιδεια but adds that it enables Ulysses to partake of Circe's pleasures with σωφρον. Note also that Mercury, the bringer of moly, is the god of prudence; see, e.g., H. M. Servius, *Commentarii in Vergilium* (Göttingen, 1826), I, 390. Cf. an interesting analogue in Marvell, "Upon Appleton House," ll. 355–60, where a prickly plant stands for conscience.

[6] Conti, *Mythologiae* (Geneva, 1651), pp. 566–67; Spondanus, ed., *Homeri quae exstant omnia* (Basel, 1606), *Odyssey,* pp. 142–43.

And temperance, which enables a man by his own inner election to act or to refrain, to combine experiences and to direct them, is the very model of an active Protestant virtue. "Wherefore did he creat passions within us, pleasures round about us" (says the *Areopagitica* again), "but that these rightly temper'd are the very ingredients of vertu?" *Comus* itself emphasizes the concept of temperance at both the beginning and the end; the Attendant Spirit in his prologue says most people partake of Comus' drink "through fond intemperate thirst" [l. 67]; and the final song declares that the Earl's children have come

> To triumph in victorious dance
> O're sensual Folly and Intemperance [ll. 973–74].

If, on the other hand, one takes haemony to represent heavenly grace and the need for grace as a central theme of the masque, one must impute to Milton the artistic folly of introducing the climactic symbol and climactic idea of the poem in a subordinate clause four hundred lines from the poem's end and of never mentioning it again.

Lastly, if haemony is a symbol of grace, yet cannot be used to release the Lady from Comus' magic chair, what shall we make of the power which does effect that release—that interesting, troublesome creature, Sabrina? Brooks and Hardy, happy to find her a water nymph, eke out a suggestion of the waters of baptism and so convert her, not without a subdued scuffle, into another symbol of grace. But a sense of economy, if nothing else, will cause us to balk at these duplicated symbols. If Sabrina is merely what she seems to be, the genius of the shore and the patroness of virgins, her influence is one step above that of temperance and one step below that of grace itself, and her function in the masque is secure. But to make haemony grace, and Sabrina more grace, and the vision of the epilogue still another aspect of grace is to destroy the very possibility of variety and development within the masque. I cannot feel that any allegory is worth the price in nonsense that one must pay for this one.

Professor Woodhouse, less undiscriminating in his response to imagery, does not try to see grace behind both haemony and Sabrina, but he does conclude for Sabrina as such a symbol and so (presumably) against haemony [*UTQ,* XIX, 218–23]. But if we bear in mind the difficulties [emphasized by R. Blenner-Hassett, *MLN,* LXIV, 315–18] which Milton faced in converting his nymph from the somewhat tainted figure who appears in Geoffrey, I think we shall feel that he did enough simply in making her a chastity symbol. If she were a symbol of Christian grace, would it not be unreasonable to invoke her by means of a long list of explicitly pagan deities [ll. 866–83]? Would it not be absurd to let her sing about willows, osiers, and cowslips, but not a word about God or grace or divine power, and so to dismiss her to Amphitrite's bower without a single hint dropped as to Christian grace? When Spenser dipped the Red Cross Knight into the Well of Life, he made the action awkward and arbitrary in itself and added an explicit moral comment. But Milton did neither of these things; neither haemony nor Sabrina is marked unmistakably as the vehicle of grace; and there is no better reason to suppose that Milton intended either identification than to suppose he intended both.

So far as there is an allegorical meaning for haemony, then, one need not look beyond temperance. But an important reason for Milton's introduction of haemony is not allegorical at all; it has to do with the demands of his story. He cannot have the young men rush in and skewer Comus on their literal, material swords because natural powers cannot be allowed to overcome supernatural ones and because the Attendant Spirit, who has already announced that his function is to convoy the good, cannot be left unemployed. Milton clearly needs haemony in order to balance black magic with white; but as for a suggestion that he is trying to tell us that "Grace and Virtue are essentially the same" or that "the plant symbolizes Virtue in a state of awareness of its own imperfection, expecting perfection only in heaven" [B & H, p. 212]—these are pure extrapolations. One might as well argue from the statement that "the leaf was darkish, and had prickles on it" that the Lady herself was thus afflicted or that virtue on earth is not merely difficult but essentially forbidding in its aspect. This Milton simply did not believe; he would not have felt Spenser to be a sage and serious poet if he had. He would not have written those many passages on the beauty of virtue which stud his work. He would not have been a Renaissance humanist but a Coptic monk.

If, then, the masque is not preaching the insufficiency of virtue without grace, there is no reason to suppose that the Elder Brother is the object of all that criticism which Brooks and Hardy impute to Milton. A priori, it is hard to see why Milton should have undertaken, in a masque which is essentially complimentary, to expose the adolescent heir of the Earl of Bridgewater as a pompous, pedantic fool; and, in fact, the evidence that he intended anything of the sort is remarkably slender.

For example, the Elder Brother's first speech is said by Brooks and Hardy to exemplify naïveté because he asks the moon to "disinherit Chaos" [ll. 330–33], and Comus has "already (on sound traditional authority) used the moon as the symbol of his sovereignty" [B & H, p. 205]. But the Elder Brother has not heard Comus talk about the moon; in fact, he has no reason for supposing that such a creature as Comus exists. The identification of Comus with the moon rests on line 116,

> Now to the Moon in wavering Morrice move,

though there seems no reason why one should not, by the same logic, identify Comus with the stars too, on the basis of lines 111–12:

> We that are of purer fire
> Imitate the Starry Quire.

But in fact there is no reason to identify him with either, for the moon is Cynthia's chariot as well as Hecate's and is associated with chastity as well as with witchcraft. As for the Elder Brother, he asks both the stars and moon for light and then says that if neither is forthcoming, he will follow a light from a house. Why this should be considered abysmal innocence is not clear. He wants light from stars, moon, or a dwelling, and an audience which is expected to find these requests naïve might well be advised what other sources of light a dark wood usually affords.

Brooks and Hardy make much of the supposed naïve confidence which the Elder Brother expresses in his sister's safety, as if Milton wanted us to consider him a brash and overconfident theorizer. But in fact he holds to the doctrine of virtue's self-sufficiency only with a very distinct qualification, which Brooks and Hardy do not so much as mention. He will not be alarmed that his sister is lost and alone,

> Not being in danger, as I trust she is not [l. 369].

If Milton intended us to consider him naïve, this reasonable restriction completely undermines the poet's dramatic purpose. The Elder Brother does not take an obviously unreasonable position in saying,

> Vertue may be assail'd, but never hurt,
> Supriz'd by unjust force, but not enthrall'd [ll. 588–89],

since, as we have seen, this principle is dramatically fulfilled by the Lady and Comus in the temptation scene; and when Thyrsis is first heard approaching in the distance, the Elder Brother is notably aware of the various ills against which he and his brother must be on guard [ll. 482–84].

In two other passages Brooks and Hardy find the naïveté of the Elder Brother expressed in an absolute opposition of good and bad. He is so much against Comus that he forgets vice may be alluring; and the audience, in hearing him, is expected to realize this limitation of his character.

> Som say no evil thing that walks by night
> In fog, or fire, by lake, or moorish fen,
> Blew meager Hag, or stubborn unlaid ghost,
> That breaks his magick chains at *curfeu* time,
> No Goblin, or swart Faëry of the mine,
> Hath hurtfull power o're true Virginity [ll. 431–36].

Of this language Brooks and Hardy say that "it represents good and evil in abstract terms of white and black rather than light and dark. . . . The 'Goblin,' the 'Faëry,' the 'Hag' are merely items in a catalogue of evil *things,* the use of the word *thing* taking from them whatever quality of 'thing-ness,' of tangibility, they might have had" [B & H, p. 208].

This argument involves several strained, not to say mistaken, assertions. "Thing" as used of spirits comes with particular force; being creatures of several different spheres, neither wholly alive nor altogether dead, they can be referred to only by a slippery, noncommittal word like "thing."

> *Marcellus:* What! has this thing appear'd again tonight?
> [*Hamlet,* I, 1, 21.]

That the passage lacks all tangibility and is "completely abstract" [B & H, p. 208] seems so lamentable a misreading that I can only appeal in silent amazement to the lines themselves.

Another example of the Elder Brother's supposed naïveté is found in lines 601 ff., where, in expressing his detestation of Comus, the Elder Brother is said to make of him "a 'simply' frightful creature, attended by such obvious bogies as Harpies and Hydras," so that the audience is intended to see in the Elder Brother a sort of "moral-philosophical Hotspur," illogical and immoderate [B & H, p. 211]. Against this view we may appeal to dramatic probabilities. Thyrsis has told the Elder Brother that his sister is entrapped by a sorcerer living "within the navil of this hideous Wood," a person skilled in witcheries, who offers to travelers a "baneful cup" which transforms them into "the inglorious likenes of a beast." Comus and his rout are called by Thyrsis "monstrous" and are compared to "wolves or tigers"; they are "abhorred" and "barbarous," and Comus, once again referred to, is a "damn'd wisard" [ll. 519–70]. After all this, the Elder Brother would have no dramatic existence at all if he were not fairly indignant at his sister's seducer—and such a seducer! He proposes direct action against the enchanter, and this idea, while inadequate, certainly is not held up to mockery. It is inadequate to the occasion, which is extraordinary in ways that only Thyrsis can suspect, but perfectly "natural" in its immediate contexts. The idea is natural in the situation in which the Elder Brother is involved, and natural in relation to the audience, which expects and sympathizes with impetuous faults in young men whose sisters are threatened with rape. A display of perfect decorum and a philosopher's wariness about all conceivable dangers would, under the circumstances, forfeit the sympathy of the audience forever.

Thus three central elements of the masque may be seen to fit together on the earthly plane without notable inconsistency or incongruity. The spiritual energies of the Lady's virtue suffice to repel Comus without any divine back-stiffening. The brothers are able to approach Comus armed not with grace, but with temperance; and the doctrine that chastity or virginity possesses special powers for its own defense is enunciated by the Elder Brother without any such backlash of ironic commentary as Brooks and Hardy have imputed to Milton. The machinery of magic is invoked to protect the Lady and her brothers, and its connection with chastity may even have been, in Milton's mind, a conviction more integral than the word "machinery" implies [see the discussion in Tillyard's *Milton* (London, 1930), Appendix C]; but in the masque it serves moral ends which can be perfectly well understood on the secular plane.

Where, then, is heaven, and where in the masque does heavenly influence intervene? Obsessed with theological ultimates, Brooks and Hardy locate heaven at least three times over. The Attendant Spirit is for them a heavenly messenger because he comes from somewhere near Jove's court [pp. 189, 192]; but then they say flatly that the "father's . . . court, in the play, symbolizes heaven" [p. 226]; however, when the Attendant Spirit, speaking the epilogue, says he is leaving the court for a new sphere, this, too, seems to be heaven [p. 228]. Is it possible that he should leave heaven to go to heaven? No, it seems that the Earl's court has only "played" for a time at being heaven [p. 230]; and thus heaven is unmade as blithely as formerly it was made.

But, in the first place, there is little reason to suppose the Attendant Spirit a proper angel. Milton's manuscript refers to him as a "daemon," and daemons, as Burton will inform us, were not angels but tutelary spirits.[7] The Attendant Spirit goes to some pains to make his nature explicit:

> Before the starry threshold of *Joves* Court
> My mansion is, where those immortal shapes
> Of bright aereal Spirits live insphear'd [ll. 1–3].

He lives before—that is, outside—the threshold, and he lives where spirits are ensphered; these two facts place his home among the planets, where "Il Penseroso" assigns the residence of daemons:

> And of those *Daemons* that are found
> In fire, air, flood, or under ground,
> Whose power hath a true consent
> With Planet, or with Element [ll. 93–96].

He represents the interests of heaven, he is a messenger of heaven, he has supernatural powers and supernatural knowledge; but his real business is on earth, and it is by no means so general a concern as one usually attributes to ministers of grace. He exists, by his own account, to provide a special protection for specially virtuous people against specially pressing perils [ll. 15–17, 40–42, 78–82]. Theologically he is a guardian spirit, dramatically a master of ceremonies; in neither capacity does he determine the events of the story, exercise any superhuman power other than his wisdom, or attempt more than the release of virtue to establish its own destiny.

The Attendant Spirit does not come from heaven, and there is no more reason to suppose the young people are going there. The court of the Earl of Bridgewater at Ludlow Castle is doubtless a good place to arrive, and heaven is no doubt the final destination of the good; but the Earl might well have been startled by the imputation that he was God the Father. The Attendant Spirit's account of the presidency of Wales [ll. 18–36] offers no allegorical significance to the scrupulous eyes of Brooks and Hardy; here, if anywhere, one would expect the symbol of heaven to be made explicit. But the allegory seems to rest entirely on two lines in which Comus tells the Lady that he has seen her brothers and

[7] "Some indifferent *inter deos et homines* as heroes and daemons which ruled men and were called genii" [*Anatomy,* part 1, sec. 2, mem. 1, subs. 2]; cf. also Augustine, *De civitate Dei,* Books VIII and IX; and Apuleius, *De deo Socratis,* "Daemones sunt genere animalia, ingenio rationabilia, animo passiva, corpore aëria, tempore aeterna."

> if those you seek
> It were a journey like the path to Heav'n,
> To help you find them [ll. 301–03].

And that a hyperbolical cajolery in the mouth of a notorious deceiver should be taken as a positive statement of fact about an unrelated matter seems a queer sort of syllogism.

No, heaven appears in the masque just where it ought to appear, as the epilogue to a story which concerns primarily the trials of this earth. The Attendant Spirit departs to that "vaguely located mansion from which he has come" [M. Y. Hughes, ed., *Paradise Regained, The Minor Poems,* etc. (New York, 1937), p. 268], a mansion not to be equated with the Christian Paradise, but symbolized by a series of pagan heavens, the islands of Hesperus, the Elysian Fields, the garden of Adonis, and the retreat of Cupid and Psyche. Whatever else these heavens represent, they are not the Christian Paradise, either symbolically or otherwise; [8] for the Spirit can fly or run only

> to the green earths end,
> Where the bow'd welkin slow doth bend,
> And from thence can soar as soon
> To the corners of the Moon [ll. 1013–16].

His heavens are of the spheres, and of the lowest spheres at that, the earth and the moon. But in his final statement to the audience he urges:

> Mortals that would follow me,
> Love vertue, she alone is free,
> She can teach ye how to clime
> Higher then the Spheary chime;
> Or if Vertue feeble were,
> Heav'n it self would stoop to her [ll. 1017–22].

Here at last is the Christian heaven, unmistakably. It is not seen or described, as it should not be; it is merely indicated as an aspiration. Its position is "higher than the Spheary chime," above that music of the spheres which echoes and complements the saintly choirs, but is distinct from and inferior to them. "In any case," Brooks and Hardy assure us, "it is clear that the final attainment is not made without the assistance of a power higher than Virtue's own" [p. 233]. What it is clear from is not apparent; all the poet says in the body of his direct declarative assertion is that virtue can teach mortals to get to heaven. No doubt Milton, like

[8] Note particularly the MS changes of l. 995, where Milton rejected successively "manna" and "Sabaean" dew for the strictly pagan "Elysian" dew.

all other Christians, understood the efficacy of another power; but his silence here is more compatible with the emphasis that grace supplements virtue than with the negative assertion that virtue is inadequate without grace. The properly Miltonic mortal actively climbs toward grace, he does not passively wait to receive it. And if long-range consistency matters at all, one might point to that striking series of lines in *Paradise Lost* [III, 309 ff.], in which Milton applied the doctrine of merit to Christ himself.

The last conditional couplet of *Comus* confirms, even as it expands this notion:

> Or if Vertue feeble were,
> Heav'n it self would stoop to her.

Taking it for granted that throughout the masque virtue has been shown as feeble and heaven as stooping, Brooks and Hardy are thoroughly embarrassed by Milton's use of the conditional in line 1021; they say Milton chose this construction "only to emphasize the paradoxical nature of the situation proposed, not to leave its existence in doubt" [p. 233]. This bit of critical patter may be worth a moment's examination. There is nothing "paradoxical" about virtue's being feeble or heaven's adjusting itself to this weakness. Even though the notion of "virtue" may include either goodness or potency, morality or strength, there is no impression of paradox in line 1021, because virtue in the first sense can obviously be feeble, and virtue in the second sense obviously cannot. When a word has two senses, the fact that one of them is nonsensical in context and the other platitudinous does not suffice to make a paradox. But even if a tiny germ of paradox were apparent at the farthest reach of one reading of "virtue," a conditional construction would not serve to emphasize it. The last word of line 1021, "were," is crucial here; and, to parse its grammar out, it is a third person singular subjunctive form used in a subordinate clause to indicate a condition contrary to fact. By writing the last couplet in this form Milton can only have intended to convey that if virtue were feeble (which he did not think she was and had not represented her as being), heaven would stoop like a falcon to help her. But in what sense virtue could be "free" if her only function, or an indispensable part of her function, were to be lifted aloft like a limp rabbit in the claws of an eagle is not clear. Active virtue is a norm in the masque; passive acceptance of grace is an exception. A glistering guardian *might* come to aid virtue "if need were" [l. 218], but such an appearance is exceptional and auxiliary. Spirits perverse have access to earth, says *Paradise Lost,* and can tempt or punish mortals,

except whom
God and good Angels guard by special grace [ll. 1032–33].

If it has any moral meaning at all, *Comus* intends something much closer to "the Lord helps those that help themselves" than to Caliban's notion of the deity, or Holy Willie's. The point is made perfectly explicit in Aurelian Townshend's *Tempe Restor'd* (1631), which tells a similar story, with several close verbal parallels, and in which the Lady Alice Egerton had already taken part as a masquer:

He finds no helpe, that uses not his owne
[A. Townshend, *Poems and Masques,*
ed. E. K. Chambers (Oxford, 1912),
p. 85].

Though it may have this incidental result, the real trouble with overreading is not that it imposes a rigid pattern on the literary work. Ardently as Brooks and Hardy have struggled to interpret *Comus* according to their own lights, the total effect they present is not of an intricate architecture but of an ingenious, perverse chaos. When Milton wrote that virtue alone is free, it appears that he meant to say that virtue alone is dependent; why he did not say this instead of the contrary remains mysterious. When Milton wanted to refer to Christ's Thorn, he hid it behind the name of rhamnus, which he hid behind the name of moly, which he hid near the name of haemony; and he was so crafty about making us think of Christ's Thorn that he never mentioned it, as a result of which three hundred years had to elapse before anyone could so much as suspect his intention. There may be carelessness in this sort of thinking, or confusion, but it is principled carelessness and confusion. The trouble is not with the critics, who are men of ingenuity, not even with the particular interpretation of *Comus,* which is wrongheaded, but with a way of interpreting it, with an image of the creative mind which produced it. Milton's was not a sly, furtive, random, cryptic mind; he did not work, like some very great artists of another breed, in indirection, innuendo, and pastiche. For every beauty which one uncovers on esoteric assumptions (and it is both odd and significant how little Brooks and Hardy make of beauty, how indifferent they seem to be whether they uncover an anagram, a pun, a grotesque fault in taste, or a relevant harmony), one sacrifices a half-dozen of the larger elegancies for which *Comus* really exists. The fault of overreading is pervasive, it corrupts everything and will sacrifice even its own best perceptions for the glare and tinsel of a bit of false wit.

This is especially noticeable when, as frequently happens, Brooks and Hardy succumb to an obvious, jangling antithesis such as Milton had within his grasp and deliberately chose to forego. The double significance of "virtue," a word which may connote either "strength" or "goodness," opens the way to many puns, all of which, though Milton passed them up, Brooks and Hardy strive strongly to foist back into the poem. Another opening for a pun occurs in one of the concluding songs:

> Heav'n hath timely tri'd their youth,

says the song; and Brooks and Hardy must forthwith wrench Milton into a timely-timeless antithesis [p. 227]. Heaven has tried the youth of the young folk in the world of time; it will reward them in the world beyond time. No matter that neither Milton nor any contemporary ever uses "timely" in any such sense; no matter that the death thought involved in "going to heaven" jars on the jubilation of homecoming. We must have the antithesis at all costs.

One useful device for creating antitheses where Milton never intended them is to treat him as a nineteenth-century poet flavored with nineteenth-century transcendental philosophy. For instance, Thyrsis prefaces his account of Comus by saying that though "shallow unbelief" and "ignorance" refuse to admit it, the supernatural beings described by poets do exist [ll. 513, 518]; and for Brooks and Hardy this comment imports "the dependence of poetic truth on belief" [p. 209]. Why they do not add that poetic truth also depends on knowledge is all too obvious. But, in fact, Milton did not think that poetic truth depended on belief; he nowhere distinguishes poetic truth from other varieties or asserts, as Blake and Keats were to do more than a century and a half later, that a strong conviction about any matter makes it true.[9] So also in line 10, where the Attendant Spirit mentions the crown that virtue gives

> After this mortal change, to her true Servants.

Brooks and Hardy read the phrase "mortal change" as "the constant change which makes mortal existence a death-in-life" [p. 189]. But a doubt or two may creep in as to whether Milton really intended a comparison between the Earl of Bridgewater's children and the Ancient Mariner. For one thing, he never uses the phrase "mortal change" or anything like it to describe life; but he does [*PL,* X, 273] use the same phrase of death, as well as a variant, "thy mortal passage" [XI, 366].

[9] *The Marriage of Heaven and Hell,* conversation with Isaiah; Keats to Benjamin Bailey, November 22, 1817.

Not having read *Die Welt als Wille und Vorstellung,* he did not think of change as aimless or delusive, and nothing in his life or writings suggests that he considered mortal existence a "death-in-life." As a matter of fact, whether "mortal change" refers to life or death does not particularly matter, so far as the argument over virtue and grace is concerned. But Brooks and Hardy cannot resist the chance for a quibble; they must assume that Milton wrote "after this mortal change" by way of saying "after this changing mortal life," at the expense of a tautology, in defiance of the words' most obvious connotations, and for no other visible reason than to bemuse explicators.

Mr. Don C. Allen, in an essay already referred to, carries this position to its logical conclusion. Having urged that *Comus* is not a masque because it lacks formality and ritual, nor yet a play because it lacks suspense and character alteration, he adds that it is written in a patch-work of styles. When he has completed his indictment with the charge that *Comus* is intellectually muddled, Mr. Allen has ample reason to dismiss the entire production as a series of faulty compromises, "a mélange of various tendencies and styles that never merge into anything intensely organic" [*THV,* p. 32].

About Mr. Allen's need for something "intensely organic" I am not sure that anything can be done; "organic unity" as an exclusive whole-sale criterion of critical judgment is a cant phrase out of eighteenth-century Germany, dependent on a sort of muzzy metaphysics with which neither Milton nor any modern critic except conceivably Sir Herbert Read is in genuine sympathy [see, for fuller discussion of these points, James Benziger, *PMLA,* LXVI, 24–48]. But some unity can be introduced into a reading of *Comus* by forgetting that the villain presents "a modified Neo-Epicurean argument" to which the Lady replies with a mixture of "stoic statements" and "the quasi-Christian concept of virginity" [*THV,* pp. 36–37]. Sly, sensual seducers are not usually held to such strict account for the exact framing of their arguments according to philosophic schools, any more than are virgins defending their virtue. If Comus is a bad man and the Lady a good girl, we shall not find their "ethical premises" mixed at all, even though our modified Neo-Epicurean had, at first sight of his victim, been charmed into standing for a moment, stupidly good.

Another device making for unity would be to disregard those elements of what Mr. Allen calls "the pre-texts" which Milton did not specifically invoke. "Comus is, of course, the son and heir of Circe and the brother of Ariosto's Alcina, Trissino's Acratia, Tasso's Armida, and

Spenser's mistress of the Bower of Bliss" [*THV,* p. 33]. Of these five familial relations, four and a half are gratuitous attributions of Mr. Allen's; all Milton says is that Comus is a son of Circe. It is odd to suggest that Milton was "attempting to unite all these motifs with their diverse interpretations"; it is a great deal odder to blame him for not following "the traditional working-out of the pre-text" [*THV,* p. 33]. If he was really trying to unite five different moral allegories, on five different themes, the least one could grant Milton, it might seem, would be the right to modify his story a bit. And if he altered Geoffrey of Monmouth's account of Sabrina, the changes may indeed "bother those who have the original history in their heads" [*THV,* p. 35] so firmly that they cannot get it out; but these people would be bothered, too, by Shakespeare's liberties, in *Hamlet,* with Saxo Grammaticus.

Mr. Allen urges further that the theme of *Comus* "is not unspottedly Christian" because some pagans believed in the virtue of chastity [*THV,* p. 38] and that the time of the action is confused as between pre-Christian Albion and the Christian present. But, on the first point, few poems of any age have been so immaculately, not to say vindictively, Christian as to celebrate no virtue of which any pagan ever partook; nor am I aware that they have suffered from their contamination. The critical criterion is an odd one indeed. What the argument points toward is the idea that *Comus* is not a particularly Christian poem. This may or may not be true; the feeling, if not the machinery of the poem, is far from pagan. But even if *Comus* is not specifically Christian, neither is Donne's "Extasie" or Marvell's "Garden" and what this has to do with the merits of these poems as poems is by no means clear. On the second point, it is true that *Comus,* being a pastoral, takes place in a world outside time; so does "Lycidas," where the poet communes now with Phoebus, now with St. Peter and compares young Lycidas now with Orpheus and now with a Christian saint. So too in Spenser's *Shepherd's Calendar,* where Christian and pagan mythologies are cheerfully scrambled into a panegyric of Queen Elizabeth. If an indeterminate date in time, involving a confusion of mythologies, mars *Comus,* surely it mars a great many other works as well. No doubt Mr. Allen can reconcile or adjust his various critical opinions without much trouble; what is interesting is his explicit recognition of the fact that, in searching for something "intensely organic" (i.e., in which the decoration is structural), he has been led to make hash out of *Comus.* It is no accident; the same principles followed with the same deadly consistency would make hash out of almost all the poetry written by John Milton, or for that matter by most English poets.

The examples could be multiplied, but conclusions are privileged to generalize. The readings of *Comus* which emerge from a close analysis of the imagery, unchecked by a larger perspective on the poem's literal architecture, may yield a series of flashing, fragmentary insights but are unlikely to co-ordinate them into a coherent whole. For good or for evil, much of Milton's imagery is strictly decorative; his overtones exist to be realized and forgotten, not to be exalted into general principles and large-scale structural devices. In point of fact, brightness and coolness do not happen to be "associated with Virtue throughout the poem" [B & H, p. 225]; but even if they were, the fact would be of dubious structural significance. Milton did not compose *Comus* in cools and hots any more than in lights and darks, louds and softs, wets and drys, or thins and thicks. He made use of these qualities as occasion required, but he did not attribute allegorical or general significance to them without explicitly indicating it; their role is decorative and subordinate, not structural and primary. Any reader who chooses may, of course, impose an allegorical significance on any element he likes; but only at the risk of having to drop it when it no longer fits. In certain sections of the masque, for example, no radical harm ensues from associating Sabrina's aquatic habits with a cool, cleansing virtue. But if water-equals-virtue be made a constant equation, the brothers' search for virtue—"som cool friendly Spring" [l. 281]—then becomes responsible for the Lady's entire plight. No doubt any respectably energetic allegorist can invent in a few minutes half-a-dozen ways of getting over, under, around, or away from this difficulty; I am convinced that it would be far less distracting and far closer to the main lines of Milton's intent to let the water-virtue connection quietly disappear the minute it ceases to help our understanding of the images and begins to make demands on its own account. It should remain on the fringe of our minds, not in the center. If this critical outlook implies a low estimate of *Comus* as a tissue of images and implications, some consolation may perhaps be found in the sleazy weaving of all the fabrics hitherto produced from these materials. *Comus* as a masque presenting a clear story, a simple allegory, and a graceful compliment embroidered with a fluid imagery seems to me worth ten fretworks of strained conceit and forced interpretation. Perhaps when the critics have learned a little temperance in the application of their Byzantine ingenuities, we shall be able to enjoy without apology the simple beauties of obvious commonplaces set in musical language.

The Interpretation of *Comus*

A. E. Dyson

Comus is a delightful work in itself, and it is also of great interest as an introduction to Milton's later poems. Many of the poet's rhetorical and stylistic techniques, and certain moral ideas which are central to *Paradise Lost, Paradise Regained* and *Samson Agonistes* can be found in this early and glorious masque. In view of this, we may be more than a little surprised that so little space is devoted to it in the many excellent critical accounts of Milton which have recently been written. A full and valuable analysis is offered by A. S. P. Woodhouse in his article "The Argument of Milton's *Comus*",[1] but this errs, I think, on the side of being too elaborate and speculative. Mr. Woodhouse discovers several levels of meaning in the poem, but he makes far too much of the closing section, and his analysis is more intensively intellectual than the text seems to me to warrant. In one positive respect, too, I think that his emphasis is wrong. He maintains that the action of the poem is set in the realm of "Nature" until the closing pages, when the entry of "Sabrina fair" raises it to the realm of Grace. But to my mind, the visions of life belonging to nature and Grace respectively are present side by side throughout the poem, the one represented by the arguments of Comus, and the other by the type of insight and strength which protect the Lady. The fact that in dramatic terms Comus's view, though plausible, is shown to be false, and the Lady's view, though austere, to be true, is central to the poem's meaning, and what it is "really about".

The student of Milton will find Mr. Woodhouse's work interesting,

Reprinted from *Essays and Studies, 1955* (published by Messrs. John Murray Ltd. for the English Association) by permission of the English Association and the author.

[1] *Toronto Quarterly,* XI, 1941: "The Argument of Milton's *Comus*". *Toronto Quarterly,* XIX, 1950: "*Comus* Once More".

but not final. There is still room, I think, for an attempt to analyse the poem more simply in terms of the probable impressions which an educated seventeenth-century audience would have formed on seeing a dramatic presentation of it for the first or second time. This sort of analysis would both avoid the pitfall of over-subtlety, and serve as a better introduction to the study of similar themes and techniques in Milton's later works. It is something of this sort that I hope now to attempt.

Among other recent articles on *Comus,* Mr. J. C. Maxwell's in *The Cambridge Journal*[2] seems to me the most helpful. The substance of this present essay was written before I had the opportunity to read his remarks, but I find that I agree entirely with what he has to say. None of the more well-known Miltonic scholars, however, has studied *Comus* in detail except Dr. Tillyard, and it is from his analysis, now republished in *Studies in Milton,*[3] that I propose to differ a little. Despite some points of interest in his article, he seems to me to have misinterpreted the main movement of the masque. Like Mr. Woodhouse, he ascribes to the Epilogue, especially in its revised form in the 1637 edition, an importance which seems to me altogether exaggerated. He finds in it a significance which only a scholar who knows the text, almost literally, backwards, is likely to consider convincing. When *Comus* is transferred from the study to the stage, the main outline of its ideas, action and moral purpose unfolds gradually from its opening words; and the total effect of the masque is not only firmly established by the time that Sabrina fair makes her appearance, but practically finished and rounded off as well. The closing moments have their importance, admittedly, but more on account of the exquisite lyrical relief which they provide after the action than for any new ideas which they introduce, or for any vital modification of the total effect.

The interpretation of *Comus* centres upon what we make of the case between Comus and the Lady. Dr. Tillyard assures us that previous attempts to consider the case have been governed by the assumption that "one of the disputants is right". This, he thinks, is a misleading idea. "The assumption is false. Comus and the Lady are both wrong, or, if right, in ways they did not perceive". He bases this assertion on the belief that to accept the Lady at her face value is to accept Chastity as a

[2] *Cambridge Journal,* Vol. I, No. 6, March 1948: "The Pseudo-Problem of *Comus*".

[3] "The Action of *Comus*" originally appeared in *Essays and Studies*, Vol. XXVIII (1942–43); a revised version was republished in *Studies in Milton* (1951).

mode of life more excellent than Marriage; and he argues from passages inserted in the 1637 version of the Epilogue, as well as from personal conviction, that Milton did not himself believe this to be the case. I hope to return to this matter later, and to offer my own tentative opinion on Milton's feelings about Chastity and Marriage. But I wish to say now (and I find that Mr. Maxwell agrees with me), that in my reading of the poem the Lady stands not so much for Chastity as for self-control, insight and moral balance—or, to put this slightly differently, that she stands not for a particular virtue but for Virtue itself. Milton does, in point of fact, choose Chastity for his particular virtue, and I think that the choice was more than arbitrary. If I am right, he regarded it as the most important virtue of all (at least during this period of his thought). But in *Comus*, Chastity is more than an isolated virtue: it is symptomatic of spiritual wholeness and the life of Grace, and it is at the same time a special case, albeit the most important one, of that larger and classical issue, the control of the passions by the Reason. The great debate in *Comus* (and "debate", as I hope to show, is a misleading word: the issue is represented dramatically, and the actual debating points made by Comus and the Lady are to be seen and judged in the context of the poem as a whole)—the great "debate" is not between Chastity and Incontinence, and still less between Virginity and Marriage, but between Reason and Passion as controlling factors in human conduct.

The centrality of this theme in seventeenth-century literature has been impressed upon us by Dr. Tillyard himself, and there is no need for any more to be said about the context of thought in which Milton came to maturity. The predominating influence upon Milton's earlier ideas was Neo-Platonism, and a few extracts from some other of his earlier poems will serve my present purpose. In the fragment *On Time,* he contrasts the dull and gross world of changing things with the purity and joy of eternity. The power of Time extends only to bad and worthless things. All that is good and true is meant for the realm of timeless perfection. When Time has purged away all that it has power to purge,

> Which is no more than what is false and vain,
> And merely mortal dross . . .
>   then that which remains will be

> . . . everything that is sincerely good
> And perfectly divine . . .

And as for the end of Man, the poet tells us that

> . . . all this earthy grossness quit,
> Attired with stars, we shall for ever sit
> Triumphing over Death, and Chance, and thee, O Time!

The word "grossness" here is typical of Milton's attitude to the life on Earth. With the Earth, he identified all human passions, and especially those that link man with the animal and lower parts of creation.

Another powerful theme in the earlier poems, helpful to the understanding of *Comus,* is the Platonic vision of cosmos as harmony and chaos as disharmony. The following passage from *Arcades* combines the two familiar commonplaces, that the heavens are filled with music, but that only the virtuous can hear it:

> Such sweet compulsion doth in music lie
> To lull the daughters of Necessity,
> And keep unsteady Nature to her law,
> And the low world in measured motion draw
> After the heavenly tune, which none can hear
> Of human mould with gross unpurged ear. . . .

The lines *At a Solemn Music* include the Christian version of this notion, which accounts for our earthly exile from the cosmic harmony as one of the consequences of Original Sin. The poet pays his tribute to the celestial music, and prays

> That we on earth, with undiscording voice,
> May rightly answer that melodious noise;
> As once we did, till disproportioned Sin
> Jarred against Nature's chime, and with harsh din
> Broke the fair music that all creatures made
> To their great Lord. . . .

Now to return to *Comus:* the Lady is, I feel, "right", and Comus "wrong", and the movement of the entire drama is intended to illustrate this. I hope in a short analysis to support this view, but first I must make clear a few assumptions which I am making. The first of these is that Milton, as a seventeenth-century Christian, did not share the view that all ideas are equally fallible, or the view that "Truth", in so far as that vexed word has any meaning, is to be found in or through a synthesis of conflicting opinions. Though he was far from being naïve, he certainly believed that such distinctions as good and bad, white and black, true and false could be made, and that they were of the most vital importance. As a Puritan, moreover, he held a profoundly theological view of human nature and human history—a view which was the basis of the political ideals and revolutionary hopes expressed in his first prose tracts, and was firm and clear enough to inspire the white heat of apocalyptic expectation to which these ideals and hopes gave rise. He believed that though certain common arguments and actions are notoriously a mixture of truth and falsehood, there is no *necessary* reason why this should be so. The confusion is a consequence of the Fall of Man, not a reflection of ambiguity and contradiction in the nature of things. In the last resort, and to the recipients of a divine revelation, truth is both knowable and known; and a great gulf is eternally fixed between God and Satan, Heaven and Hell, Pride and Humility—between, in fact, Good and Evil, when considered in their final and absolute forms.

Milton further believed that the Devil and his emissaries were deceivers, and that the evil which they advocated was seldom without strong arguments and inducements in its favour. Their arguments, moreover, were not only subtle and well thought out, but also not without the support of plausible though misguided analogies drawn from the natural order. Satan in *Paradise Lost* is at pains to convince Eve that God really wants her to eat the apple, and that a correct consideration of the circumstances in which she has been placed should lead her to this conclusion. Comus, in the masque, argues with great power that the whole of Nature is in conformity with his view of life, and that the Lady, by her abstemiousness, is out of tune with her cosmic environment. Both of the deceivers do much more than to tempt the emotions; they tempt the mind itself to confound good with evil.

Milton believed, in addition to this, that the arguments of devils were particularly likely to appeal to fallen man, whose understanding is clouded by the effect of sin, so that he cannot clearly distinguish truth from error, and his will infected, so that he is more than half in love with sin. The notion of "truth" as a discovery made by the intellect alone would no doubt have shocked Milton deeply. "Truth" on the spiritual level was reserved for the pure in heart to know. Those who relied upon their intellects alone would fall ready victims, he would have supposed, to the rationalizations and sophistries of devils.

Milton did not, therefore, make the mistake of underestimating the diabolical mind. In his representation, which is also the traditional one, evil is not unsubtle, but unrealistic; not unintelligent, but wrong. To an age like our own, which tends to equate "truth" with the findings of the intellect and intellectual prowess with the result of an I.Q. test, this may seem puzzling: but our modern view is at variance with the Christian and Platonic one, that purity and moral discipline are the doorways to knowledge concerning good and evil, and that this is a knowledge which no exercise of the discursive faculties, however capable, can hope to discover.

When Milton gave a devil or tempter his intellectual due, we must remember, then, that he was very far from admitting that there might be "something in" what was being said; and when he gave them their emotional due, in that their temptations really are tempting, and not mere *tours de force* of abstract logic, he was not revealing an inward sympathy with the sins that were being advocated. This may seem a very obvious point, yet it is often overlooked by respectable critics.

To some people, indeed, it seems, if we can believe them, that Milton is hardly worthy to be thought of as a serious artist if he was entirely out of sympathy with Comus (and, after Comus, of course, with Satan). The very idea of an artist seems to them to imply some pagan and diabolical affinities. The view is surely plausible, however, that Milton proved himself an artist, if not by some Bohemian affection for his devils and tempters, at least by giving them a proper run for their money. No one can accuse him of making Comus less than attractive, or of creating a devil who is too obviously unacceptable in human eyes to be dangerous. Comus, like Satan, is a splendid creation, with striking arguments to help him in his work of tempting, and with splendid verse in which to dress them out. This is not the place to debate whether poetry is more at home in Hell than in Heaven; but on a practical level we must remember that no poet can afford to deny his full gifts to any of the characters he creates, and that richly sensuous verse is more appropriate in a moral work to the bad dramatis personae than to the good ones.

My assumption, therefore, bearing all this in mind, is that in a moral or theological debate Milton would be almost certain to believe one side of the case, despite his ability very forcibly to present the other. Dr. Tillyard rightly points to the use of rhetoric in *Comus,* and to the poem's affinities with an academic disputation, but wrongly concludes that Milton is in an impartial and midway position between the two chief disputants. On some issues, no doubt, Milton suspended judgement, and found the technique of arguing more interesting than the arguments themselves. But in matters of the sort which are at issue in *Comus* he would inevitably have been deeply involved. The arguments which he gives to Comus (and to Satan) are not exercises in rhetoric but insights into evil. To suppose for a moment that they can be thought to be anything other than this is to get the whole of his poetry out of perspective.

An example of Milton's rhetorical powers used more or less for their own sake is to be found in *L'Allegro* and *Il Penseroso,* which, as Dr. Tillyard has shown, can be regarded as academic exercises, the one in praise of day and the other of night. But even here, Milton is dealing with moods which are familiar to all men, and the poems are more imaginative and delightful than the view of them as "academic exercises" naturally suggests. *L'Allegro* expresses the desire for a full, pagan and sensuous life, and might be one of Comus's songs. *Il Penseroso,* in contrast to this, embodies the longing for a sober, scholarly existence, far from the madding crowd. Milton knew quite well that these were only moods, and that his fanciful idealization of the thoughts to which they gave rise into a whole way of life was nothing more than a pleasing fantasy. The poems are only day-dreams, and no attempt therefore is made to link them, or to adjudicate between them in the context of a larger framework of thought. Milton does his best for each mood in turn, devoting his intelligence, fancy, and skill in using words to the task of "making out a case" for them. This looks forward, therefore, to the technique in *Comus,* but we must bear in mind this important difference—that whereas these earlier poems are so slight and fanciful that Milton can afford to be unimplicated, the speeches of Comus and the Lady respectively are not. It is also of importance that whereas *L'Allegro* and *Il Penseroso* exist on their own, the speeches in *Comus* are set in a dramatic context, with reference to which they are to be judged.

There are a few other general considerations relevant to *Comus,* which I shall do little more than list. One of them touches a point which Professor C. S. Lewis makes in his "Preface To *Paradise Lost*", that an artist finds it easier to depict a bad character than a good one. For the former, he has only to look within, and to report the promptings of all those instincts and desires which in his own life he tries to suppress. For the latter he has to look outwards to a moral balance and perfection which he has not as yet attained, and which is less attractive to fallen man than ideally it should be. If we are tempted to think of the Lady as being less attractive than Comus, at least we should bear this in mind.

A related fact to remember is that a poet finds it easier to portray the passions than the reason. His richer verse rhythms are more appropriate to the former than to the latter. In my own opinion, the bareness and austerity of Milton's verse when he is writing speeches for the Lady (and later on for God the Father in *Paradise Lost* and for God the Son in *Paradise Regained*) is not necessarily inferior, when seen in perspective, to the sort of verse which he creates for Comus and Satan. But the verse spoken by Comus is undoubtedly more *immediately* attractive than that of his intended victim; and no doubt the emotional nature of his appeals makes this more or less inevitable.

We should remember also that it is easier for Milton to create an advocate of falsehood than an advocate of truth, and easier to create Comus's frivolity than the Lady's "high seriousness". Comus and his crew, like Satan after them, are liars, and can say anything that comes into their heads. As long as they have a practical aim in view, they can rationalize and defend it as freely as they wish. Saving only that their arguments must be intelligent, plausible, and at least superficially attractive, they can range in their discourse as freely as they will. This allows very great scope for passionate declamation, rich sensuousness, persuasive logic and all the poet's other arts. But God, and the angels, and the good characters, in contrast to this freedom, are limited very severely to true statements and respectable modes of presentation. They have to be not plausible and attractive, but right—and right in a way that would satisfy a seventeenth-century audience with an inordinate taste for theological niceties.

The consequences of this are widespread. The good characters cannot invent freely. They must always be wise and judicious, the reverse of passionate. Their arguments must appeal to the mind by way of the moral sense, not by way of the emotions. They cannot clothe their words in suasive language without undermining the supposed power of truth to stand in its own light, unaided by stylistic devices. They cannot, above all, attempt to ally themselves on the sly with those "weak and beggarly elements" in man's soul out of which tempters and devils make good capital. They have to be as innocent as the dove without being as cunning as the serpent.

As far as *Paradise Lost* is concerned, Milton had further serious obstacles in his path, and not least among them the intractable and very probably contradictory nature of his myth.[4] The lesser difficulties which I have just been considering, however, apply as much to *Comus* as to the

[4] In *Paradise Lost,* too, I think that the existence of a major "split" in the poem is much more probable than is the existence of such a split in *Comus.* The tragic intensity of some of the speeches of Satan and Adam really does transcend, and perhaps weaken, the already precarious theological framework. But in *Comus,* the framework is less complicated, and more intrinsically acceptable as a whole, and no hint of anything as serious as tragic feeling enters into the speeches of Comus himself.

later poem, and if we study them here we shall perhaps improve our understanding of Milton's work as a whole. I am taking now as a working rule that in any of Milton's poems, whenever God, or an unfallen angel or spirit, or a character embodying Right Reason speaks, then he must be considered "right" in this sense: that the views on religious or moral problems which he expresses correspond, as Milton understood it, to the landscape of reality, and are unequivocally accepted by him as "true". The good character is not partly right and partly wrong, and the truth does not lie somewhere (or even nowhere) between his views, and views expressed by other characters. Likewise, when a devil or a fallen spirit, or an advocate of the passions against the Reason speaks, he is always warped in outlook, and subtly wrong in every detail. His views though intelligent, and embodying arguments which might, in a slightly different context be valid, do not correspond to reality, and if heeded, can produce only disastrous results. His whole concept of reality is out of touch with the facts, and he is unable, quite literally, to say anything that is untouched by distortion.

In *Comus,* the characters seem to me to be grouped as follows. The Lady, as "a most wonderful piece of virtue", is right, and Comus, as a tempter, is wrong. The Attendant Spirit is a visitant from the purer regions far away from our fallen Earth, and can, therefore, be taken to be fully reliable. The two brothers are ordinary humans, but their lengthy deliberations are informed by the spirit of understanding, and are in many ways a reiteration of what the Attendant Spirit has to say. The Lady herself, touching her status, seems to me to be both allegorical and real. She is Chastity (or Virtue) incarnate, and her purpose is to illustrate the immutable nature and wisdom of this virtue. She is not, like Eve, an entirely real person, likely to be overcome by temptation and ruin herself. But at the same time, because Milton thought that the attainment of virtue was not impossible to flesh and blood, she is not entirely allegorical. She is an attempt to portray an actual, if rather rarefied mortal, reacting properly to a difficult and trying situation. I hope now to show that this reading of *Comus* is the only one possible in the light of the action as a whole.

The first character to appear is the Attendant Spirit, and his opening words amount to a presentation of credentials. He is, he tells us, one of those "bright aerial spirits" that lives in a serene and calm peace, far removed from the corrupt world beneath the moon:

> Before the starry threshold of Jove's court
> My mansion is, where those immortal shapes

> Of bright aerial spirits live ensphered
> In regions mild of calm and serene air,
> Above the smoke and stir of this dim spot
> Which men call earth. . . .

He is, therefore, someone on whose word we may rely; and he comes, not without personal inconvenience, to aid that minority amongst mankind who seek to escape from their sordid terrestrial prison and to climb to those purer heights where virtue alone ("that golden key") can open the way to mortal flesh:

> . . . some there be that, by due steps, aspire
> To lay their just hands on that golden key
> That opes the palace of Eternity:
> To such my errand is; and, but for such,
> I would not soil these pure ambrosial weeds
> With the rank vapours of this sin-worn mould. . . .

The phrasing here is Platonic, and Platonic thinking is at the root of all Milton's theology, deeper than his Evangelicalism, deeper than his Puritanism. Behind these opening words of the Spirit is the belief that Virtue is Knowledge, and that an unclouded understanding is both the condition of Virtue, and its reward. Temptation, in Milton, always begins with an attempt to cloud the understanding as a prelude to perverting the will.[5] In *Paradise Lost,* for example, Satan first leads his own mind astray with false arguments arising from pride, and then he rebels against God. Adam and Eve are later subjected to a similar (though more complex and plausible) onslaught upon their understandings, with the result that they, too, fall from grace. The actual sin which Adam and Eve commit is disobedience: they assert their supposed right to ignore the dictates of God. The result of their sin, theologically, is death—a permanent separation from God brought about by their own chosen and irrevocable action. The result of their sin, in practical terms

[5] Milton believed, I think, that sin was fundamentally an act of rebellion against God originating in wilful disobedience. Eve is distinctly told not to eat the fruit, and Samson not to reveal the secret of his strength; and the clouding of their minds with false ideas, though it gives psychological probability to their defection, in no way serves to excuse them.

One of the great problems which faced Milton in *Paradise Lost* was to show how creatures whose happiness lies in obedience to God, and whose intellects are perfectly aware of this, can ever be supposed to fall. This is a very difficult thing to show indeed, and I do not think that Milton succeeds. In *Comus,* however, he is concerned only to show how a clear and virtuous understanding protects its possessor against false representations. This is an easier task, and I think that he meets with greater success.

(and this is the result of Satan's sin also) is that their Reason is overthrown, and lawless passions are unleashed which will bring their whole being—body, mind and spirit—into degradation, disintegration, and decay. Their minds are no longer illuminated with insight, but move in a maze of unfounded illusions and impossible hopes. Their spirits are tormented with uncontrollable passions (in Satan's case, envy and bitterness,[6] in the case of Adam and Eve, lust).[7] Their bodies are mirrors of the troubled souls within, and begin soon to show, visibly and unmistakably, signs of the hell that rages there. Of Satan, as he is shaken with envy, Milton records the following:

> Thus while he spake, each passion dimmed his face
> Thrice changed with pale ire, envy and despair:
> Which marred his borrowed visage, and betrayed
> Him counterfeit, if any eye beheld:
> For heavenly minds from such distempers foul
> Are ever clear. . . .

And it is at this moment in the poem that Uriel, whom Satan has recently deceived, catches sight of the fallen angel's face, and knows him for what he is. Adam and Eve, after they recover from their bout of lust, also see in one another's bodies the evident marks of a fall from grace:

> Our wonted ornaments now soiled and stained,
> And in our faces evident the signs
> Of foul concupiscence. . . .

The loss of Virtue, then, is followed by loss of self-control, and by growing conformity with the environment of a fallen world. This condition can be mended only by a gradual purification and discipline of the soul, undertaken in the desire to transcend this corrupt and transient world, and to seek reunion with the spiritual and intellectual realities beyond.

This, of course, is public doctrine, and one small aspect of the familiar medieval synthesis of Christian and Platonic ideas. The doctrine is central to the meaning of *Paradise Lost,* and it is implied, with the Platonic elements predominating, in the Spirit's opening speech in *Comus.* When the Spirit speaks of an ascent "by due steps" to the eternal world, he is thinking in terms of the ladder of love in the *Symposium,* with the meaning adapted to a Christian context. His first words, therefore, give a clear indication of the masque's context of ideas,

[6] *Paradise Lost,* Book IV, lines 1–120.
[7] *Paradise Lost,* Book IX, lines 1011–66.

and he goes on without a pause to say that he has come to protect the Lady, who is wandering in the allegorical wood of human perplexities, from an enemy who is most likely planning to tempt her. This account of the situation at once removes what follows from the level of a debate, and fixes the Lady as "Right" and her enemy as "Wrong". The Spirit goes on to talk about Comus, and now, not only the masque's ideas, but its symbolism also, is employed to enforce Milton's main intention. Comus is the son of Circe, and nothing could be clearer (as Dr. Tillyard points out), than the allegorical significance attaching to his magic cup,

> Whoever tasted, lost his upright shape,
> And downward fell into a grovelling swine. . . .

The victims of the cup are those who are degraded by unbridled sensuality to the status of beasts. They are travelling down the ladder of creation towards the brutes instead of upwards towards the angels. The Spirit's description of their plight is in keeping with the Neo-Platonic and Christian synthesis of ideas which I have just been referring to. Participation in animal pleasures has so blinded their minds, that they mistake their degradation for enlightenment and their wretched and godless state for the best of all possible worlds.

> Soon as the potion works, their human countenance,
> The express resemblance of the gods, is changed
> Into some brutish form of wolf or bear,
> Or ounce, or tiger, hog, or bearded goat,
> All other parts remaining as they were;
> And they, so perfect is their misery,
> Not once perceive their foul disfigurement,
> But boast themselves more comely than before;
> And all their friends and native home forget,
> To roll with pleasure in a sensual sty. . . .

The Spirit's Introduction helps us, therefore, to get our bearings, and it is followed by the stage direction:

Comus enters with a charming-rod in one hand, his glass in the other; with him a rout of monsters, headed like sundry sorts of wild beasts, but otherwise like men and women, their apparel glistering; they come in, making a riotous and unruly noise, with torches in their hands.

We note here (and if we are at a performance we can scarcely miss it) the "riotous and unruly noise", symbolizing chaos, sin, disharmony. The Lady, in contrast to this, is always associated with music and concord, and her singing ravishes with delight all who have the good fortune to hear it. This is one of the several ways in which Milton involves the claim of Comus to "imitate the starry choir" in a sustained irony, and keeps the true facts of the matter firmly before us.

Comus opens with some gay and infectious verse, in the manner of *L'Allegro.* The idealized picture which he presents of pagan joy is immediately attractive, as it is intended to be. We are so enchanted by it, that we are almost glad to hear him dismissing some of those more tiresome virtues, which could only spoil the fun—"Rigour", "Advice", "Strict Age", and "sour severity". (The unobtrusive but effective use of suasive adjectives, "strict", "sour" and so on, is a routine piece of trickery.) But Comus goes on without a pause to make a claim which directly contradicts the view of the situation presented by the Spirit, yet one which the Spirit's words have warned us to expect:

> We that are of purer fire
> Imitate the starry choir,
> Who, in their nightly watchful spheres,
> Lead in swift round the months and years. . . .

He asserts, in fact, that the discords emanating from his rout are indistinguishable from the celestial harmony. Dr. Tillyard notes this claim, and calls it "impudence", but he does not integrate its far-reaching implications with his reading of the poem as a whole. Actually, of course, Comus is illustrating the type of blindness which the Spirit has just been alluding to:

> And they, so perfect is their misery,
> Not once perceive their foul disfigurement,
> But boast themselves more comely than before . . .

He is involved in the doom of nonsense.

Comus now hears the Lady in the wood, and resolves to tempt her. He explains, with the directness and reliability of a pre-Shakespearean soliloquy, what his normal procedure in such circumstances is:

> I, under fair pretence of friendly ends,
> And well placed words of glozing courtesy,
> Baited with reasons not unplausible,
> Wind me into the easy-hearted man,
> And hug him into snares.

This should be more of a warning than it is to some of the easy-hearted critics whom Comus has also hugged into snares. The tempter says that he is going to be plausible, but deadly. Any sneaking suspicion which we have that the Lady would have been more normal and agreeable if she *had* taken just a moderate sip from his cup should be firmly rejected. Upon her power to give the correct answers to his "reasons not unplausible" depends the whole of Milton's vision of reality.

The Lady enters, meditating on her predicament in rich and moving verse. Those who complain that she has the worst of the poetry do not sufficiently consider this speech. Even on the naïve assumption that the more sensuous the verse the more worth-while it is, this speech is among the finest in the poem. The Lady calmly reviews the dangers surrounding her, and is confident that a moral and religious armour will protect her from even the worst assaults of the enemy:

> O welcome pure-eyed Faith, white-handed Hope,
> Thou hovering angel girt with golden wings,
> And thou, unblemished form of Chastity. . . .

These, except that Chastity replaces Charity, are the theological virtues, and the reference to them reinforces the allegorical structure of the action.[8] The Lady now breaks into a song, to the excellence and harmony of which Comus himself bears ecstatic witness:

> Can any mortal mixture of Earth's mould
> Breathe such divine enchanting ravishment?
> Sure something holy lodges in that breast,
> And with these raptures moves the vocal air
> To testify his hidden residence. . . .

Comus bears witness also to the Lady's serenity and peace of mind: the evidence of a spiritual wholeness which, ironically, he cannot really understand, and is able only to destroy.[9]

> . . . such a sacred and home-felt delight,
> Such sober certainty of waking bliss
> I never heard till now.

[8] Kenneth Muir has based upon this replacement of Charity by Chastity his belief that the Lady's virtue is criticized in the poem (*Penguin New Writing*, No. 24, 1945: "Three Hundred Years of Milton's Poems"). But the replacement seems to me quite natural in the circumstances, and I agree with Mr. Maxwell in finding Muir's argument unconvincing. Certainly, when so much evidence points in the other direction, this point seems a very slight one.

[9] So also, in *Paradise Lost* does Satan bear witness to the alien and detested joys of Paradise.

The first stage of Comus's attack on the Lady now occurs, and meets with success in that she believes his words and entrusts herself to his guidance. She is deceived, of course, only on a matter of fact, not culpably. The insinuating and courtly over-tones in his speech ("And left your fair side all unguarded, Lady?") have made no impression upon her innocent mind, and she has accepted him on his own showing as a simple shepherd. She is in his power, therefore, but only physically so.

The scene shifts to her two brothers, who are naturally disturbed when they reflect upon the possible plight of their mislaid sister, but are enabled by the allegorical nature of the danger to pause for a discussion of its moral implications instead of rushing off at once to look for her. This section is intellectually the most concentrated in the poem, and to try to adjudicate between the Lady and Comus without giving due weight to it is to miss the point rather badly.

The elder brother sings the praises of Virtue, and insists that no harm can befall those who are protected by their purity. The inner nature of a man, the heaven or hell which he has made for himself within, cannot be changed by any danger or influence from without. Only an act of free will can effect such a change, not the mere exigencies of environment or outside suggestion.

> He that has light within his own clear breast
> May sit in the centre and enjoy bright day:
> But he that hides a dark soul, and foul thoughts,
> Benighted walks under the mid-day sun;
> Himself is his own dungeon. . . .

This looks forward to one of the important themes in *Paradise Lost* upon which I have already touched, that Hell, although for allegorical purposes it is given a local habitation, is more essentially a state of mind—or, more accurately perhaps, a gradual disintegration of mind, body and spirit following upon an initial act of disobedience towards God. When Satan has left the physical Hell far behind, he is in no whit released from the reality which its monstrous and shifting images symbolize:

> . . . horror and doubt distract
> His troubled thoughts, and from the bottom stir
> The Hell within him; for within him Hell
> He brings, and round about him, nor from Hell
> One step, no more than from himself, can fly
> By change of place. . . .

In a similar way, a good man can walk among any evil things without being touched by them. This is the theme which the Elder Brother goes on to speak about when he reviews his sister's defences. The power of Chastity is absolutely invincible.

> So dear to Heaven is saintly Chastity,
> That when a soul is found sincerely so,
> A thousand liveried Angels lackey her,
> Driving far off each thing of sin and guilt;
> And, in clear dream, and solemn vision,
> Tell her of things that no gross ear can hear,
> Till oft converse with heavenly habitants
> Begin to cast a beam on the outward shape,
> The unpolluted temple of the mind,
> And turn it by degrees to the soul's essence,
> Till all be made immortal. . . .

Chastity here, as I said earlier, is only one example (though the supreme one) of self-control, Reason, and the life of Grace. It is the entrance to that world of spiritual realities from which Comus and his crew are totally excluded. The Brother goes on to deal with the other side of the picture, the world in which Comus and his followers move:

> . . . but when lust,
> By unchaste looks, loose gestures, and foul talk,
> But most by lewd, and lavish acts of sin,
> Lets in defilement to the inward parts,
> The soul grows clotted by contagion,
> Imbodies and imbrutes, till she quite lose
> The divine property of her first being.
> Such are those thick and gloomy shadows damp
> Oft-seen in charnel vaults and sepulchres,
> Lingering and sitting by a new-made grave,
> As loathe to leave the body that it loved,
> And linked itself, by carnal sensuality,
> To a degenerate and degraded state.

This passage sums up many of the themes I have been dealing with, and properly considered, makes nonsense of the notion that the Lady is partly wrong. The Younger Brother is so impressed by the realities with which it deals that he exclaims:

> How charming is divine Philosophy;

and as though to confirm this view, the Attendant Spirit arrives a few moments later to say most of it over again, but with the peculiar authority which belongs to him as a good Angel:

> Within the navel of this hideous wood,
> Immured in cypress shades, a sorcerer dwells,
> Of Bacchus and of Circe born—great Comus,
> Deep skilled in all his mother's witcheries;
> And here to every thirsty wanderer
> By sly enticement gives his baneful cup,
> With many murmurs mixed, whose pleasing poison
> The visage quite transforms of him that drinks,
> And the inglorious likeness of a beast
> Fixes instead, unmoulding Reason's mintage
> Charactered in the face.[10]

The Spirit then tells of how he has heard the Lady in the wood, using imagery which once more compares the melodiousness of her singing with the dissonance of her enemy:

> The wonted roar was up amidst the woods,
> And filled the air with barbarous dissonance;
> At which I ceased, and listened them awhile,
> Till an unusual stop of sudden silence
> Gave respite to the drowsy-flighted steeds,
> That draw the litter of close-curtained sleep;
> At last a soft and solemn breathing sound

> Rose like a steam of rich distilled perfumes,
> And stole upon the air, that even Silence
> Was took ere she was ware, and wished she might
> Deny her nature, and be never more
> Still to be so displaced. . . .

Milton is now almost ready for his central dramatic episode. The Elder Brother still finds time, however, to improve the occasion with a few further divinely philosophic reflections, which serve also as a programme note to the scene about to follow:

> Virtue may be assailed, but never hurt,
> Surprised by unjust force, but not inthralled;
> Yea, even that which mischief meant most harm
> Shall in the happy trial prove most glory:

[10] This is the clearest statement in *Comus* of the belief which I have already mentioned, that the body is an outward and visible sign of inward and spiritual disorders.

> But evil on itself shall back recoil,
> And mix no more with goodness; when at last,
> Gathered like scum, and settled to itself,
> It shall be in eternal restless change
> Self-fed, and self-consumed: if this fail,
> The pillared firmament is rottenness,
> And Earth's base built on stubble. . . .

This phrasing echoes passages which have already been quoted from Milton's earlier poetry, and amounts to an impressive declaration of faith. The ultimate value of life is said to depend upon the certainty that Good is stronger than Evil, and that Good will necessarily triumph at the last.

The central scene is prefixed with the direction:

The scene changes to a stately palace, set out with all manner of deliciousness: soft music, tables spread with all dainties. Comus appears with his rabble, and the Lady set in an enchanted chair, to whom he offers his glass, which she puts by, and goes about to rise.

Comus's first speech is a polished and luxurious statement of victory. He has the Lady as firmly "in his power" as any villain in Victorian melodrama, though only touching her physical captivity and on the level of allegory.

> Nay, Lady, sit! if I but wave this wand,
> Your nerves are all chained up in alabaster,
> And you a statue, or as Daphne was,
> Root-bound, that fled Apollo.[11]

The Lady answers vigorously, claiming to be free in mind, despite the captivity of her body. And here we must allow, I think, that though her manner seems ungracious, she has no cause for it to be otherwise. The position in which she is placed does not lend itself to social graces and charms. Also, she is not a maiden of ordinary flesh and blood defending her honour with greater or lesser enthusiasm in a Mayfair drawing-room, but the embodiment of that vital and perennial conflict between chastity and lust. The outstanding qualities of her answer to Comus are clarity of diction, precision of thought, and rightness of moral content. These qualities are set in balance against the sensuous, suasive and

[11] Of incidental interest here is the syntax, which looks forward to *Paradise Lost.* Grammatically, it is involved and "unEnglish"; poetically, it is an example of that rich "placing" of ideas and images which is characteristic of Milton's creative use of language. This point has been developed, I believe, by Mr. Rajan, in his excellent study *Paradise Lost & the Seventeenth Century Reader.*

insidious style of Comus, and are dramatically very fitting and appropriate. Only the critic who is unwilling either to believe in the spiritual values of which Milton is writing, or to suspend his disbelief, will find the Lady's style less artistically acceptable than that of Comus.

Comus now begins his first temptation, which is an invitation to the Lady to escape from the toils, perplexities and hardships of endless moral warfare, into the warm, refreshing easefulness of surrender. The first half is a direct appeal to the sensual appetites, which, as a human being, the Lady will be certain to experience:

> . . . here be all the pleasures
> That fancy can beget on youthful thoughts
> When the fresh blood grows lively. . . .

Then comes a call to surrender, which combines Comus's supposed concern for the Lady's happiness with the implied reproach that she is being unnatural:

> Why should you be so cruel to yourself,
> And to those dainty limbs which nature lent
> For gentle usage, and soft delicacy?

This is supported by the strong emotional enticement of the idea that "everybody does it"—an idea which is one of the strongest weapons in any tempter's hands. Comus speaks of "the unexempt condition, By which all mortal frailty must subsist", infusing great suasive force into his placing of the words "unexempt" and "must"; and follows this with the narcotic lotos-music of a "dying fall":

> Refreshment after toil, ease after pain,
> That have been tired all day without repast,
> And timely rest have wanted. . . .

The Lady's reply to this is as sharp and unenchanting as a douche of cold water, and exactly what is required by the drama. If we are not ourselves victims of Comus's spells, and are responding to the work as it exists in Milton's intention, we shall be filled with relief and austere joy by what she has to say, and the way she has to say it. She states, quite unequivocally, that Comus is wrong. She sweeps away at one stroke the seductive and evil plausibility of his temptation. She looks at the mixed rabble who have heeded him in the past, and sees them not as they are fallaciously represented to be, but as they really are:

> . . . What grim aspects are these
> These ugly-headed monsters?

This is to see things steadily and to see them whole. The Lady's words mark the place where her victory becomes actually, as well as theoretically, certain. With this unimpaired view of the situation, she is unlikely to be impressed by anything further that the tempter has to say. When she goes on to tell him, in no ambiguous terms, that

> . . . None
> But such as are good men, can give good things,
> And that which is not good, is not delicious
> To a well-governed and wise appetite . . .

we shall accuse her of being "priggish" [12] only if we totally ignore the masque's meaning; and we shall accuse her of being "unpoetic" only if we have a very naïve view of the nature and function of dramatic verse.

Comus enters now upon his main temptation, which makes explicit the view of reality behind his attitude. He develops the claim that the whole of Nature is on his side, and by drawing extensive and powerful analogies, provides a congenial "interpretation" of the message which the natural order has for man. This is a great piece of diabolical advocacy, and is at daring and conscious variance to the traditional religious modes of thought. The stoics, and others who preach temperance, are represented as soured, foolish, and out of sympathy with Nature's express example of fertility and abundance.

> Wherefore did Nature pour her bounties forth
> With such a full and unwithdrawing hand,
> Covering the Earth with odours, fruits and flocks,
> Thronging the seas with spawn innumerable,
> But all to please and sate the curious taste? . . .

He draws from his own reading of Nature the great lesson,

> . . . if all the world
> Should, in a pet of temperance, feed on pulse,
> Drink the clear stream, and nothing wear but freize,
> The Allgiver would be unthanked, would be unpraised . . .

The entire tenor of the masque, as I have been attempting to prove, is a demonstration of the falseness of this argument. Milton has been creating a dramatic and poetic context in which this classic but misguided interpretation of Nature can be seen to be not Reason, but

[12] A misleading word at the best of times, which tends to prejudge moral issues according to personal tastes instead of to clarify them in the light of reason.

Unreason "Baited with reasons not unplausible". We hold our breath as Comus sweeps on to his inevitable conclusion, that the Lady should descend to bestiality, and so be ruined. Only during the temptation of Eve in Book IX of *Paradise Lost,* when our foreknowledge of what the outcome will be adds unbearable irony to the situation, does Milton work up greater excitement in a temptation scene. The temptation of Christ in *Paradise Regained* is a tamer (though not less interesting) affair, which moves for the most part on an intellectual and unemotional level, and which is predestined to very certain failure. The temptation of Samson is nearer to this in type, but Samson's bitter disillusionment and almost paranoiac self-reproach do not allow Delilah much of a chance to be effective. Comus, however, even though he has met his match in the Lady, has all that is most natural and pagan in man on his side, and is more likely to find sympathetic ears among uncritical hearers than any of the Miltonic "enemies of man" who come after him:

> Beauty is Nature's coin, must not be hoarded,
> But must be current. . . .
> If you let slip time, like a neglected rose
> It withers on the stalk with languished head.
> Beauty is Nature's brag, and must be shown
> In courts, at feasts, and high solemnities. . . .

It is a great relief, though no longer perhaps a surprise, to find the Lady still unmoved by all this, and very vigorously in her right mind:

> I had not thought to have unlocked my lips
> In this unhallowed air, but that this juggler
> Would think to charm my judgment, as mine eyes
> Obtruding false rules pranked in Reason's garb . . .

Her verse has exactly the right qualities to offset that of Comus—short, decisive words, clear syntax, sharp diction, and firm structural control. She proceeds to deliver a brief and reasoned defence of temperance, in words which sound, at this stage of history, a shade too much like socialist propaganda, but are none the less salutary for that: and she ends by reaffirming the faith which both the Attendant Spirit and the Elder Brother have placed their hope in:

> . . . To him that dares
> Arm his profane tongue with contemptuous words
> Against the sun-clad power of Chastity,
> Fain would I something say,—yet to what end?

> Thou hast nor ear, nor soul to apprehend
> The sublime notion, and high mystery,
> That must be uttered to unfold the sage
> And serious doctrine of Virginity. . . .

Comus, as I have insisted already, is not on the same scale as *Paradise Lost.* It is altogether slighter and more pastoral, and the Lady, as Virtue Triumphant, has a different, and less melancholy role to fulfil than that of Eve as our first parent. When her victory is indisputably won, Comus admits in an aside

> She fables not; I feel that I do fear
> Her words set off by some superior power,

and his return to the attack,

> Come, no more,
> This is mere moral babble

is half-hearted, and speedily terminated by the arrival of the rescue party. The victory is won, and the rest of the masque, as Dr. Tillyard remarks, is in the nature of a coda—an enchanting pastoral close (for now that Virtue has triumphed, it can afford to display enchantments of its own), but not of sufficient significance seriously to modify our awareness of the main events, which are now over and done with.

I said at the beginning of this essay that though I consider Chastity to be chiefly important as an example of Virtue and Right Reason, I do not think that Milton chose it in any arbitrary spirit. In the Platonic scheme of things, purification is an essential preparation for insight, and the aim of mankind must be to transcend material and transient things altogether, and to seek to rise "by due steps" to the world of pure spirit. In this type of pilgrimage, any earthly ties and affections are likely to prove a hindrance, whether they are within the bands of wedlock or not. Later on in his life, no doubt, Milton came to terms with the more specifically Christian view (which Spenser expresses in *The Faerie Queene*), that Marriage is an estate as honourable as Virginity, and equally compatible with chastity, temperance and Reason. But in his earlier work (and certainly before the 1637 insertion into the Epilogue of *Comus*), I think that he regarded Virginity as superior to Marriage, both because it is more in keeping with the Platonic view of Virtue, and because it is an aspiration more capable of inspiring and sustaining a white-heat of idealistic fervour than is its humdrum and widely practised alternative.

We must always remember the stern and exhilarating heights of idealism among which Milton dwelt in his youth, and the passionately uncompromising moral dicta which he was in the habit of delivering from his happy vantage-point—"Virtue which wavers is not virtue, but vice revolted from itself, and after a while returning." Whereas Temperance and a due respect for the marriage vows are intellectual and often rather tired conceptions, Virginity can be a shining and exalted ideal. Milton's appetite for wholeness was, on any showing, more robust than anything to which we are accustomed by modern literature. It is also an important aspect of his particular genius and greatness.

To my mind, therefore, the Lady is an exponent of Virginity in its most absolute form, and I do not think that she would have felt the need to water down her opinions for the benefit of less aspiring mortals. But whether she would have taken kindly to an honourable proposal of marriage or not, it is certain that she stands for unswerving Virtue and for the life of Grace, and that her position is totally vindicated in the masque as a complete work of art.

I should like, in conclusion, to return to the article by Mr. Woodhouse, "The Argument of Milton's *Comus*". Mr. Woodhouse distinguishes four different virtues in the Lady's make-up; Temperance, Continence, Chastity and Virginity. He maintains that the first two of these belong to the order of Nature, the third to the orders of Nature and of Grace alike, and the fourth to the order of Grace alone. Upon this division he bases an elaborate analysis of the poem, but one which seems to me unduly complicated by the somewhat arbitrary divisions which he has drawn, and by the posing of problems which I agree with Mr. Maxwell in feeling to be "pseudo". If I am right, Nature and Grace do not need to be thought of as separate orders with a tendency to overlap, as Mr. Woodhouse suggests, but as two different modes of cognizing and responding to the human situation. The philosophy of Comus is that of the "natural man" in the Pauline sense: he is wholly pagan in outlook, and "knoweth not the things of God". The Lady belongs to the world of Grace, and her entire attitude, even at points where it overlaps with the beliefs of stoics or other "natural philosophers", springs from a true and spiritual vision of reality. We should not make the mistake of thinking that she and Comus are arguing at any point in the masque on the same "level", or that the arguments of one can be thought of as "positive" and those of the other as "negative". The Lady's attitude is positive, and unified, and "right", and Comus's position is positive, and unified, and wrong. The differences between them are of an entirely fundamental nature, and the masque consists of a straight battle between the two in which the Lady, as I have already insisted, comes off wholly triumphant, winning a victory which is not just a personal affair, but very much wider in its significance. This, it seems to me, is a simpler and more clear-cut issue than Mr. Woodhouse's article suggests; and it is central to the interpretation of *Comus.*

Image, Form, and Theme in *A Mask*

Rosemond Tuve

Milton's own title for what we call 'Comus' attaches it to a genre which has been dead nearly three hundred years. Dramas, odes, lyrics, sonnets, elegies, and even epics—all Milton's other forms are still written and still read; the masque is not a living form. It is true that students of the period have read a considerable number of masques,[1] but since masques were rather to be seen, and to be heard, even this is rather like saying that a limited number of persons have listened to several other ballets, or read several other operas. This reflection is one to give confidence a salutary shake, when it comes to authors of an era like the seventeenth century, when genre was a factor governing all manner of small and large points of decorum. What was a major factor in determining their style will be a major factor in our understanding it.

We cannot see court masques. But this need not cut us off from quite all the pleasures which a taste for them adds to *Comus.* What we perceive through an awakened sympathy toward the form is—no small point—that the nature of the genre governs the kind of relation between abstraction and the concrete in a masque. This relation is the heart and secret of an image.

Reprinted by permission of the publisher from *Images and Themes in Five Poems by Milton* (Cambridge, Mass.: Harvard University Press, 1957), pp. 112–61.

[1] That Professors Percy Simpson and Allan Gilbert, Enid Welsford, D. G. Gordon and certain others have in recent years made something better than this possible and attractive is important to a reader of *Comus,* even if one mentions here only the superb essay on the form in the Herford and Simpson edition of Ben Jonson (vol. II).

Of course it is obvious that a masque has imagery which is visual in a special way, the element of spectacle being used as a component actually necessary to convey part of the figurative meaning of an action that is not acceptable literally. Although we might say with some truthfulness, 'less is lost by reading, instead of seeing, *Lear,* than *Comus*', we should rather say that something different is lost. Comus—who is an image, for this is not a play—is partly *understood* through the eye, the antimasque dancing is an important *completion* of images verbally commenced, the brightly lit banquet *scene* is part of the posing of light against darkness (op-position, not conflict). Usually we only read 'Noble Lord, and Lady bright. . .' with its image of 'triumph in victorious dance O're sensual Folly, and Intemperance', and no one now can be part of a function where the three children dance before their parents the continuation and conclusion of this Song—itself a musical image of the action's outcome, recalled in free and swelling cadences by the voice of the Attendant Spirit. If we have watched the motionless Lady as a 'prison'd soul', unable to make any movement other than speech, we are ready to see in these free dancing figures an *image* of what 'Heav'n it self' has stooped to protect, the ordered Freedom conjoined with light of the many abstract statements concerning Virtue. But these are simple points, close neighbors to those additions made by the inward eye of any trained reader 'staging' any read drama, or related to our realization that no sung lyric may be quite understood without its music.

This last reservation holds for all the songs, which are portions always rich in imagery, and especially for the Lady's Echo song. Since two large images are given to the effect of the latter, in speeches by Comus and by the Spirit, it is the more possible to be specific about some aspects of the music's contribution to the effect of images, with these for examples. It is chiefly hearing the music which makes us share the judgement and thence concur regarding the significance which these two hearers of the Lady's song point out. They do so through subtly phrased images which differ only within their similarity; these are not concert-room flatteries of the Lady Alice's voice, but precise judgements of the song's qualities *qua* music. Even ill-managed, the young voice singing those words to that music would be for us an image of what the Elder Brother is to speak of: 'noble grace that dash't brute violence With sudden adoration, and blank aw' (450). We should have seen the protection afforded by the armor of Diana work, upon Comus, before the Elder Brother ever proclaims his trust in the sacred rays of Chastity, and would have felt that no other armor could be so fitly eulogized for fifteen-year-old Alice Egerton.[2] It is musically accurate that even Circe's son sees the difference in *her* kind of music—lapping prison'd souls (even her victim Scylla) in a false Elysium, 'in sweet madnes' robbed of themselves. His words after the Lady's song, 'Ile speak to her And she shall be my Queen', show as Milton's usual (and very Spenserian) emphasis on the perverted, not the rejecting, response of the impure to the beauty of the pure. 'That might create a soul Under the ribs *of Death*' is the Spirit's phrase for this attracting power; 'smoothing the Raven doune *Of darknes* till it smil'd' is Comus's (560, 250; these are like another famous instant when a dark force is momentarily 'stupidly good', and Comus had that first moment too). This power, which here has little to do with sentiment but much with musical form, needs to be felt by us *before* it is described. Without the music, though affected by youth and beauty in straits, we are scarcely persuaded of certain ideas that are to become important, but with it we are; it is heard as integral part and completion of the second speech after the riotous antimasque, and stands out frail but clear against the ironic fact of the hidden listening Comus. In forgetting Lawes's part in *Comus* as an artistic whole we do not copy the masque's author.

It is in subtler ways than these, however, that the genre of the piece has most affected the imagery of *Comus.* Masques, as a kind, are inescapably symbolical. The peculiar relation borne by the work of art to real happenings and meanings—symbolized, rather than described, or dramatically viewed—is borne by the action itself, by what we call in a play the plot. Masques do not have plots, but designs, 'devices'. Jonson's words are better than any: '*Upon this hinge,* the whole Invention moov'd'. He concludes thus in his Preface to *Chloridia,* 1630. When Her Majesty had purposed a presentation to the King, 'It was agreed, it should be the celebration of some Rites, done to the Goddesse *Chloris,* who . . . was proclaim'd Goddesse of the flowers'; by a decree from Jupiter she 'was to be stellified on Earth', because he 'would have the

[2] Under 'the circumstances'—which are to be forgotten in plays, remembered in masques—the unsubstantial strength of untouched purity is certainly a better vehicle for Milton's symbolizing of the strength to be trusted in by this endangered creature in the dark wood of the world than Fortitude's shield or Prudence's serpent, and a quality in the singer is re-enforced by a quality in the song, a pure clarity as of light. Commentary on the music may be found in the edition by Visiak and Foss, 1937, and in Willa Evans, *Henry Lawes* (New York, 1941), ch. v. See also E. Haun's 'An Inquiry into the Genre of *Comus*', with relevant citations I do not repeat (*Essays in Honor of W. C. Curry,* Nashville, 1954).

Earth to be adorn'd with starres, as well as the Heaven'. This 'hinge' is a good example of the fact that a masque's *device* is (as its name emphasizes) itself a figure; here it is a large and simple, but metaphorical, identification of living persons with the symbolical personages of myth (the Queen of course comes down with her stars, her ladies the masquers, to adorn and fructify England). What corresponds to plot is thus provided, and largely out of the listeners' minds, for these symbolisms were familiar to the cultivated audience—the only kind masques had.

Although both a morality and a masque dramatize an idea, in the device of the latter the *datum* is an idea comprised in a figure. *Everyman* to be sure becomes, as we read, a vast figurative statement about man's earthly sojourn and its end, but it is figurative in that, universalizing it, we read of ourselves and all men in a pure *moral* allegory (which I prefer to call by its ancient name, tropology, to avoid certain confusions we shall notice). *Comus,* like many other masques, shares this character of 'moral allegory', but initially by virtue of its device, a myth which is figurative in other ways though it also had come to have a certain moral-allegorical force to everyone.[3] Most masque devices are basically an extension or unanticipated exploitation of some myth; they use the great known figures—the Golden Age, the Isles of the Blessed, the Golden Apples of the Hesperides, Eros and Astraea and Venus and Hymen and Diana. They *start out as* great Images or speaking pictures and are by definition figures given 'application'.

This is the first respect in which the relation of abstraction to concrete vehicle is determined by the nature of the genre. Upon the great hinge of the Circe-Comus myth Milton's whole invention moves; out of its known connoted meanings the pervasive imagery of light and darkness springs quite naturally, and this is elaborated with the greatest originality by Milton, with conceptual refinements and extensions impossible to a lesser genius.

Another aspect of the relation which obtains in masques between abstraction and the concrete is more peculiar; so astonishing it is, in fact, that I do not believe it can be understood other than historically, for in this pure form it flourished and died with the court masque. One can

[3] No one looking at the history of sixteenth-century drama could deny a close relation between morality play and masque, but differences will become apparent as we proceed. When *Comus* is too strictly related to the moralities, the sequel is usually either condemnation of or apology for Milton's narrow asceticism. This word might fit *Comus,* read purely tropologically, but its allegory is so written as to ask a further reading, and it will not stay in the category.

think of no other genre that exhibits it, and pleasure in it is a learned response.

Certain ones of the characters are not characters but masquers; they are not court personages *acting* parts in a play, but have, as themselves, been written into a dramatic piece, and play in it without ceasing to be themselves. In Jonson's *Pleasure Reconciled to Virtue,* 1618, the twelve Masquers are the companions, literally as well, of the Prince of Wales, son of Hesperus, with whom they appear suddenly out 'from ye Lap of' the mountain Atlas who had bred them up in all knowledge. When Virtue gives them entrance to the Garden of the Hesperides, and Daedalus instructs them in ways through the three Labyrinths of men's actions, of beauty, and of love (which three mazeful ways they *dance* out), they are at once these mythical persons and themselves as English courtiers, and when they enter the Garden (Hesperus the King looking on from his 'State') it is to dance with the ladies of the court who indeed did daily present them with the labyrinthine mazes of amorous intrigue for which they needed Daedalus' tutoring. The young courtiers who in Jonson's *Vision of Delight* are 'the glories of the Spring', sons of Favonius, not only personate but are, shining in favor, the glories of the spring of 1617, soon on its way. Or compare the pyramid of young men in Shirley's *Triumph of Peace,* dressed as silver 'terms' or pillars with heads; they are explained by 'a Genius or angelical person' who speaks to the King in person—'I . . . here present you with *your own*'. Being created by the King's virtue they are without life until, at the moment the Genius says 'That very look into each eye Hath shot a soul', they break into movement, and dance before the King. These young men are their literal selves, Gentlemen of the four Inns of Court, and equally they are the King's means of 'keeping' that very *Law* and *Justice* (Eunomia, Diche) who have just come down to his earthly realm and danced, and they are his way of 'ordering' that *Peace* (Irene) whose triumphant chariot we have just watched descend in a cloud.[4] There is no jerk back to 'reality' when the Attendant Spirit turns from blessing

[4] For economy and pleasure I use masques Milton surely knew, and throughout emphasize Jonson for reasons of accessibility (even to non-courtiers) and eminence. Evidence for Milton's knowledge and use of both these Jonson masques is given in Herford and Simpson's Commentary (vol. X) and in II, 305 ff.; see also Welsford, *The Court Masque* (Cambridge, 1927), pp. 307 ff., 314 ff. W. Evans, *Henry Lawes,* pp. 81 ff., gives some details on Shirley's masque (with William Lawes's music), in which Henry Lawes took part, as did the Egerton boys, Milton's Elder and Second Brother; given twice in February 1633/4, printed 1633.

the brimmed waves of Sabrina to 'Com Lady . . . not many furlongs thence Is *your Fathers* residence'. For the friends there 'met in state' are present for the same reason as the masquers who hasten to 'double all their mirth and chere' by joining them; all are met 'to gratulate His wish't presence'—that is, to share in the *whole* masque's 'occasional' *raison d'être.* And the perplex't paths of the drear Wood in which his children lost their way have been the enchanted woods in which men meet Evil without ever ceasing to be the woods of Shropshire.

The odd but definite pleasure we take in the double reality of scenes and of persons in a masque is simply a variant upon the usual pleasure in metaphor, where two ways of seeing things to be 'true' are constantly and delightfully present, and yet seen as one. When Thyrsis answers 'my *young* Lord' and the Second Brother interrupts with ' 'tis my father Shepherd sure', he says what every listener knew, that Lawes was musician in the Egerton household, and this does not in the least disturb the 'belief' we and the listeners gave to the figure of an otherworldly guardian of endangered youthful innocence, who states that he takes the likeness of this same swain 'That to the service of this house belongs'. The three young people, 'nurs't in Princely lore' and on their way to wait upon their father's first court and 'new-entrusted Scepter' (36), had 'their youth, Their faith, their patience, and their truth' tried through hard assays, and proving themselves proved Virtue's strength, so that Heav'n has thought fit to 'send them *here* . . . *To triumph*' (971) in victorious dance over Folly—the 'device' is all one with the total purpose of the evening's celebration of virtue *in* her servants, from the 'noble Peer' who is holding his first 'state' as Lord President of 'An old, and haughty Nation' on down through all those whose 'revels' are an extension (after the manner of masques) of the full meaning of the piece.[5] When 'the Scene changes' from the wood to 'Ludlow Town and the Presidents Castle' we are not fetched back from this other world of ideas; we have been in both all the time. Sabrina was to everyone present the neighboring river they knew, which watered that westward-looking tract on the border of which the whole action is specifically set, and which, moreover, Lord Bridgewater has in charge from the god of

[5] The evening ball ('revels') is of course normally enclosed within the masque proper, with the final speeches kept until, after the listeners' dancing, they close at once both the action and the evening. Since a masque always honors someone, this peculiar unity of participating groups, one 'assisting' as at a ritual, bears resemblance to something we know chiefly in services of worship. Certainly it makes for differences from the ordinary play that the 'audience' should be thus *within the image* or device.

all waters and island kingdoms. Hence she has not only maidenliness and that 'local propriety' Warton notes but with triple fitness joins her assistance to that of the other non-human or superhuman figures whose allegiance is given to such human creatures as share their virtuous nature. She is no less the actual Severn, for all that.[6] The Lady does not represent but presents virtue, and presents it in that one of its aspects most suitable to her literal self, for she does not cease to be Alice Egerton though she is equally the human spirit partially in the power of insidious evil.

Such a dramatic kind, in which *some* of the 'characters' are both their fictive and their literal selves, and in which imagery consistently functions to point this out, could not develop ripely, I suppose, except at such a period of history as this; an audience thoroughly accustomed to taking things allegorically occurred contemporaneously with a social situation that called for elaborate works of courtly compliment.[7] I have emphasized the topical references because it is so easy to forget the special piquancy of the pleasure they afforded; few literary genres provide poets with a situation in which double entendres are at every moment possible and expected. Some are moving, some gay.[8]

In these two ways, then—the central controlling figure as a 'hinge' upon which the whole invention moved, and the constantly possible

[6] She has other meanings to be noticed later. The kind of pleasure given by Milton's mythologizing of the local landscape where his literal action is taking place is given amusingly in reverse in the antimasque added by Jonson to his *Pleasure Reconciled to Virtue,* and called 'For the Honour of Wales' (the Prince was chief masquer). Here Welsh speakers produce comedy by taking the masque's figures literally. They put forward a string of Welsh mountains as tall and of as good 'standing' and 'discent' as 'the prowdest *Adlas* christned', suggest that Owen Glendower would do 'very better, and twice as well' as Hercules, and maintain that there 'is a thousand place in *Wales* as finely places as the *Esperides* every crum of him'.

[7] Unless the piece is simply a poor one, judgements on masques which take offense at the 'adulation' of their 'courtly flattery' show misreading of imagery. For masque devices do not just fasten sets of classical or abstract names upon James or Charles or Anne; they turn all the latter (as Milton turns his Lady) into *figures for* the virtues, powers or situations presented. Meanwhile the persons retained their literal validity and complexity.

[8] Further examples are: Comus's 'Hail forren wonder', certainly not bred in 'these rough shades', 264; the Lady's thrusts at tapestry halls and courts of Princes, 323; Comus roving the Celtic and Iberian fields and at last betaking himself to the new Lord President's Welsh marches; Thyrsis-Lawes's pastoral tasks and Orphean powers; the Lady's condemnation of pampered Luxury; the local description in the Sabrina scene. Serious meanings are merely salted by such fleeting double flavors. But *Comus* is not so bleakly grave a piece as some read it. It is deeply serious at its center.

double reference to two equally but differently real worlds—the nature of the genre strongly influenced the writer's choice and use of imagery. That it is not a representative example of its form one would grant, but it came late. However, it is not only longer and more comprehensive like other Caroline examples, but also deeper and more permanently intelligible. Milton touched no form that he did not remould, yet he did this from within, working on the basis of a profound and respectful knowledge of the essential nature—but also of the full capacities—of ode, elegy, epic or masque. Certain other influences I shall mention rather in the form of expectations which we form as readers of masques, each with its important corollaries touching the imagery of *Comus.* As one follows the other, we shall see most of the famous complaints about the piece fall away, for when the imagery is rightly read *A Mask* comes close to the perfection of *Lycidas.*

Given the genre, we expect pastoral elements in the action, and the pastoral imagery is neither artifice nor falsity. We expect (indeed must demand) allegory, and images allegorically read are the heart of the piece. We expect debate, not 'drama'. We are meant to listen, which causes Dr. Johnson to complain, 'without anxiety'—but not 'without passion', for in each of the two major debates we see the figuring forth of clearly opposed mental positions which do not conflict in any stage personality because we ourselves are that personality; the Lady (though imperfect) does not here hesitate and 'choose', we do. So with the Elder as against the Second Brother; and this is the proper nature of a contest carried on by opposing image to image, which is neither opposing idea to idea, nor personality to personality. As 'personalities', these are the three Egertons, and Comus (unlike Iago, or Satan) is not given such being. We expect the instructive, and if we find that 'tedious' must avoid the form—yet surely it is tedious only to those who miss the figurative nature of the whole invention and, hence, mistake a revelation for a struggle and symbolic detail for splendor of decoration. We expect some great simple contrast between Vice and Virtue; we expect some such expositor and guide of the action as the Attendant Spirit, expect long speeches, expect mythological personages used to convey Christian ideas like that of grace, expect archetypal amplitude and simplicity in the basic figures, expect even stichomythia. We experience the fulfillment of all these expectations in *Comus* with delight, excitement, and surprise.

The pastoral aspect of *Comus* may seem at first not to have been structurally inevitable, a mere habitual varnish. It has been joined, in some critics, to certain petulant denigrations of Spenser. It is instructive to read *Comus* with an eye to what Milton could do only because Spenser had written. For one thing, he had as contemporary audience those only who had read and understood the great Spenserian images. It is in this area of the possibilities and use of the larger structural figures that we come upon one of Milton's greatest debts to his predecessor; his way of using the pastoral is a related but minor debt. True, it is in the most obviously pastoral section of *Comus,* on Sabrina, that he honors Spenser as the truest poet 'that ere pip't' (822), and he speaks of what he has learned from this 'Meliboeus' under the name of the noble old apologist for the shepherd's life in Spenser's pastoral Book, VI. The poetic habits shown in this whole complex of imagery—the river myth and the use made of it, the fit relation to the symbolical Neptune figure, the way of handling the conventional masque motif of a disenchantment, the quality of language and picture, the epithetic economy of the invocation with its charm-like succession of mythical persons recalled with a single 'tinsel-slipper'd . . . wrincled look . . . lovely hands'—these are pastoral and Spenserian habits, but others had them. In these and other connections it is the pastoral imagery and pastoral incident of Fletcher's *Faithful Shepherdess* which strike us, as do portions of Browne's *Inner Temple Masque,* as having the very tone and movement we hear in parts of *Comus.* Fletcher, dealing with the nature of chaste fidelity in a context which aims primarily at defining love (through the inter-action of those who impersonate various forms or deformities of it), can even furnish us with a touchstone by which to discern the very real differences of all these English pieces from Tasso's *Aminta,* though that has been declared 'the real model' for *Comus.*[9] This comparative exercise would re-emphasize a principle fundamental for study of imagery: that comparable images accompany comparable 'causes', themes, temper, conceptions of the range of a subject. Fletcher and Browne and Spenser (*FQ* III and II) all concern themselves with questions which are central in *Comus.*

Accordingly, Milton's greater debt to Spenser is to these latter Books, though they are not pastoral. Milton's great controlling device, the

[9] By Praz, in 'Milton and Poussin', *Seventeenth Century Studies Presented to Sir Herbert Grierson* (Oxford, 1938), p. 202. These two pieces cannot but differ stylistically as they do, having such dissimilar subjects; neither takes up what is the chief issue in the other. Similarly, Peele's *Old Wives' Tale* cannot illuminate for us any character or image in *Comus,* and earlier emphasis upon it exemplifies how deceptively the noting of parallel situations or story-motifs can deflect 'source' study. Browne of course has the special similarity of a parallel in the initial metaphorical 'device'.

Circe-Comus figure, is involved with pastoral by historical development not by origin (and is not pastoral in *FQ* II for example), and for the first 70 or 80 lines of his Attendant Spirit's opening speech we may think he is simply going to be Homeric-Christian, in good Renaissance fashion, moving from Jove's starry threshold to the seats where sit the crowned saints, from Neptune to Wales, from daemon to guardian angel, in the way to which his predecessors have accustomed both him and us. He does not choose to follow his main image into the companion figure of the Earthly Paradise (the Fortunate Isles, the Garden of Venus) to which it was so commonly allied, as in Spenser, Tasso, Ariosto, and of which Jonson's Hesperidean Garden in *Pleasure Reconciled to Virtue* is a variant. What he does do is no more of a surprise than that would have been, for pastoral imagery had found a natural home in the masque.

Nymphs, satyrs, Silenus, Pan, Flora, 'sylvans', graces, seasons, Geniuses of woods and fountains, are there our expected companions, as they are also in the nearest neighboring small kind, the 'entertainment', where they often have more structural point. The way to praise James on his birthday is to write of *Pan's Anniversary* (by Jonson, 1620) and make him leader, singer, hunter, protector, shepherd *par excellence.* Arthurian or chivalric romance materials are pastoralized (see Jonson's *Oberon,* 1611), as they had long been in fiction and poetry; we think of such links in Drayton's *Pastorals* and Spenser's *Shepheardes Calender,* or of Sidney's *Arcadia,* especially of the pastoral games which close the Books. The reasons for the affinity between masque device and pastoral imagery are not alone those of literary history, date, fashion, fitness for 'scene' and production, common classical origin. They are alike with respect to their metaphorical base.

In the pastoral as a kind, that easy interaction between mythical or semi-mythical beings and actual human characters, noticed above as essential to the masque, had been maintained time out of mind. An Attendant Daemon is no stranger to a pastoral. The commingling of heavenly story and specific human situation is usual; topical reference is the very hallmark of the genre, and all the variations of allegorical double meaning are known to it. Pastoral's greatest hold upon the imagination of its users and readers proved to be that sense of unifying harmony between all creatures of 'Nature', human or not, which is the foundation of the so-called pathetic fallacies. When these are not vulgarized or ineptly parroted by insensitive poetasters, they are not fanciful 'humanizing' of unsentient things; they are figures of speech by which non-human things are meant to express a total natural sympathy, for which expression we sentient beings have no mode but the sentient.[10] To such figures, and with them all the Geniuses of streams and places, the chaste Sabrinas and mourning dryads, it is almost impossible to respond, with immediacy, at our moment of history; that Englishmen of the sixteenth and seventeenth century felt their truth seems to me clear from their literature—and quite consonant with both their classicism and their theology. Pastoral figures could not stay pagan. Secular they often remained, yet, when a work takes on seriousness, nothing is more common than that the pastoral images begin to show as informed with Christian feeling; they need not be Biblical in order to work in a poem as support for Christian moral or ontological assumptions.

Such remarks do not take entire care of the figure of the Attendant Spirit; he is pastoral as a disguise, ostensibly, and is many other things besides. But the pastoral element, perhaps initially brought into *Comus* for him, slips into it (by way of the imagery) the usual pastoral conception of a strong web of support provided for human goodness of various kinds by the very existence of a harmonious natural order. There is a kind of common front of all natural things;[11] all unperverted nature stands with the human creatures against the dark forces of *un*natural, *in*temperate *dis*harmony.

The wood is 'hideous' because it is enchanted, taken over. The Lady calls upon Echo, the mountain and water nymph and favorite of pastorals, lover of human creatures and revealer of the lost. To Echo is nightly addressed the nightingale's lament, that singer who is the type of all that have lost those they love ('And O poor hapless Nightingale', the Spirit is later to say of the Lady singing, 565); for answering, Echo will be 'translated' like the saints to echo forever as they do the songs of love in Heaven. The entire Sabrina scene, as well as the Spirit's prior explana-

[10] This metaphorical aspect of pastoral imagery is more carefully treated in the essay on *Lycidas* [elsewhere in *Images and Themes*]. It is not Wordsworthian.

[11] To avoid complications, I have not brought in here the uses made of disturbances to this harmony (see p. 147 of this essay [p. 153 herein]). Obscure connections with *un*natural evil are felt in such images—from the 'bleak *un*kindly' (against nature) Fog, that stops growth or the mere 'urchin blasts' and 'shrewd medling Elfe', to the ill-intentioned '*inchanted* Iles, And rifted Rocks whose entrance leads to Hell' (268, 845, 516). Though 'such there be', the malevolence is not ascribed to their nature, like the benevolence. One should note that the line is not sharp between 'pastoral' (real sheep) images and others which happen likewise to give beneficent sentience to natural things; use of the latter will give a 'pastoral' temper to works not in the genre.

tions of her protective care and of the shepherds' grateful tributes thrown into Severn's smooth and healing stream, elaborates upon the same pastoral conception of a concord which makes both natural and heavenly protectors available to the virtuous human creature in misfortune or in danger.[12] Image after image has this function; nature, like heaven, watches over its own, and loves in all creatures the image of its own virtue. The answer to Comus's fraudulent 'naturalism' does not end with the Lady's speeches to him. That chastity should be a 'natural' virtue of the Lady presents in this respect no problem; Comus's stereotype of an Earth-mother or a Venus *genetrix* for great all-encompassing Natura (one he shares with some moderns who find him convincing) is shown to be as insufficient as his cliché of plenitude 'naturally' inviting excess is illogical.

The Lady's plea to Echo for other-than-human (but natural) assistance is to be obliquely if too tardily answered by the following action. But it is part of the pattern of ironic disordering of things that her song brings to her 'aid' Comus, the sorcerer and disturber of nature's ordered ways. So also, the Spirit's assuming of 'the Weeds and likenes of a Swain' (best fitted to the task of safe convoy which high Jove has assigned him, 81) is given an ironic faked parallel a hundred lines later, by Comus's so distorting the Lady's vision that to her *he* appears in the weeds and likeness of a swain, whom she addresses as 'gentle Shepherd' and accepts as convoy—already partly blinded by the magic dust.[13] So also, Comus's definitions of Nature and of her manifest intentions constitute a travesty of the true unity that holds all creatures together

[12] This does not contradict or otherwise interfere with an interpretation of the symbolism of water as connected with divine grace; see p. 152 of this essay [p. 157 herein]. One symbolism does not destroy another—that is, not unless the *meanings* they assist us to grasp are in conflict, and in such a case an author with a conscience will have muted one symbolic possibility and magnified the other. The necessity for this *second* kind of congruence is our chief brake against a tempting and very familiar abuse in the reading of symbolic imagery, but symbolisms may be very incongruent as to *provenance* without leading us to draw in meanings that injure or refuse to cohere with those clearly indicated.

[13] The irony was marked to the eye. Comus's 'quaint habits' were far from pastoral, and Milton has him comment on their suspiciousness. All the images that occur within the irony are affected by it—a quiet example is the Lady's remark about where true courtesy is less soon found and most pretended, made to a true 'Prince' himself, more's the pity. And there is some comedy in this unshepherd-like personage claiming that he is so early about as to anticipate the *lark* getting up from her thatch't pallat, considering his preceding lascivious descriptions of Night and Morning. With several images thus enacting a brazenly open deception, the Lady's five-times-repeated address shows her as partially giving herself into the power of evil.

interdependent within one harmonious order, so that it is a parody of 'Nature' that asks the Lady to substitute ravin, presumptuous self-love and indulgence for those 'sober laws' which *she* claims are the intent of 'most innocent nature'. Images play their part in this contrast between definitions of 'Nature', from the beginning. Of course particulars pin-point the illogicality of definitions of the natural, in Comus's argument (the most amusing example being that eminently unnatural drink, 'the clear stream', indulged in by petulant man in a fit of priggish ungrate-fulness). But much more important is the fact that previous images (especially pastoral ones) have given us a different conception of nature, against which Comus's sophistical definitions appear as contrast, before the Lady ever speaks. The physical presence of the rabble—not beasts but perverted Men and Women, 'Monsters'—is not always felt, when reading, as a constant comment on the truth of Comus's lines about Nature; that visual presence goes some distance toward making 'sober laws' look rather more natural and attractive, more humanely dignified, than they commonly do.

The strain Milton is later to sound so often, that evil works by assuming the very form and reasons of the good, charming first the eye and then the judgment, is sounded so clearly in *Comus* that it is hard to see why there has been so much comment on the attractiveness of Comus, as if this were unintended. It is a deliberate part of the imagery's truth to life as we know it that Fraud acts as like Jove's messengers as it can—to start with. That very pastoral disguise, so natural and so reason-able, which the Attendant Spirit took on that he might succeed, Comus takes on and does succeed—so long, that is, as hypocrisy is all he need add to the magic dust which is a masque's way of indicating delusions the virtuous reason could not counter. Men cannot be enabled by virtue always to see through to the true nature of that which, without other sign of evil, simply says it is other than it is; hypocrisy is a vice in the creature seen, not in the judgement behind the seeing eye—which is faulty but not guilty—and Una could not recognize Archimago, nor Uriel Satan. Both 'shepherds' in *Comus* are followed. When Thyrsis' and 'the Villager's' different ends begin to show themselves and give to Comus's advice (as well as to his 'cottage') a character which the virtuous reason is able to see the flaws in, *then* must the Lady see, by her own 'virtue', the Wolf in the pretended Shepherd she has followed. Thyrsis *is* a Shepherd. He came down to be one, and his disguise is his meaning. Nothing could be more useful to Milton than this pastoral imagery which can move easily from literal to metaphorical sense and back again, and tacitly make these discriminations. They are not subtleties which ask for reflection, a turning back to study out, or analysis (until we attempt to restate them); they enter the mind, at least the mind accustomed to pastorals, through eye and ear, swift as the sparkle of a glancing star. But it is the *mind* they enter.

Milton's structural use of the pastoral tradition has thus a quite magnificent economy, and it is this, not its occurrence, that gives surprise. One other delightful virtue should be remarked. It is so astonishingly neat. Now appears what a stroke of wit it was to put Lawes the Attendant Spirit into the disguise which, in its accepted metaphorical sense, was his actual position in respect to his interlocutors. The Orpheus image, comfortably domiciled of course in both pastoral and masque, is compliment to Lawes (86, *cf.* 493), and what light-hearted compliment! There is of course none of the easy condescension to his father's musician which one critic finds in the Elder Brother's talk of strayed sheep; Pan and Christ watched sheep. It causes trouble when one runs in and out of a pastoral metaphor's *meaning* thus. But part of the pleasure of metaphor is that meanings literally true remain as really part of the situation as what is being metaphorically said, and the Second Brother's ' 'tis my father Shepherd sure' is charming because the number of ways in which it was and it wasn't his Father's Shepherd both amuses us and startles us into insight. A similar pleasure in the mere suitability of the pastoral imagery to the actual setting of this masque, simpler than the double entendres we noticed earlier, frequently shows through the slighter traditionally pastoral touches: the telling of time by the 'swink't hedger', and the ox (a superlative Virgilian English ox), the brothers picking grapes (a likely story; Comus's), the loose unletter'd Hinds that 'thank the gods amiss' (these 'late Wassailers' of whom the Lady fears to ask her way are the Shropshire drunks of Michaelmas 1634, and that the voices of Comus's retinue can be mistaken for their 'swill'd insolence' is a wry compliment to Gryllus's lost letters), the benighted brothers' wish that they could see some rush candle's 'long levell'd rule of streaming light' from a shepherd's hut, or even hear the flocks in their wattled cotes. Seventeenth-century rural England, where their author expected these lines to be heard when he wrote them, was still pastoral, and still unlighted, and still wooded.

But these are extra pleasures. The chief virtue of the pastoral figures in *Comus* is the special decorum with which their full metaphorical force works to carry out the great central device of Circe's powerful son.

The hinge upon which Milton's whole invention moves is the great and famous allegorical figure of Circe, and he has caught and deepened every important phase of the significance she had borne in the many appearances which had made her one of the best-known symbolical figures of the Renaissance. Milton's originality in extending so many of the clustered multiple significances of Circe to her son we owe partly to the 'occasional' aspect of his piece, to such given conditions as the age and sex of his masquers, and so on. Of course he knew the earlier Comus figures, from Philostratus' Bacchus-like and delicate young man to Jonson's Belly-god and (probably) Puteanus's sensualist, and they are relevant but not limiting. Hence I shall save circumlocutions by speaking here about 'the Circe myth'. Comus, in being her son, is as much the son of Spenser's Acrasia and Ariosto's Alcina as of Servius' and Plutarch's and Gelli's and Vives' and Landino's and Bruno's and Pico's and Conti's Circe. For of course Homer is only the beginning.

This essay will provide no sketch of this ancient figure's development, nor yet of its 'meaning'. The first can be found elsewhere.[14] The second of these is impossible; no form of paraphrasing poems is more outrageous in the eyes of a student of images, for a poet could himself have eschewed the precariousness of traditional figurative language if he had 'meant' such a capsule-summary as we might make apart from the discussion of his poem. What is possible and pertinent here, however, is an indication of how such knowledge of the history of *Comus*'s central image applies as we read the masque. There is no doubt of the relevance of the knowledge. The allegorizing of Circe took place early,[15] and such renowned texts as Boethius' *Consolation of Philosophy* are concerned in it. It long antedates the mythographers of the Renaissance, whom recent

[14] See Douglas Bush, *Mythology and the Renaissance Tradition,* Minneapolis, 1932, ch. xiv and cf. ch. ii; Merritt Hughes, 'Spenser's Acrasia and the Circe of the Renaissance', *Journal of the History of Ideas,* IV (1943), 381–399; and such references as are relevant in the Variorum edition of *FQ* II. I omit direct reference to relations with Plato, to be found here and elsewhere. Bush chooses much the same material as I present from Sandys, and on the background of Renaissance development of mythological images see his first four chapters.

[15] For example in Heraclides Ponticus' *Allegoriae;* Milton owned this book (Columbia *Milton,* XVIII, 577). The story is moralized in Holcot's *Moralitates* (no. xvi; there were many MSS., and I used the edition of 1586, ?Basel). More important are the moralizations of Boethius' *Consolation,* iv. metre 3. The textual problem is tangled (see *Histoire litteraire de la France,* XXXVII, 1936–38), but numerous commentaries, translations with 'gloses', a vast spread of MSS., plentiful editions, early made the Circe story as a Christianized allegory something to be quite taken for granted—with allegorizing of the moly, of Mercury's divine assistance, Ulysses as reason, wisdom, virtue, in the soul, and as man sailing the sea from the orient of his birth to the occident of his death.

researches have taught us to consult if we wish to understand any classical myths used metaphorically by a sixteenth- or seventeenth-century author—and this, not decoration, is commonly their use. But if I quote from two such Renaissance books, one certainly and both probably used elsewhere by Milton, we shall like the Brothers have a sprig of haemony in the hand enabling us to see into the nature of Milton's damned enchanter.

Natale Conti's *Mythologia*[16] has a long treatment of Circe (vi. 6), and his conception of her as nature, especially the generative principle in nature, is relevant to Comus's presentation of the usual arguments of Renaissance naturalism (these last are commonplaces, as Bush points out). Conti often, like Bacon, prefers natural-philosophy allegories to 'mystic' or even moral ones; Circe, daughter of the Sun and of Oceanus's daughter, of heat and moisture, which engender physical pleasure, allures men to the indulgence of all intemperate appetites. She tempts each human being according to the character of his special inclinations. I quote here only Conti's definition of the 'beasts' who made up the rabble of Milton's antimasque: 'faculties of the mind conspiring [*complottans*] with the body's affections and breaking their harmony with reason'—and Reason he sees traditionally enough as the faculty that makes human beings approach the divine nature, being creatures with souls divine and immortal by the grace of God. Sandys's famous commentary (1632) on Ovid's *Metamorphoses* (Book xiv) refers to both Servius and Conti, in the three or four lengthy pages that are of special interest and convenience to the student of *Comus.* After his habit, he eclectically provides the 'naturall sence of this fable', the other 'philosophicall' senses, and gives authorities.

> . . . Ulysses could not loose his shape with the rest, who being fortifyed by an *immortall* power, was not subict to mutation. For the *divine and coelestiall soule,* subsisting through the bounty of the Creator, can by no *assault of nature* be *violated,* nor can that bee converted into a beast, which so highly participates of reason . . .
>
> [Circe is daughter of Sol and Persis in that lust proceeds from heat and moisture; and luxury, getting] the dominion, deformes our soules with all

[16] This, and the extreme numerousness of its editions, is so well-known to students of the period that I merely refer to the citations in n. 14 above, adding J. Seznec, *La survivance des dieux antiques* (London, 1940). The remarks about reason and the soul come from Conti, transl. Montlyard, *Mythologie* (Lyon, 1612), p. 591. On the use of Conti for the Circe story of the splendid *Ballet comique de la reine* (1582), see F. Yates, *The French Academies of the Sixteenth Century* (London, 1947), esp. pp. 240 ff.

bestial vices, alluring *some* to inordinate Venus; others to anger, cruelty, and every excesse of passion . . . [Circe's charms] are not to bee resisted, but by the *divine* assistance, Moly, the guift of Mercury, which signifies temperance. So the fortitude and wisedome of Ulisses, preserves him in the midst of vices . . . [Some of his companions are destroyed, others are] converted into beasts by Circe: their headstrong appetites, which revolt from the soveraignty of reason (by which wee *are onely like* unto God, and armed against our depraved affections) nor ever returne into *their Country* (*from whence* the soule deriveth her coelestiall originall), unlesse *disinchanted,* and *cleansed* from their former impurity. For as Circes rod, waved over their heads from the right side to the left: presents those false and sinister perswasions of pleasure, which so much deformes them: so the reversion thereof, by *discipline,* and *a view of* their owne deformity, restores them to their former beauties. (pp. 480–481; my italics)

Even this pedestrian summary shows the power of symbolical images to convey complexities not by any subtlety of story or 'character' (the Circe story never lost its primitive simplicity), but by developing for us a multiple metaphor, some elements pulling in conceptions it would take a treatise to discuss. The complexities so introduced are not only psychological. What Sandys calls 'the Philosophicall sense of the fables' generally involves not only ethics but a conception of man's nature and destiny.

Even here, we read the figure as something other than tropology; poetry based on it would go beyond the 'moral-allegory' effect of swaying powerfully toward a right choice between the pleasures of sense and a virtuous temperance, for this has become a myth of temperance allied with God-given and celestial reason. (The Lady's *holy* dictate of spare Temperance eventuates in harmonious order throughout nature, justice to all, and due 'praise' rather than 'base ingratitude' to 'the giver', 766). The fable has got to this un-Greek destination by informing the notion of Wisdom with the traditional Christian interpretation of reason as that in which we are made in God's image—thus 'onely like' him. (In the place where there was once a 'human count'nance, Th' express resemblance of the gods', Comus's drink 'the inglorious likenes of a beast Fixes instead',—'unmoulding reasons mintage Character'd in the face', 68, 527). In this myth about the admixture of reason and unreason in the human psyche, her godlike nature is seen as armor against her depraved nature—it is a myth about what *is* 'natural', and what is 'deformity'—and indeed about the *'violation'* of the soul's chastity by 'nature' in the Circean sense. It does not even stand far from a notion of the celestial soul as belonging chastely to God alone, admitting as it does in Christian terms the idea of the soul's return to that 'Country' whence she had her celestial origin. The return is by liberation from thralldom and by purgation—'disinchanted, and cleansed'—'restoring them to their former beauties'. (When defilement is let in to the inward parts, the soul 'Imbodies, and imbrutes, till she quite loose The divine property of her first being'; whereas a soul 'sincerely' chaste has such converse with heaven that the outward shape, 'The unpolluted temple of the mind', is turned 'by degrees to the souls essence, Till all be made immortal', 453–468). In a 'classical' myth which has admitted the conception of a divine soul possessed through the gift of the Creator and 'subsisting through His bounty', the conventional Moly of Temperance has become so very divine an assistance, fortifying 'by an immortall power' the celestial soul, that we could scarcely find ourselves surprised if something 'yet more med'cinal then that Moly', as Milton says haemony is, could be none other than grace.

I have interlarded these comments on Sandys's summary of a well-known image with references from Milton not because of any point about source (Sandys does not pretend to singularity, and would tell a falsehood if he did), but because it makes certain observations possible without discussion. One is that when images have taken on symbolical force they maintain a kind of integrity, and stubbornly go on meaning something similar from piece to piece. Idiosyncratic or eccentric meanings attached to them are suspect, because that which is symbolized takes command and transmutes a figure, and it is poets who wish to talk about *that* who choose such an image; they do not willingly waste its main energies, and they know how it will be understood. One is wary, for example, of intricate psychological analysis of 'a character' which instead of deepening destroys the image at its center, and leaves us with a Lady worsted, and rightly, in the encounter of the cup.[17] Also it seems too late in the day for Milton to manipulate the Circe myth in order to show 'that both the Lady and Comus were wrong: that there *was* another meaning' in her gift of feminine beauty and that 'the meaning

[17] See J. E. Hardy's essay in Brooks and Hardy, *Poems of Mr. John Milton* (New York, 1951). This handles almost every image in the work, and is often acutely observant, but interpretations and general conceptions suffer, as here, from lack of historical sophistication (see for example also the points about a 'classical creed' or about 'condescension', *infra* pp. 137, 129). On the other hand, R. M. Adams, criticizing over-analysis of *Comus* in an extremely amusing extravaganza, leaves us with a fairly thoughtless work for tired practical minds (*Ikon: John Milton and the Modern Critics,* Ithaca, 1955, re-using an essay from *Modern Philology,* LI).

was marriage'.[18] Even though the matter of chastity as fidelity is certainly in the piece, we are leagues away from problems of social or religious contract or some single human institution, are led by this image into questions that touch constantly every man's total moral life; nor could the great type of Heavenly Visitant [19] come down to advise this or that girl to marry—such a one as he comes down to guard Jove's sheep. The same caveat, that the profounder meanings of traditional images have great staying power, is pertinent in connection with a general tendency in criticism to proceed as if Milton's entire presentation could be summed up as a chastity-test. We can hardly find a time when the Circe image has not figured intemperance very broadly conceived—'Lust' itself being almost figuratively used as a way of typifying every excess of passion. Certainly this is Acrasia's meaning, and it is partly because Spenser is our great instructor in the comprehensiveness of allegorical figures that one is ready to claim that *Comus* best opens itself to ardent readers of *FQ* II; everyone knows the famous sentence that proves it written by one such.

It seems even more necessary and wise to call attention, against the background of all that Conti and Sandys represent, to the impossibility of watching 'pagan' and 'Christian' suggestions and meanings separately at work in such traditional symbols. 'There is little that is Christian about *Comus*', says Saurat; one must respond that 'there is the central figure and device'. No kind of writing, in the year 1634, could succeed in getting the Christian senses *in which it was read* out of the Circe myth, and could enable it to symbolize 'the strictly non-Christian character of this value given to chastity.' [20] Saurat is referring to chastity's 'magical'

[18] E. M. W. Tillyard, *Studies in Milton* (London, 1951), p. 94. See the note on variant versions appended to this essay. Much turns on the 'marriage imagery' of the Epilogue, and Milton's changes in this respect.

[19] Important to an understanding of the figure of the Attendant Spirit are: the Platonic elements confirmed by the name *Daemon* in the Trinity College MS.; the nature of his errand from Jove; suggestions that arise through use of Incarnation imagery (in the soiling by taking on flesh, 'this Sin-worn mould, 17); all the imagery of enthroned saints, Hesperidean Gardens, Adonis, and celestial Cupid, which describes the archetypal place whence he comes and goes. On Milton's various conversions of the idea of the Guardian Angel into a 'philosophical symbol of great speculative import' see J. H. Hanford, 'That Shepherd, who first taught the chosen Seed', *University of Toronto Quarterly,* VIII (1938–39), 403–419.

[20] See D. Saurat, *Milton: Man and Thinker* (New York, 1925), p. 16. Nor is D. C. Allen's point that the poem's virtues and conceptions are 'Christian only by adoption' a tenable one (see ch. ii of *The Harmonious Vision,* Baltimore, 1954); if the Lady's stoic arguments exemplify how 'the characters in general speak *like pagans*', we shall be hard put to it to find historical Christians who do

and 'supernatural' powers. But the conceptions of reason's origin and workings, even in the bare explanations I have quoted, Christianize the choosing soul's very nature as well as the 'immortall power' that assists it, and a super-Natural power granted to the chaste soul is the Christianized heart of the myth as it is read in Milton's contemporaries and himself. A. S. P. Woodhouse's reading of speeches and symbols that relate the doctrine of Chastity to conceptions of the Christian mind 'grounded in nature and illuminated by grace', is thus much more consonant with the whole development of the poem's imagery.[21]

It is in the gradually developed emphasis upon that special meaning for 'chastity' which allies it to 'the sage And serious *doctrine* of Virginity' that Milton extends the traditional image, but he extends rather than remakes it. Chastity as inviolable 'fidelity to God' had already entered the symbol, as was unavoidable; it is the natural converse of *Luxuria,* when *luxuria* is not one vice but figures all—and this meaning is also inevitable, given the differing beasts Circe turns men into. There is no place in a masque with this 'device' for speaking of that fidelity to God in the usual *imagery* (of each soul seeking, and finally wedded to, its heavenly bridegroom), and the Lady is right in saying that to unfold the *doctrine* of Virginity, which would require the extreme of that language, is impossible in a debate with one who is the very type of appetitive natural man. Even man, who is not just a Comus, can barely understand the faithful chastity of the search, and presumes still less to comprehend the virginity of those mystically married. Milton openly used the traditional imagery only in his elegies. But the fervor of this passage, which has made the Lady so many enemies, is entirely proper to 'The sublime notion, and high mystery' that would have to be utter'd in order to unfold the doctrine—for it is nothing less than that which the doctrine depends upon, the central Christian mystery of the soul's eventual union with the source of love. The Lady's rapt spirits are kindled by the 'worth

---

not, from John onward. It will be noticed that I do not say in the text above, 'Christian senses *read into* the Circe myth', but 'in which it was read'. The assumption we do not share with those readers is that truth is veritably *in* the pagan stories, veiled, but to be seen *in its Christian shape* when they are *read* as *figure.*

[21] Many images are illuminated by Woodhouse's especially original point, the distinguishing of continence, chastity and virginity in the poem, relating the last to the order of grace, and chastity to both orders, of nature and grace. For connections also with *FQ* III, with the celestial Cupid, with 'Freedom', and for the interpretation of the Sabrina imagery mentioned below on p. 151 f. [p. 157 herein], see 'The Argument of Milton's *Comus*' and '*Comus* Once More', in *University of Toronto Quarterly,* XI (1941), 46–71, and XIX (1950), 218–223.

Of this pure cause', but she makes no claim (nor anyone for her) to a place among those who, already symbolically joined to a Heavenly Bridegroom, vow virginity. That Milton does not examine this underlying connection (between the 'chastity' of all faithful souls and the virginity of the celibate spouse of the divine), and that he keeps primarily to the traditional purport of the Circe allegory—the reasonable soul's freedom from sensual enslavement—neither makes it 'less Christian' nor introduces a 'pagan-Christian issue' nor gives the Elder Brother a 'classical creed'. For in the figure, as that was a *datum* for Milton, reason and freedom and temperance and wisdom have all been converted to Christianity, and suiting both the figure's story and ordinary usage they all come under *chastity:* the chaste principle in man's total nature unseduceable by that which would alienate it from its celestial original, tempting it to substitute idolatries for the love of God.

The key to these complications and distinctions is simple. It has to do with a firmer definition of what kind of figure of speech Milton has used. The whole myth had already become figurative, and *in it* chastity even as literal continence is a type of something, shadows forth meanings as they operate in another order. The terms for this other order can sound more, or less, specifically Christian. The faithful soul that for love of the supreme good keeps an unstained purity of devotion, at last to be perfectly reunited with that whence it came, is a commonplace of Platonized Christianity. The Elder Brother's long Platonic image, 452–468, speaks about a *gradual,* not single, loss of this purity, and speaks about the '*soul*' being 'found' to have 'Saintly chastity' ('found *sincerely* so'); the image begins with the thousand liveried angels that attend the chaste soul and drive from her (she is of course *anima* in either sex) 'each thing of sin and guilt'. Chastity in our present limited meaning, which will not cover many seventeenth-century uses of noun and adjective any more than it covers Spenser's, is of course frequently spoken of in a piece with this particular 'device'. Yet if each time the Elder Brother speaks about a state of the body *and* a quality in the soul which is as armor to protect virtue, and each time the virgin (and also chaste) Lady speaks about seeking the unblemished *form* of Chastity which will be a guard to her honor, we read solely about some literal condition, we of course will move in a world of meanings in which one brother is deluded, the other stupid, their sister self-righteous, and Milton's concern obsessive. So many have found them. But, among other things, this is very unhistorical of us. The very transmutation by which fidelity came to be a way of figuring all virtue is a thing which happened in history. Nor can we rip out of a figure the metaphorical meanings which history puts into it. Often this comes to pass by the mere development of new ideas (as 'His service is perfect freedom' has both changed from within and left in some ways unchanged the seemingly 'classical' statement, 'vertue is free'). No more rapid and subtle form of these transmutations can be found than that historical phenomenon, the allegorizing of classical myth.

This phrase is technically precise, and so far as it goes accurate. The term 'allegorizing' goes beyond 'moralization'—if we may use our terms with as strict a historical care as possible, in order to define differences there is no other way of catching in a statement—to indicate a resemblance to that which happened to Moses and Samson. They became types of a Christian truth, were Christianized—so was the Circe story. The long history of *Comus* criticism would not be so full of contentions if Milton had kept to *moral* allegory, but not even his master Spenser could do that; both perplex the ears of an unallegorical generation with nice speculations of *divine* philosophy. Hence we must observe that these 'classical' figures, in becoming metaphors (the nature of allegory) have taken on an additional way of being true, and that their new reference is to a Christian understanding—not of behavior but of the metaphysical structure that determines the meaning of actions. This is a point about both poetics and history. Phrases like 'the conflict of pagan and Christian ideas in the poem', 'intrusion of a Christian theme into a pagan context', 'the shock of the sudden juxtaposition', are historical observations, but insufficiently accurate as history.[22] Christianity had long ago planted the flag of its sovereignty within the mind of 'Ulysses'.

Happily, good poets use symbolic images with long histories just as they use others, that is, taking care for their integrity and clarity. Milton must keep to the terms supplied by that device upon which his invention moved, but they are truly figurative, one term happening to be confusingly literal in the case of his particular human Lady; she happens to have both kinds of chastity to lose. In a myth where a seduction has come to convey, metaphorically, seduction by one's own appetites, the

[22] These phrases are Hardy's (see the book cited in n. 17), but the point of view is extremely common. We should probably relate the frequency with which 'pagan versus Christian' springs up in Milton criticism of the last thirty years to the increased popularity of 'the approach through imagery'. The question of *when* an image is 'pagan' is not in the least a simple one, though discussion sometimes seems to use the assumptions which suffice for distinguishing a paynim in chivalric romance—one who says By Mawmet. The question of when an *idea* is pagan is not simpler.

non-desire which arms and protects the soul can easily take this form of her literal untouchedness. We have to accept the literal terms, as well, of Milton's image in which the figurative chastity of the untouch*able* soul is to be read. But we may not rest in them. The Lady's virgin state is not defined as her virtue; it is the 'armor' which provides 'a hidden strength' against the particular kind of assault upon the virtuous soul that is made by a Circe-figure. It comes into the Brothers' colloquy when the Second Brother fears for her as 'helpless' against that theft to which the erotic image of the golden apples traditionally refers. The Elder Brother's denials of the word *helpless,* in the form of all the images of armed nymphs whose chaste austerity was that armor, only say of the Lady what is true, that she too has that defence and that it is a bow, a shield, and made Diana 'queen oth' Woods'—of those very dark places which in this masque figure forth all danger. A distinction is clear when he says (421) that she, like a quiver'd nymph, has 'Arrows keen' and can therefore go safely alone in the wilderness, where *through the sacred rays of Chastity* none will dare soil her virgin *purity.*

What he says with such confidence turns out to be quite true. One of the thousand liveried Angels comes within forty lines to pursue his own way of driving off each thing of sin; the Lady perfectly typifies 'Vertue . . . assail'd, but never hurt', 'Surpriz'd' but not 'enthrall'd'—Comus never does 'touch the freedom of [her] minde', and it is *exactly* what he wishes to take possession of, as the whole myth clearly figures. He argues for interior consent—giving this is what would make her his thrall, and it is what the rest of the rabble have given. Were she to accept his claim that man is by nature intended for the sumptuous banquet instead of the clear stream and the pulse, this would be a rape, and her chastity would have succumbed to his temptation of voluptuous self-idolatry. Toward this rape of the mind every step in his argument is directed, the music and the banquet, every image that supports every form of sensuous gratification as nature's proven sole intention—the spawning seas, the silkworms at work, the ore and the gems, the beauty not to be hoarded, the vermeil-tinctur'd lip; and the sleight-of-hand image that makes wearing silk instead of frieze and eating cates instead of pulse into a form of gratitude to 'Th'all-giver' is as much a part of the seduction as is the attempt to make Virginity look—not pleasureless, but absurd.

Each single step in the Lady's answer shows her 'chaste', and what this chastity keeps inviolate is her freedom, specifically her free and uncharmed judgement; her 'Temperance' is not a disjoined rational prelude to her impassioned acclaim of the 'Sun-clad power of Chastity' but constitutes a similar stand against 'Luxury' based on a parallel recognition of man's proper fealty. This is shown in her answer: that nature, innocent and herself law-abiding, means her provision only to those of her children who are thus also (excess being lawless, disproportionate, and unjust), that indulgence is *ingratitude* and intemperance *blasphemy,* and that praise is due to the giver because *he* is man's 'feeder'. This chastity, like this attempted rape, is what the traditional figure provided: a way of imaging the problem of man's freedom, within nature of which he is a part. The Lady's position is the completely Christian one (she takes one, not two): that Comus does not fully describe 'nature' and 'man's nature'. She acts according to another allegiance, and what she has that he cannot shake is fidelity. The consent Comus cannot get from her is an agreement with his postulate: 'Scorning *the unexempt condition By which all mortal frailty must subsist,* Refreshment after toil, ease after pain . . .' (684). Her response to this 'you are by nature a body' is simply to act as if man's nature is to be a soul incarnate in a body. ('Subsisting through the bounty of the Creator', was Sandys's plain phrase for her very different postulate). There are those who think that the Lady should show some signs of being tempted. It would destroy the *figurative* device of the masque, and prevent it from enclosing these problems of the relation of virtue to freedom, of man's nature to 'nature', to reason and to the divine; these concerns furnish the intellectual interest of many another presentation besides Milton's of the meaning of Ulysses' stand.[23]

We ought, I believe, to resist strenuously the idea that Milton, influenced by earlier understandings, states in *Comus* that 'the divine and celestial soul (Lady) can by no assaults of nature (Comus) be made to yield'. (Comus might say disgustedly that this unpenetrating half-truth is what *Comus* means). Allegory does not work this way at all. We watch the Lady and Comus as they reveal to the understanding

[23] In Iden's 1557 translation of Gelli's *Circes,* as Ulysses has his amusing series of dialogues with the 'Grecians' turned into oyster, lion, mole, goat and the rest, we are gradually shown that man's distinction and glory is his conceptualizing power, his capacity to 'understand the universals', not merely apprehend particulars. Hence his 'elective' temperance, freely chosen by a free will, and his self-awareness. All the distinctively human power (the 'very operation' of 'human nature') is seen as man's unique form of knowing and worshipping the first mover, now imperfectly known but later to be seen in perfection, who loved his creature man—the sole creature who is 'naturally bound' to give honor to God (see esp. dialogues 10 and 8, and the dedication to Cosimo de Medici).

the meanings we try to capture in such rough statements. The value of such a great traditional metaphor, as a hinge upon which the total invention can move, is that it can allow of a revelation of the nature of the opposition between good and evil. It is not a matter of 'triumph over' after 'conflict with', for the myth has become rather a way of looking at what the human moral predicament is. We do not watch a struggle-between but a discovery or uncovering-of; and in fact it is a great strength in the figure that its metaphorical base is not a fight but a seduction. We have imaged before us in the entire piece the greater beauty, superior reasonableness, and the naturalness, of all that we can lodge within the insufficient word *virtue* (the figure *castitas* is better), and imaged also all the dark perversions that can betray it—disorder, intemperance, voluptuous self-love, *libertin* naturalism, the beast in its relation to the beauty. 'Imaged'—that is, we see what things look like; and see the real not behind the apparent but in the apparent.

The masque as a genre is peculiarly suited to this unveiling or discovery of the true nature of things through images; its high moment is commonly a sudden disclosure of the masquers, when as in a vision the key to full meaning and application opens the image wide. The conditions precluded this, for Milton, but in his as in other masques the accoutrements, speech and behavior (properly kept stylized) of symbolic personages slowly open up his main image.

'Revelation' describes the functioning of the images from the very beginning of the poem. They do not describe, and seldom argue. Comus is the incarnation of disorder, yet the ordered loveliness of his moonlit images is not a mistake. The woodnymphs are decked with daisies trim, the brooks dimple, 'The Sounds, and Seas with all their finny drove Now to the Moon in wavering Morrice move', and he and all his followers merely join all fertile and amorous things, that worship what seems to be the cause of their being; this *is* order, he says, the order of Nature. The rout of monsters is there, and their noise is just as 'unruly' as it is to sound later when the Spirit calls it that 'wonted roar' which fills 'the Air with barbarous dissonance'. The difference is simply that it does not seem to us unruly, rather only 'merry' as Comus names it, the tipsy dance seems not uncontrolled or unattractive but merely more like life than ballet, the shout and the revelry seem to be what midnight asks for, as it also demands 'better sweets'; what hath night to do with sleep? Comus claims, 'We that are of *purer fire Imitate the Starry Quire'*, and though every word of the five is an irony, what he says is true, they do; this is no time for us to notice that his 'we' is a crew of beast-headed yahoos, and that if their 'imitation' of the 'swift round' with which the dancing spheres roll Time endlessly away seizes the full meaning of that heavenly dance, then the vast skiey system is nothing but one grand and idiotic whirligig. Not 'purpose', but life and beauty, disappear. Making Time pass; round and round—'orderly' enough, if that is what one means by order. The dark ritual worship of lasciviousness does not look very beautiful, or even very free and pleasant, even as Comus describes it; but the distinction escapes our notice, for we know what he is saying when he says this is Pleasure. This secret flame is the very type, if that is what one means by pleasure.

These are not persuasions; we merely see that what is said is true, while we are within this mind and seeing the world with its postulates (and of course consent to that kind of taking-possession is the rape the Circe-figure commits upon men). In the same way the Lady reveals a different total conception of what all things are and mean; the images she uses speak of the same objects and simply replace the way we have seen them with something quite different. The woods (Comus's 'dun shades' conniving at couplings) were 'kind and hospitable', and only the invasion symbolized by the raucous noises made them the 'blind mazes of this tangl'd Wood' which present to her and us the *selva oscura* in which the human creature is lost. Evening had been a gray-hooded Votarist, Phoebus's last dim attendant clad like one holy and devout. Long before Comus argues for exploiting nature's wealth of gifts we have seen him at it; before the Lady ever overtly sees in this self-indulgent exploitation a perversion of nature's own soberer plan, we have heard the drunken riot as her ears heard it—frightening insolence and grossness that is a skewed way of thanking the gods for abundance. For this image (176) she has often been called priggish; none in the piece turns out to be more accurate—the noises are being made by those who did believe Comus's later-given recommendations for the Forms of Thanksgiving.

Before we hear any discussions about reasonable temperance, imagery of two kinds, one visual, reveals to us the exact case of the men-beasts: 'their human count'nance, Th' *express resemblance of the gods,* is chang'd Into som brutish form', some '*in*glorious likenes', 'unmoulding *reasons mintage'*. All but the psyche is still 'human'. Man's *glory,* the divine image that is part of Milton's definition of *human,* is what is at stake; loss of this is what loses them self-knowledge, so that they 'Not once perceive their foul disfigurement' (68, 527, 74). Seeing an image of this loss of freedom is quite as important as hearing of it from the

Attendant Spirit; between his two descriptions we have seen the dance—not a cavorting, but The Measure's aped courtliness—of the ridiculously inglorious crew, so 'fair a herd'. Therefore we take in without analyzing it as such a converse demonstration of the same aspect of the central device; the Lady safely and chastely keeps the freedom of a mind which fully accepts alliance, but knowingly and only to 'that which is good'. It is the Elder Brother's prophecy come true—he had said, 'Yea even that which mischief meant most harm, Shall in the happy trial *prove most glory*' (590). That the unseduced virtuous reason, free to choose what it gives itself to, is man's most glory (and hence the very eye of the target) is part of what the traditional figure could reveal through, rather than despite, the emphasis on chastity. The Brother quite naturally goes on: 'But evil on it self shall back recoyl, *And mix no more with goodness*'. One could find great numbers of these echoes and patterns in which images again and again uncover rather than expound. As always such designs present (imitate) the coherence and integrity of that which is symbolized, and upon this, the true Pattern, all 'image-patterns' depend. It cannot be paraphrased.

The nature of the issues has made one ancient symbol—Light—consistently important throughout the masque, and many subtleties and profundities are made open and powerful through Milton's supremely imaginative control of such symbolism. It is not possible to follow this with any completeness, for a reader or hearer knows the infinite variety and speed of that play of changing light over line after line of the thousand-odd, from the first 'Before the starry threshold . . .'[24] to the last light at 'the corners of the Moon' melting into that wherein the sphery chime escapes a mortal ear and eye. I shall accordingly notice only some of the radical symbolical powers of this image, whence many lovely others are born. No analysis will catch the deep reasons for the way they stir us, and though we speak with gratitude of Milton's unearthly sureness touching all that makes verse like music, we have in the end to sit silenced.

Some of the ways in which light's symbolic power is caught in form can be helpfully spoken of. First and simplest, this masque (like a dozen

[24] Or, of course, of the light-filled description of the world whence he comes, with which the Attendant Spirit opens the masque in the Bridgewater MS., and which reflects a cancelled original beginning in the Trinity MS. I have placed at the end of this essay a note too long to include here, with the references most necessary to those interested in how differing versions of *Comus* affect study of its imagery. Some of the most important recent interpretations of *Comus* have been based on evidence of this kind.

others) uses the ancient enmity between Jove and Night, physical darkness being used as symbolic of radical moral evil and protectress of its exponents. The thick lustful dark in which the lascivious goddesses move becomes that of a psychic and moral abyss: the dragon womb of Stygian darkness that spets gloom, the very upper element of air one blot, dark vail'd Cotytto worshipped with the sultry licking flames of lust, the ebony chariot of Hecate, all these moon images that give the lie to the seeming innocence of the earlier ones. Both the worship of evil and evil's envious hatred of good are put in terms of this symbolism: the 'nice Morn', 'the tell-tale Sun', and the marvellous spiteful denigration in 'the blabbing Eastern scout', all demote Light the ancientest of all figures for divinity to the only role Comus sees divinity as playing: ' 'Tis onely day-light that makes Sin'. Yet there is no plain equation of Comus with the dark and the good personages with the light—if we except perhaps the angelic and shining figure of the Attendant Spirit, who speaks of his own place and of all good things in the very language of light. His images always use dark in a pejorative sense, from 'this dim spot' of Earth to the cypress shades at 'the navil of this hideous Wood',[25] which he parallels with the storied rocks 'whose entrance leads to Hell' (real, though to their reality 'unbelief is *blind*'). But this consistency is unusual.

To be sure, the darkness is the consistent character of the enchanted wood (*ominous, black, dun*) and there is a related figure in the fogs and 'black usurping mists', for whatever prevents man illegitimately (as in 'usurping') from *seeing his way* is ranged among evils—again just part of the whole point. But not only is there much imagery of light in the speeches of Comus himself, there is also no indication that natural darkness is evil. The Lady says 'O theevish Night' because an unnatural 'single darknes', 'envious', had supplanted the starlit night in which a *natural* ally would give *due* light to the misled and the alone:

> Why shouldst thou, but for som fellonious end,
> In thy dark Lantern thus close up the Stars,
> That nature hung in Heav'n, and fill'd their Lamps
> With everlasting oil, to give due light . . . (198)

The same moon that was Hecate to Comus makes the sable cloud itself become the Lady's help: 'Was I deceiv'd, or did a sable cloud Turn

[25] That Comus is there *immur'd,* 520, though master, is only another example of the recurrent link between *darkness* and *prison;* this springs from the way in which the relations between *virtue* and *freedom* are conceived in the whole piece. Cf. note 26.

forth her silver lining on the night?' It was the eerie unnaturalness of finding no one and no lights in the place whence came the noise she had reluctantly followed that made the Lady fear she had stumbled into a darkness where unnatural things possess and use nature's night—beckoning shadows dire, and bodiless tongues that can call by name and secure mastery over one. She has, of course.

Hence it is the more ironic and courageous when, 'startled' but not 'astounded' (209; we hear always this note of the free mind in control), she calls on the ideas she thinks her *champions.* There is no mystery in their not being Faith, Hope, and *Charity.* Not only are *Castitas* and Agape-Caritas related, and certain Platonic conceptions entirely pertinent, but she is seeing the very form and essence of the only *protection* she has. It is, as is usual in allegorical images, *seen* in two ways, *form* in two ways, and *protection* in two ways, and all are equally true. All three guardians are imaged in words suggesting light, but the third ('And thou unblemish't form of Chastity, I see ye visibly') she sees also literally with her physical eyes. And when we see the literal moon edge into sight from behind the sable cloud, and see it as chaste Diana, and both as the type of the Platonic-Christian fidelity between the human soul and the 'Supreme good' who 'would send a glistring Guardian if need were', we feel not only the excitement of the poetry but the gratitude for light in this dark place which stirs the Lady's next lines. This is allegory. And I suppose that no reader who thus reads the passage can do so without some sense of his own darkness and light. This does not turn the Lady into us, for she is what, when, and where she was; it merely takes care of everything at once, as profound metaphors always do. She 'did not err', the silver that lightens the natural dark 'casts a gleam' over the unnaturally possessed dark grove, and she has also seen, though not 'visibly', faith and hope; she can now believe, that is, that even 'all things ill' are but as unwilling officers that inescapably do the bidding of 'Him, the Supreme good'. When she then sings to wake Echo, the irony of Comus's appearance in answer plays again on these strings of natural, supernatural, unnatural, and we take in complex notions of the relations between them long before any such are stated.

That the symbolic use of darkness is thus closely and firmly prevented from denying the Lady's later 'most *innocent* nature', and that it yet constantly raises the question what-is-nature, is simply one case among many where analysis would show how images uncover the unified and consistent meanings presented to us later in other ways. If we had not already taken in through the symbolism the profundity of 'Light' as an issue in the action, we should not feel the strange beauty of 'Unmuffle ye faint Stars . . .'; terror would not catch at us, unexpected and as if for no great reason, when the Elder Brother says 'Stoop . . . And disinherit *Chaos,* that raigns here In double night of *darkness,* and of *shades*' (332). It is not only the irony of the fact that we have just seen the very spirit of disorder take over full authority and that the speaker does not know what he is saying—his *shades* an unrealized pun, and his allusion to old Night's opposition to Cynthia a fable but no lie. But also, when it all happens over again—the stars, and 'thou fair Moon', and the traveler's benison, the pale visage through a cloud, the mists and the villagers and the rest of it, but happening now against the background of that previous scene with Comus which had ended with the Lady's prayer to Providence and the wild irony of her 'Shepherd lead on'—as we hear them again, the poignancy of all these innocent appeals for light becomes connected with a troubling sense that we are seeing in a mirror the whole human condition. The conversation that follows between the Brothers is kept very particular and local, and the symbolic use of light bears the whole burden of this symbolical extension, but it gives reality, fitness and power to the outburst of radiance accompanying the most famous image of light in the masque:

> Vertue could see to do what vertue would
> By her own radiant light, though Sun and Moon
> Were in the flat Sea Sunk. . . . (374)
>
> He that has light within his own cleer brest
> May sit i'th center, and enjoy bright day . . . (381)

Certain powers which this symbol has always possessed will work more openly, from here on. An image especially moving used of good and evil becomes, also, one especially translucent used of wisdom and unwisdom, insight and blindness. We have already seen too many symbolic appearances of light to rate this trust in it as self-sufficiency, even if the passage on Wisdom and Contemplation were not there; moreover, the continuation, by contrasting the enslavement of the man of dark soul, clarifies the fact that this inner light which keeps the will free to elect virtuous action is scarcely to be confused with stoic pride.[26]

[26] The image does not read 'He that has *virtue* within his own breast may sit and enjoy being virtuous.' Light is a symbol, virtue partakes of the nature of *that which it symbolizes,* has therefore her own light and can see and freely do what *she would;* and the man who has *light* within (still symbolic of the

This is made quite clear by the following development in Platonic and Christian terms of the imagery of light in the soul (the angels, the 'beam' cast on the outward shape by the 'oft convers with heav'nly habitants'; the 'souls essense' and 'divine property' passages re-emphasizing Christian conceptions of the soul's destiny, 454 ff.).

The radiance of this image, in which the Elder Brother gives virtue 'her own light', is not dimmed but strengthened by the fact that it shines within an irony; that we have just seen the virtuous Lady blind to Comus's real nature does not make nonsense of it. His sister has willed no evil, done or thought nothing unvirtuous, nor will she, and this image shines uncontradicted by the action through to the end, to 'Love vertue, she alone is free'. Yet as that end too shows, though virtue has her own radiant light, can teach man 'how to clime', virtue is not equated with all that Light symbolizes in the poem. The Lady did see, and do, what virtue would, but that she was, even so, insufficient and could be blinded by a charm that touched the outer sense if not the moral judgement or the rightly choosing will, is surely an intended part of the action and meaning.

It does not take care of the situations man gets into in the dark wood that he can 'do what vertue would'. Light as his human wisdom and virtue manifest it is not enough illumination to see completely the nature of reality, still less to save himself from the consequences of blindness. Moreover, the Lady is not Virtue; one does not say of allegory 'The Lady is Virtue'—she *figures* it. We therefore do not see her unvirtuous, but we do see her not 'free'—for we see a mortal and limited creature. We see her in the common human state: '. . . this corporal rinde Thou haste immanacl'd, while Heav'n sees good' (663). And in her incapacity to transcend such fetters (they can be worn by a soul however virtuous, living in nature), and in the incapacity of others to do this for her, we see figured what the Epilogue states: that if Virtue, that strength which teaches mortals how to climb toward the realms of light itself, should be feeble, *Heav'n it self would stoop.*

---

unstatable) enjoys day though he sit at the dark center of the universe. The man within whom is hidden a *dark* soul makes of his self a *dungeon,* in which, mock-free, he *walks*—under nature's high noon sun, yet overtaken (*benighted*) by the setting of the inner one. I can not embark on the history of the Light-as-wisdom aspect of the symbol though it would clarify some of these uses, as commentary (usually on *PL* iii) shows; I have chosen instead to scrutinize exactly in relation to the central figure those images which are read with wide differences, in interpretation after interpretation of *Comus,* with the result that evaluations of the poem show the most extreme disparity.

That Heaven must stoop to the aid of strength is far from being nonsense. Two major images at least carry the burden of this idea, the Attendant Spirit and the Sabrina episode. Here Woodhouse's exposition of the relation of the Sabrina episode to the Lady's insufficiency as well as to the incapacity of the others for action seems exact and sound (see n. 21 above). Not only is need shown in *Comus* for the greater *illumination* of grace, but the symbolic use of water suits with the demonstrated need for 'a new infusion of divine grace' before the Lady can be freed (as no human creature can free another) from what Comus represents, and from every resulting bondage. It is to be noted that haemony, carefully distinguished from the moly of temperance, protects the brothers from one aspect of the enchantment here in question; they know *what Comus is* and can therefore enter his spells and yet come off—as the Attendant Spirit promised: 'for by this means I knew the foul inchanter though disguis'd' (644). That there is a relation between haemony and grace seems probable,[27] though another symbol bears (quietly; it is not to be labored) the burden of completing Milton's Christian argument and Christianized 'device'—the symbol of water, perhaps the most ancient and untranslatable of all, and here used with truly symbolic force. The most meticulous rereading will show that such use as Milton chooses to make of the old symbol of the rod or wand does not conflict but is fitted in with all this, for the cure of the rod waved in reverse—'by discipline, and a view of their owne deformities'—can be beyond the unaided reach and power even of virtuous human creatures, de-formed from their 'coelestiall originall'. Their insufficiencies are circumvented.

To the student of imagery watching the operation of a symbol with manifold powers, like that of light, through a long and complicated work, no impression is more powerful than that he receives of a symbol's sureness and dependability. It does not lie, never has to be excused for inconsistency or incoherence, but retains a purity and translucence which make symbolic imagery the foe of obscurity. One's conviction grows that this is not the result of calculated subtleties on the part of an author, but of a true symbol's profound but stubbornly orderly relation to that which it presents. The logic of this relation varies from symbol to symbol, and its history usually uncovers this logic, but once grasped (the

[27] This is E. S. LeComte's suggestion in *Philological Quarterly*, XXI (1942), 283–298, where it is presented with extreme care and very interesting detail. For phrases quoted from Sandys in the next sentence see above, p. 132 [p. 142 herein].

lines are generally large and simple, but plunge deep), it shows as capable of sustaining almost infinite complexities of meaning without ever producing confusing ambiguity. Multiple meanings and seeming ambiguity are on the other hand common. 'Who knows not Circe *The daughter of the Sun?*' That Comus is the grandson of the very source of natural physical light is in perfect accord with the symbolic meanings of light just examined, with the ideas conveyed about wisdom, nature, man's relation to the rest of nature, and to the generative principle working throughout it, to chastity and desire, to fertility and fulfillment. The sentence rather illuminates than conflicts with that other, 'though Sun and Moon Were in the flat Sea sunk', and even the *unsun'd heaps* of miser's treasure (a seemingly opposed pejorative reference) falls into its dark and proper place. The translucent and flowing light seen through water, of the Sabrina songs and speeches, tinsel, golden, diamond, or glassy and cool, is loveliness itself; yet the earlier burst of light when the Scene changed to Comus's Palace (the first we have seen; all the good characters have moved hesitantly through darkness), glowing 'with all manner of deliciousness', presents a double meaning with perfect sureness and speed—through all the symbol remains entirely unambiguous and pure. One is only warned not to put 'good' or 'bad' beside any object or quality and then follow some 'pattern of symbols', but rather to watch the symbols infallibly develop before us complexities we had not suspected, in a pattern which they do not provide, but follow.

These complexities bear an interesting relation to the nature and possibilities of the masque, as compared with the drama or play. The one is characterized by subtleties of idea, conveyable by images; the other by subtleties of psychological motivation and personality, conveyable by characterization. The first of these two is the ground for the second, though that statement does not describe the process of artistic creation. But in a masque psychological refinements are implicit in the meaning of the great images, not inter-acting before us in complete people. Welsford's generalization in another connection so suits *Comus* that it can direct us, providing both illumination and warning, to a central fact about the nature of that work:

> . . . For classical drama . . . is concerned with the final phase of a conflict, and the interest is concentrated upon the last few hours of uncertainty which must soon be terminated by irrevocable choice and decisive action: but the masque deals, not with the last phase of a conflict, but with a moment of transformation; it expresses, not uncertainty, ended by final

success or failure, but expectancy, crowned by sudden revelation; and even when the opposition of good and evil is symbolized by masque and antimasque, this opposition is shown as a contrast rather than a conflict.
(*The Court Masque,* p. 339)

The damage done to Milton's *A Mask* by looking at it as a play (and the history of this aspect of *Comus* criticism is a history of damage done) is related to an essay on its imagery only at two or three points.

We miss thus what is a chief pleasure in this as in any masque: the pleasure of watching the central image unfold, display itself, dance before us. Plot is simple, already known or guessed, surprise at a minimum, situations are slight, almost negligible, adventitious, unagitating because warmth is not the quality of the sympathies awakened; but the image which is the heart of this frail action slowly opens out one meaning after another, never disappearing, never standing still, looking at us with one face out of the long and leisurely speech of one stylized personage, with another face out of the songs and declarations of another, is seen in this position and in that. All is serene, tranquil, and slow; speakers do not push their personalities into the tone of their lines, as we can test by noticing the extreme vulgarisation that results from allowing it; there is time for whatever elaboration will reveal the nature and distant arising of the meanings which move as in orbits of their own, and only finally come together, posed, in contrast but still without struggle, and then fall away, one regnant and one vanished. To roughen and tear this surface with fussy differentiation of personalities, with conflict between heated and emotion-torn people, is to deny the true feeling that moves beneath it; polyphony rent and jagged by Wagnerian dynamics. Our involvement is of a different character; we do not respond to meanings by way of our sympathetic identification with living persons, but directly.

For a masque imitates life differently, and we directly experience 'understanding something'; we do not as at a play re-live that whence understanding wells up or will accrue. Differences in the kinds of things understood are proper to each form. The transformation which 'crowns expectancy' may seem less sudden and less important in Milton's masque than in many. But Sabrina's release of the motionless central figure is not the climax of a suspense-filled action; it is the quiet completion of meanings which have slowly unfolded and shown themselves to us, mirrored in images. The gradual opening up of the complete meaning of a symbolical device offers no single crisis. Though the cup scene is by far the most important posing of contrasts, the masque form would lose its figurative character, which is its great beauty, if such scenes, instead of uncovering without haste a radical opposition, were so written that we watched in anxiety and doubt for the question 'will she drink? or not?' to be answered by the act of a person herself in doubt which to choose.

Over-emphasis upon the scene in Comus's palace as a 'conflict' or 'temptation' scene has many sources; among the results of it are a hectoring but frigid Lady, and a discontent with the 'debate' character of the scene. This is the burden of very much early, and some present-day, criticism of *Comus.* The true Lady is in the lines, if we read them without intrusive 'drama', and have come to their overt statements prepared by the previous expression of these same profound concerns through imagery. The debate in a masque is expected and watched for, if two irreconcilable conceptions must meet.

Some hint of this element enters any masque based on a device related to the 'triumph', Petrarchan or otherwise; the *debat* is so traditional and proper an element in all pastoral kinds that the word 'eclogue' all but calls for one (pastoral 'choice', pastoral 'invitation', and pastoral emulation in song, all take form as debates). The special sort of masque known as 'the Barriers' can be an outright debate; the second part of Jonson's *Hymenaei,* a debate between 'Truth' and 'Opinion', upholding and opposing marriage, is instructive concerning long speeches, their tone, the symbolism, the audience's expectations.[28] Of all dramatic kinds, certain types of masque best suit our current phrase 'the dialectic of drama'. The date of the form's greatest successes is not an unrelated fact. Even that characteristic of the dialectical method, an independent statement of two positions each in its most impregnable form, will hold for a masque whose device makes this form of the expected 'contrast' feasible.

This is not to say that *Comus,* in its character as a masque, is some sort of play in which ideas are the characters, and which we can sum up as the exposition of a philosophical doctrine. Because it is allegorical, it does not expound, but presents. This character it shares with all pre-eminently symbolical writing, and a masque has no being except as such a piece. That an audience expected to 'read' a masque allegorically goes without saying. Masques as well shallow as deep were written, by men

[28] Some conventions which make the masque too little like drama to be congenial to modern taste arise from its history, for example from its connections with the tournament-like Challenge and response, and stylized apposition of tilting forces. Cf. also *A Challenge at Tilt. Prince Henries Barriers* (not a debate) has one speech of 200 lines for Merlin; the Lady of the Lake has begun with 63.

of varying powers. But still the 'device', whether it be a story, a situation, a notion, an interpreted myth, symbolizes meanings uncapturable in exposition; philosophically slender these may well be, but falsely flat in plain statement. Likewise the meanings—in the piece—of personages are not caught by any name of an abstraction which may be our only way to refer to them (though indeed such naming is not to be disdained, as one of the few ways men have found to lay hold upon what is real). True of all allegory, and especially of Spenser's from whom Milton learned most, this suits *Comus* as well, and is the source of the excitement felt at seeing into the nature of things. It is not magnificence of spectacle but the sense of having viewed an image of life itself which kindles Jonson's words as he speaks of the 'Presentments' 'stealing away the spectators from themselves' in the first *Hymenaei:*

> Onely the envie was, that it lasted not still, or (now it is past) cannot by imagination, much lesse description, be recovered to a part of *that spirit it had in the gliding by.* (VII, p. 229)

But it is an *image* of life; personages, story, action, and often scene,[29] are metaphorical.

This describes *Comus,* and denotes the relationship of its large images to reality. Metaphor, allegory, and symbolism are linked in respect to the nature of their relationship to the real, and such distinctions as we should make between the last two (not necessary for *Comus*) *do not have this as ground.* In its greatest days, an essential element in the definition of allegory, which rhetoricians call briefly a metaphor continued, was the reality of the first term. In typology or strict allegory, this could be understood as the literal historical reality of the types—of Moses the type of Christ, or of the Giving of the Manna, type of the Last Supper. When allegory is secularized, and when myths are allegorized, the first term is not an historical Circe or Red Crosse who existed (or was thought to have) like Samson, something which historically took place like the leading of the Jews through the wilderness. Nor is it a

[29] An important though innocent-looking question is raised by D. C. Allen's remark: 'There is every reason to believe that Milton thought of the action as taking place in pre-Christian Albion' (*The Harmonious Vision,* p. 38). It—not masque but *action*—took place in one important sense near Ludlow as of 1634, also in more times and places than Milton could mention, taking place where all metaphors do, wherever universals exist. If the non-Renaissance-Platonist wishes to say, 'in the mind of man', this will do for a start. It makes the figure a little too purely psychological (too limited to a psychomachia eternally repeated) for one who believes Sidney's understandings historically more suitable, and it does not fit Milton's pronounced Platonism in the early poems.

'personality', Comus, encountering a 'personality', the Lady, whose realness consists in their being *individuals,* living and singular people. That is not metaphor, nor symbolism. The first term's historical and literal reality consists in its being a true account of every man's innumerable encounters with unregenerate natural man as he meets him in himself, every man's potential capacity to wed himself to Una, and his openness to despair, and need for release from whatever enchantment illusion leads men into. It resides in individuals, to be sure; we may call Belphoebe Elizabeth and the Lady Alice, and be right, as we may call Una Jane and Comus Alfred, if we know two such good enough and bad enough—but these are but *one* of the places of residence of a first term to which we would better attach the names of all individuals we know including ourselves. To make these identifications in a given story, if we move from single event to endlessly recurrent meaning, not merely from single event to endlessly repeated event, we use our minds as metaphor requires.[30] But allegory is not any series of little metaphors; it contains many such within *a* metaphor, which is 'continued'. And we have not yet arrived at what makes these allegorically figurative, in anything resembling the older sense, which though it did not suit all materials or artistic purposes lingered on where it did suit; we have not yet arrived at that reality which all these literally extant, real, first terms figure forth.

Here readers part company according to their philosophical postulates, but there is no doubt of which company Milton belongs in. It has

[30] We are reading tropologically. I doubt if anyone ever read *Comus* without thinking it to have some moral-allegorical force. But in the era when these figures were common, there was another element even in the 'moralization' (or Dante would not have conflated the three figurative senses). For all were based on similar metaphysical assumptions; a distinction was made, however, according to end (and thence nature) of the figures. When the Prodigal Son eating husks is seen as ourselves wasting all we are and have and eating our husks in tears, we think metaphorically in aligning all such bitter foods of error under one abstraction and seeing all in the first husk. When the Jews wandering in the wilderness are seen as a type of ourselves wandering in This Wilderness, the same process takes place, but we do not learn not to be prodigals, we see what to believe about the nature of the human state, fallen, lost and waiting to be led to its Promised Land. And that involves directly the beliefs and the Christian doctrines (*quid credas*) which the tropologically read figure, instructing us (*quid agas*) only assumed. Both secularization and certain philosophical changes mentioned below took place extremely slowly; of course not every extended metaphor could be, or ever was, read allegorically, and the possibilities surely varied with subject. The reader may test the difference for himself by saying, as he looks at the first example above, 'God the Father'—it will immediately become as *strictly* 'allegorical' as the second.

long seemed to me that profound allegory is written by (hence read sympathetically by) those who can look with the eyes of the mediaeval realist, or the Platonist (we must cover by our term the 'Plato' of later men). The deep-dyed nominalist (or positivist) can find no second term. He is left with merely a series of recurrent psychological happenings, which his interpretation of one man's covetousness proliferates when he calls it Covetousness and sees it as resembling all other examples of men being covetous, or which his interpretation of one Lady's rejection of Pleasure's Cup proliferates when he sees it as like all other such refusals. For Sidney as for Spenser's greater figures, we must take out that last *like*. Both, like those I have opposed to the nominalist, would find a metaphorical identity in the refusals by virtue of their being significant of a second term real in another sense than they. The reality which Una and the Lady (and any of us who can) make manifest, which the dark offers of Comus and Despair and our own betraying minds 'present', has its being as the 'forms' of things have being for Sidney, as the ideas have being for Spenser. The simultaneous presentation of the two modes of reality is the real excitement of allegory.[31]

When *Comus* is so read it has a date (1634), any date past or future, and no date, being a figure for timeless realities. The term that is in time is real; this is one reason why the allegorical mode has always attracted the satirist and the wit, and can make an entertainment out of those disheartening subjects, our virtues and our vices. Not everyone will read *Comus* allegorically; nor is this disastrous. It will outflank our contentions; its image encloses them.

[31] Compare C. S. Lewis, *The Allegory of Love* (Oxford, 1938), ch. ii; distinguishing allegory from symbolism, he gives us to understand that our choice is between: invented *visibilia* to express the immaterial (which I should not find necessarily metaphorical), and sacramentalism, with some form of denial of the reality of the phenomenal world. There is a third possibility, and there allegory lies. No one in modern times has done brighter and ampler service to allegorical writers than this critic. But in this definition (though not usually, it seems to me, in application) he does take away from allegory that metaphorical dimension it has by definition and history, and less well-read followers have not been slow to literalize allegory, turning it back again into the nineteenth-century naming-game. The gross misdefinitions of allegory to which we are accustomed are far from Lewis's sympathetic reading, or deep understanding (see for example pp. 358 ff., 329–339). They have been common in criticism since Coleridge took them over from German Romantic criticism, involve a complete misreading of Spenser, and fit no allegory by any master in the kind. They especially deny the nature of mediaeval and Renaissance allegorical reading and writing as readers and writers show that they understood it.

A NOTE ON SPECIAL PROBLEMS

(*see note* 24)

I have not thought it wise to take cognizance throughout in text or notes of differing readings in the Bridgewater and Trinity College MSS. and the 1637 and 1645 editions. A different and interesting essay would concern the relation of Milton's changes to his full intentions as stages in the few images affected could disclose them. Some interesting suggestions appear in C. S. Lewis, 'A Note on *Comus*', *Review of English Studies,* VIII (1932), 170–176. I believe no point of mine is changed by information in J. S. Diekhoff, 'The Text of "Comus", 1634 to 1645', *PMLA,* LII (1937), 705–727; I have found it dangerous to draw conclusions by analyzing given single images without consulting his data and his analysis of Milton's composition of *Comus.* But the simplest way to keep one eye on the Bridgewater MS. (of the masque as produced) is to have Todd's edition by one (IV, 180 ff.). A famous large variation (the nonappearance in Br. of Comus's taunts about Virginity, 737–755, and the Lady's rejoinder about the 'doctrine of Virginity', 779–806), does not affect my point about Milton's extension of the main image touching chastity.

The chief crux for a student of images which is affected by a comparison of the versions is that regarding the interpretation of the Epilogue-Prologue (especially the marriage of Cupid and Psyche, which to me seems an emblem, rather than a fully metaphorical allegory, of the fidelity between Platonic celestial love and the soul). I have stated that Tillyard's hypothesis in this connection, relating the imagery to conjugal love and involving a change in Milton's conception of the total action's meaning, seems to me suspect on other grounds (see n. 18 of this essay), and the special student may follow his arguments against other interpretations in *Studies in Milton,* pp. 97–99, where I find his answer to Woodhouse's interpretation of the celestial Cupid unconvincing. Celestial Cupid is too well established an image to allow of idiosyncratic wrenching of his meaning. See E. Panofsky, *Studies in Iconology* (New York, 1939), ch. iv, v; a case in point is Jonson's assured use of the distinction between blind Cupid (' . . . him, which they fayne, *caecum Cupidine*') and the Cupids who are 'chaste Loves, that attend a more divine beautie' than Venus (*Masque of Beautie,* p. 192; the imagery of this masque is of interest to the student of Milton—that of the tree with gold apples which these *chaste* Loves pluck, of 'new Elysium' with its Orpheus and its fountains of 'Youth' and 'Delight', and so on). There is comment on Tillyard's point in A. E. Dyson, 'The Interpretation of *Comus*', *Essays and Studies,* 1955 (this appeared after the present study was written, and I find in it, besides differences, several similar defenses and observations, though general considerations are his concern, rather than my strict examination of one kind of evidence for Milton's intentions and meanings). I should also mention a study whose length and inclusiveness I did not suspect until too late, nor read until this one was in press, and which I therefore do not try to include, thinking it unwise to interpolate comments from another full-length study of *Comus* into one completed and ready to appear (see John Arthos, *On 'A Mask Presented at Ludlow Castle',* University of Michigan, Contributions in Modern Philology, 1954). I have also not attempted references to notes etc. in editions of the poems, although my debt to them, especially to those of Merritt Y. Hughes, is of long standing.

The Subject of Milton's Ludlow *Mask*

Sears Jayne

I

The interpretation of Milton's Ludlow *Mask* is circumscribed on one side by the occasion of the *Mask,* on another by its textual history, on a third by its genre, on a fourth by its fable, and on a fifth by its allegorical subject. Every one of these boundaries is currently under dispute.[1] In this essay I shall deal with only one of them, the problem of the *Mask's* subject. In particular I want to explore the extent to which that subject may be said to be Platonic.

Not many people have thought it was Platonic. J. S. Harrison thought so in 1903,[2] and Douglas Bush thought so in 1954; [3] but in 1968 neither of the two tracks of the main line of "Comus criticism" runs in the direction of Plato. The first of the two most widely accepted interpretations of the *Mask* regards it as a philosophical allegory [4] showing how the soul (the Lady) can triumph over passion (Comus) by exercising the faculty of reason (haemony), which God (Jove) has provided (sent down by the Attendant Spirit). This interpretation

Reprinted, with substantial revision by the author, from *Publications of the Modern Language Association,* LXXIV (1959), 533–43. By permission of the author and the publisher.

[1] A useful summary of the literature on *A Mask* to 1956 is provided in Merritt Hughes, *Complete Poems and Selected Prose* (New York, 1957), pp. 86–89. Line references in this essay are to Hughes's edition, a reprint of the 1637 edition of the poem.

[2] *Platonism in English Poetry* (New York, 1903), pp. 47–57. Harrison thought the masque was based on Plato's *Phaedo.*

[3] *English Literature in the Earlier Seventeenth Century* (Oxford, 1945), p. 363.

[4] Among the most vigorous defenders of a philosophical interpretation of the *Mask* are J. C. Maxwell, "The Pseudo-Problem of *Comus,*" *CJ,* I (1948), 376–80; A. E. Dyson, "The Interpretation of *Comus,*" *Essays and Studies,* VIII (1955), 89–114; and John Arthos, *On "A Mask Presented at Ludlow Castle"* (Ann Arbor, Mich., 1954).

draws its chief strength from the fact that another well-known myth, the story of Circe, was interpreted in exactly this way by Renaissance mythographers.[5] The chief weakness of this interpretation is that Milton's fable is not the story of Circe, but a story which Hollywood might have called "Son of Circe," involving characters (especially Sabrina), action, imagery, and moral issues which go far beyond the traditional reason-passion dichotomy.

The second most widely accepted interpretation of the *Mask* is that it is a theological allegory [6] showing that man's salvation involves not only the realm of nature but also that of grace. Thus man (the Lady) is not able to triumph over evil (Comus) by reason (haemony) alone, but must have the assistance of Grace (Sabrina). This interpretation has the great merit of accounting for the presence of Sabrina in the masque, but it does not account very well for her relation to Neptune, for the Attendant Spirit's being called a "daemon," for the various references to the doctrine of pre-existence (e.g. "The divine property of her first being," l. 469), and several other details of action and imagery. The subject of the *Mask* is certainly theological, but its theology would probably have seemed strongly Platonic to a seventeenth-century reader.

Such a reader would in any case have been looking for Platonic doctrines in any masque of the 1630's.[7] Carew, Davenant, Townshend, "willing Walter" Montague (he exhausted his muse by writing a seven-hour Platonic monstrosity called *The Shepherd's Paradise*), Thomas Heywood, and even tired old Ben Jonson all ground out Platonic masques and plays to gratify Henrietta Maria's passion for Platonism; and when current production flagged, the tireless Inigo Jones

[5] The Renaissance authorities are listed by Robert M. Adams, *Ikon: John Milton and the Modern Critics* (Ithaca, N. Y., 1955), pp. 14–15. See also his "Reading *Comus*," *MP*, LI (1953), 18–32. Rosamond Tuve, in *Images and Themes in Five Poems of Milton* (Cambridge, Mass., 1957), pp. 112–61, regards the Circe myth as the "great hinge" on which the meaning of the masque turns.

[6] See A. S. P. Woodhouse, "The Argument of Milton's *Comus*," *UTQ*, XI (1941), 47–71, and "*Comus* Once More," *UTQ*, XIX (1950), 218–23.

[7] See especially G. F. Sensabaugh, "The Milieu of *Comus*," *SP*, XLI (1944), 238–49; and his other articles in *HLQ*, I (1938), 277–304, and *SP*, XXXVII (1940), 457–81. Platonism had also been associated with the masque in the Jacobean period, by Ben Jonson. See D. J. Gordon's article on the *Masque of Blackness* and the *Masque of Beautie* in *JWI*, VI (1943), 122–41. Jonson's Platonic masques are also discussed in two unpublished 1963 dissertations, one by J. P. Lucier (Michigan), the other by J. C. Meagher (Princeton). G. W. Whiting discusses Milton's debt to Jonson's masques in *Milton and This Pendant World* (Austin, Tex., 1958) pp. 3–28.

revived earlier Platonic plays, for example Fletcher's *The Faithful Shepherdess* in 1633, to fill the breach.

As a composer and performer in the King's Private Musick, Henry Lawes had participated in several Platonic masques; the two in which he had most recently been associated with the Egerton children [8] were among the most Platonic of them all: Townshend's *Tempe Restored* and Carew's *Coelum Britannicum.*

Alice Egerton had danced in *Tempe Restored* [9] in 1631/2, the year of her father's appointment to the Lord Presidency. This masque is a Platonic allegory of the soul's rejection of the material world (Circe) for the ideal world (Minerva) and a corresponding rejection of Circe for Minerva by the whole of English society (Tempe). The Tempe figure is only one of many conceits which Henrietta's writers employed to represent the Platonic reform which she fancied she had wrought in the English court. *Coelum Britannicum* [10] involves another conceit on the same theme, with the usual Platonic opposition of deities representing the ideal and material worlds (here Mercury and Momus) and the usual feverish ascending and descending between the two. Carew outdoes his rivals, however, not only in the length of his speeches, but in the macrocosmic scale on which he projects the theme of Platonic reform; here the inversion affects not merely Tempe but all heaven and all earth. All the lecherous deities in the mythological heavens look down to learn Platonic virtue from the court of Charles I, and the ideal beings inhabiting that court are stellified in the heavens. In this masque, produced earlier in the same year as Milton's (1634), not only Lawes and Alice Egerton, but also John and Thomas Egerton had all performed.

Just as the characters, actions, and devices of these and other Caroline

[8] See especially Willa M. Evans, *Henry Lawes* (New York, 1941); and Lady Alix Egerton, *Milton's Comus* (London, 1910). For a persuasive reconstruction of the first performance, see Marjorie Nicolson, *John Milton* (New York, 1963), pp. 68–70. For critical comment on the genre of the work see especially Eugene Haun, "An Inquiry into the Genre of *Comus,*" *Essays in Honor of W. C. Curry* (Nashville, Tenn., 1954), pp. 221–39; Gretchen L. Finney, "*Comus,* Dramma per Musica," *SP,* XXXVII (1940), 482–500; Rosamond Tuve, *Five Poems;* D. C. Allen, "Milton's *Comus* as a Failure in Artistic Compromise," *ELH,* XVI (1949), 105–19, and *The Harmonious Vision* (Baltimore, Md., 1954), pp. 409–40; and Enid Welsford, *The Court Masque* (Cambridge, 1927).

[9] See edition by E. K. Chambers (Oxford, 1912).

[10] See edition by Rhodes Dunlap (Oxford, 1949). The machine used in Milton's *Mask* was probably the device which opened a cloud revealing its inner lining (see Milton's ll. 221–24).

masques have left their imprint on Milton's text, so the Platonic themes of the Caroline masque may also be seen in that text. Several Platonic doctrines which appear in the *Mask* are obviously only peripheral, or indeed were added only as afterthoughts in later versions of the work, but there is one Platonic concept which seems to lie at the heart of the allegory. I shall discuss this central concept first and then point out some of the lesser details which seem to me to give the subject of the *Mask* a Platonic dimension.

II

The great appeal of Platonism to Renaissance thinkers was its service of reconciliation between traditional Christianity and the new classical learning; there are signs in the *Mask* that Platonism would have had exactly this appeal to Milton. One can see here and there in his text traces of an Ur-*Mask,* the kind of thing he might have written if he had received no instructions from Lawes. The subject of this shadow-masque is the triumph of Virtue over Vice conceived in terms of Christian theology. The three children represent Faith, Hope, and Charity (or perhaps, better, Chastity).[11] Chastity, age 15, with the help of her brother-virtues, Faith, age 11, and Hope, age 9, fights off Vice in a valiant struggle which shows that they thoroughly deserve the rescue

[11] There are traces of this idea elsewhere in the poem, as well. See especially ll. 411–12 and l. 971. Some modern critics, e.g. M. M. Ross, *Poetry and Dogma* (New Brunswick, N. J., 1954), p. 190, have ridiculed Milton for alluding to this trinity (ll. 213–15), but the idea of substituting the word *castitas* for *caritas* was a commonplace of the period based partly on the appeal of the similarity in spelling, partly on the logic that every step toward God is also a step away from the flesh. Christian painters and sculptors of the Renaissance often identified *caritas* with *castitas,* sometimes for Platonic as well as Christian reasons. (See Edgar Wind, *Pagan Mysteries in the Renaissance* (New Haven, Conn., 1959), esp. pp. 121–28.) Milton himself, in the *Apology for Smectymnuus,* identifies true love (the love of virtue) as chastity, citing Plato as his authority:

> Thus, from the laureate fraternity of poets, riper years and the ceaseless round of study and reading led me to the shady spaces of philosophy, but chiefly to the divine volumes of Plato and his equal, Xenophon: where, if I should tell ye what I learnt of chastity and love (I mean that which is truly so, whose charming cup is only virtue, which she bears in her hand to those who are worthy—the rest are cheated with a thick intoxicating potion which a certain sorceress, the abuser of love's name, carries about) and how the first and chiefest office of love begins and ends in the soul, producing those happy twins of her divine generation, knowledge and virtue—with such abstracted sublimities as these, it might be worth your listening, readers. . . . (*Apology for Smectymnuus,* Hughes ed., p. 694)

which they then receive from Lawes (Divine Grace). If Alice's older sister Penelope[12] had to be fitted in, she could be Grace, and Lawes could be simply an omnipresent Guardian Angel.

But the instructions which Lawes gave Milton must have ruined all this. The Whitehall version of the conflict between Virtue and Vice involved no Pauline abstractions, but only the triumph of Reason over Passion, with these elements figured forth as Roman gods or at least as pastoral sub-deities. The allegory of *Tempe Restored,* the masque in which Alice and Lawes had once played, reads as follows:

The Allegory

In the young Gentleman, who Circe had first enamored on her Person, . . . is figured an incontinent man, that striving with his affections, is at last by the power of reason perswaded to fly from those Sensuall desires, which had formerly corrupted his Iudgement. Circe here signifies desire in generall. . . . That divine Beauty . . . should dissolve the inchantments, and Circe voluntarily deliver her golden rod to Minerva, is meant that a divine Beame comming from above, with a good inclination, and a perfect habit of vertue made, by the harmony of the irascible and concupiscible parts obedient to the rationall and highest part of the soule. Making man only a mind using the body and affections as instruments, which being his true perfection, brings him to all the happinesse which can bee injoyed heere below. . . . So that Corporeall Beauty, consisting in simetry, colour, and certaine unexpressable Graces, shining in the Queenes Maiestie, may draw us to the contemplation of the Beauty of the soule, unto which it hath analogy.[13]

Here one sees the terms in which Lawes and the children would have expected Milton to work: Minerva confronting Circe, Hercules confronting Comus, Mercury confronting Momus, always Reason confronting Passion, and always the soul moving triumphantly from the Vice of Passion to the Virtue of Reason. One can easily imagine Alice's dreaming, as she danced in *Tempe Restored,* of one day herself playing the soul, haughtily scorning the seductions of Circe, and turning to Minerva in the person of her own older sister, Penelope.

One can also easily imagine Milton's toying with the idea of adapting the Minerva-Circe story from *Tempe Restored.* Alice will play the soul; she can overcome Circe by using moly, brought down by Lawes as Mercury, and Penelope can play Minerva. No, that won't work; the Circe story worked in *Tempe* because the soul was a man; if Alice is the

[12] Penelope, an older married sister, had also danced in masques at Whitehall. She is not named as one of the performers in the printed editions, but that does not mean that she did not participate. The reasons for supposing that she may have played Sabrina are given by Miss Nicholson, *John Milton,* p. 69.

[13] Townshend, ed. Chambers, pp. 96–99.

soul, we'll have to have a male Vice.[14] Who is a male Vice in classical mythology? Whom did Jonson use in *Pleasure Reconciled to Virtue?* An obscure drinking-deity from Philostratus called Comus.[15] But if I use Comus, what happens to Lawes and his moly? Better call Comus the son of Circe. But what has Minerva to do with Comus or Circe or any of it, and what shall I do with the two boys? I still think my idea about Faith, Hope, and Charity and Grace was better.

In some such way as this Milton might have begun with the materials which Lawes and the Egerton children knew best and realized almost at once how alien were their ideas to his own. But he might also have seen, in the same text from *Tempe Restored,* a way out of this impasse. The allegory of *Tempe Restored,* though mythological, was also heavily Platonic, and it might easily have occurred to Milton that the best compromise between his theological notions and Lawes's mythological ones was the mythologized theology of Renaissance Platonism.[16] The logical place for Milton to turn for material on Platonic theology was the *Theologia Platonica* of Ficino, but he might as easily have been led to the Platonic theology in a number of other ways.[17] Let us suppose, for example, that in an effort to find some material on Minerva or Mercury he had turned to one of the standard illustrated handbooks of symbols and allegorical figures, the *Symbolarum quaestionum* of Achilles Boc-

[14] Not only Spenser's Britomart and Busyrane showed this to be so: even St. Jerome realized it: *Castitas truncat libidinem, et femina vincit viros, PL,* XXII, col. 293. Only experience was against it; all learning was for it.

[15] The fullest scholarly discussion of the Comus myth is that by Frederick T. Welcker in the edition of the *Imagines* of Philostratus by Fridericus Jacobs (Leipzig, 1825), pp. 202–215; see also the very full notes on the text itself, pp. 215–21. Philostratus' brief description (*Imagines* I.2) is the only classical account of the god, and is the origin of Renaissance accounts such as those of Baldini (1565) and Giraldi (1565). Most of the better-known mythographers, including Boccaccio, Comes, and Cartari, ignore Comus altogether. Milton could have borrowed some details about Comus from the Latin *Comus* of Puteanus and from Jonson's masque, but most of what Milton said about the god had to be invented.

[16] See especially Douglas Bush, *Mythology and the Renaissance Tradition* (Minneapolis, Minn., 1932); Erwin Panofsky, *Studies in Iconology* (New York, 1939); Jean Seznec, *The Survival of the Pagan Gods* (New York, 1953); André Chastel, *Ficin et l'art* (Geneva, 1954); and Wind, *Pagan Mysteries in the Renaissance* (New Haven, Conn., 1959).

[17] Milton's own knowledge of classical Platonism is best described in Irene Samuel, *Plato and Milton* (Ithaca, N. Y., 1947). On Milton's attitudes and ambitions during this period see especially A. S. P. Woodhouse, "Notes on Milton's Early Development," *UTQ,* XIII (1943), 66–101; J. W. Saunders, "Milton, Diomede, and Amaryllis," *ELH,* XXII (1955), 254–86; and G. F. Sensabaugh, "The Milieu of *Comus,*" cited in note 7 above.

chius (Bonn, 1555). In that volume he would have found not only a Platonic allegorization of Mercury, but also a perfect Platonic allegorization for his *Tempe* situation of Minerva-Alice-Comus. Emblem 68 in Bocchius [18] shows, in picture and poem, the middle part of the soul, reason, repelling the passions, while above on a cloud waits the higher part of the soul, the *Mens,* ready to lead the soul up to heaven as soon as the passions have been put down. This three-part conception of the soul as including passions, reason, and *Mens* was evidently reasonably well known to Renaissance readers. Another example of the concept is an allegorical painting by Bandinelli, entitled "The Combat of Ratio and Libido," which shows a battle between two armies of Roman deities, one representing Reason and the other the Passions. In the clouds above sits a female figure, *Mens,* holding a torch and waiting to direct the soul to heaven as soon as the battle is over.[19]

The background of this emblem of the soul Milton would probably have recognized as Ficino's Platonic theology, and he could probably have turned at once to the relevant passages in the *Theologia Platonica* where the theory is expounded. The modern reader, however, needs to recover this background more gradually. We may begin with a short account of the history of the soul as the Platonists conceived it:

The soul is at first in the presence of God, where it is satisfied and happy. Then, because of its desire for, and love of, the body, it falls into the body and is united with it. There, like a person drowning in a stormy sea, the soul is overcome with oblivion, the lack of knowledge [of heaven] whence all evils spring. This physical world embodies reflections of that divine world; by these visible signs we are advised to conjecture [the nature of] things invisible. The soul is easily aroused [to a desire for heaven] because it tends in that direction by reason of its very nature. The soul is plunged into shadow, as is to be expected when it is in a dense body, but the soul easily passes out of the dense shadows into a remembrance of truer things. At length it recalls its own nature, and, recognizing and despising the meanness of the body, it seeks to return to its natural home [i.e., heaven] and feed once more on nectar and ambrosia, that is, the vision of Truth, and to rejoice in the possession of the Good. It discovers and beats its wings; it comes to life again in its dead body; it is awakened from sleep; it emerges

[18] Pp. 144–45. The figures are labelled Logos, Metanoia, and Aphrodites, but the title is *Rationis et Libidinis Certamen.*

[19] An engraving based on the original is reproduced by Panofsky in *Studies in Iconology,* Plate LVIII. Panofsky's interpretation of the work (pp. 148–50) is based on an explanation given by the artist himself at the bottom of the engraving. The work is also reproduced in Seznec, *Survival of the Pagan Gods,* p. 133.

from the river Lethe, and stretching the long-unused [wings of] goodness and wisdom, tries to fly back to heaven.[20]

Thus Platonic theologians saw human life in three stages: (1) the descent of the soul from heaven into the prison of the flesh; (2) the struggles of the soul against the demands of the flesh; and (3) the return of the victorious soul to heaven. These three states of the soul are called by various names by various Platonists.[21] Ficino himself employs several different sets of terms in his own writings; perhaps the least obscure of the Ficinian terms are the triad: *emanatio-raptio-remeatio.*[22] The idea of describing the stage between descent and ascent as a seizure or imprisonment was common among Platonists, and the term *raptio,* or *raptus,*[23] or any of its several equivalents, such as that in *Tempe Restored* itself,[24] could have given Milton the idea for the paralysis which the Lady experiences in the enchanted chair.

In any case, it is clear that Milton's *Mask* is concerned primarily with only the middle of the soul's three states.[25] We are not told in the *Mask*

[20] Ficino, *Epistolae* (Venice, 1495), fol. iii^{v}. The text given is my own translation of a marginal Latin paraphrase by John Colet. See *John Colet and Marsilio Ficino* (Oxford, 1963), pp. 89–90.

[21] See especially the association of the three stages with the three Graces, and the various names given them, discussed by Wind, *Pagan Mysteries,* pp. 31–56 and associated Plates.

[22] See references in Wind, *Pagan Mysteries,* p. 40.

[23] A typical definition is that of Cornelius Agrippa: *Raptus est abstractio et alienatio et illuminatio animae a deo proveniens, per quem deus animam, a superis delapsam ad infera, rursus ab inferis retrahit ad supera.* Quoted from *De occulta philosophia* by Wind, *Pagan Mysteries,* p. 48 n.

[24] See the Soul's speech in *Tempe Restored*:

> Yet there was in me, a Promethean fire,
> That made me covet to be man againe,
> Govern'd by Reason, and not rul'd by Sense . . .
>
> Tis not her Rod, her Philters, nor her Herbes,
> (Though strong in Magicke) that can bound mens minds;
> And make them Prisoners, where there is no wall.
> It is consent that makes a perfect Slave . . .
> 'He finds no helpe that uses not his owne.'
>
> (Chambers ed., p. 85)

[25] It is a significant measure of the limits of Milton's interest in Ficino's Platonism that he did not adopt another widely known set of Ficinian terms for the three states of the soul: *Castitas, Pulchritudo,* and *Voluptas.* Here *Chastity,* by inversion, stands for the soul's emanative love of the Body; *Beauty* stands for the soul's sojourn in the foul flesh; and *Lust* stands for the soul's desire for God. This triad illustrates a principle which is central in Ficino's thought and an

any of the details about how the children became lost in the woods, and we are not given any details about how they reached home after leaving Comus' palace. Insofar as the *Mask* is about the life of the soul, it is about the middle stage only, that stage in which the soul reaches the turning point of its *circuitus spiritualis,* rejects its love of the body and recalls its love of God.

Ficino lists seven ways in which the rejection of the flesh, withdrawal from the physical world, may be accomplished before death: dreams, fainting, melancholy, temperance, solitude, shock, and chastity.[26] In this view, chastity is not so much a condition as a specific event, the achievement of a turning point in the history of the soul. The means by which the soul achieves chastity we have already seen described in Bocchius and Bandinelli: first the reason, which is the middle part of the soul, masters the lower part of the soul, the passions (Ficino calls this part the *Idolum*); then the higher part of the soul, the *Mens,* leads the soul back to heaven. The primary function of the *Mens* is to preserve the memory of divinity which the soul brings with it into this world.

How might Milton have come upon this Ficinian conception of "chastity"? Perhaps, as I have already suggested, through Bocchius, or, simply by turning to Ficino as a possible *tertium quid* between Lawes's desire to "make it mythological" and his own desire to "make it Christian." In any case, he would certainly have found in Ficino's chapter entitled "How the soul masters the body is shown in many ways" [27] at

---

important mark of Platonism in English poetry, the concept of inversion. The basic principle is that in order to preserve the secrets of Platonic truth, those who are initiate deliberately invert their terminology. An example in English poetry is Chapman's inversions in "The Shadow of Night" and "Ovid's Banquet of Sense." For a good discussion of the principle in Ficino see Wind, *Pagan Mysteries,* p. 69. Milton mentions inversion in the *Mask* (l. 682), and to some extent practices it (e.g., in inverting the Circe story), but if he had really been interested in it as a poetic theory (as Chapman was), he would probably have seized the opportunity afforded by the Ficinian inversion of the term *chastity* explained here.

[26] *Verum quando ita vacamus, ut huius modi advertamus influxus, septem sunt vacandi genera: somno, syncope, humore melancholico, temperata complexione, solitudine, admiratione, castitate vacamus. Theologia Platonica,* XIII.2 (*Opera,* p. 292).

[27] *Quantum anima corpori dominetur, a multis ostenditur signis. Theologia Platonica,* XIII.2 (*Opera,* pp. 288–92 especially). See also *Theologia Platonica,* VIII.16 (*Opera,* p. 200), and Ficino's *Commentary on Plato's Symposium,* tr. S. Jayne (Columbia, Mo., 1944), pp. 158–59. For secondary comment see P. O. Kristeller, *The Philosophy of Marsilio Ficino* (New York, 1944), pp. 171–99, 235–88. Walter Dress devotes a whole monograph to this aspect of Ficino's philosophy in *Die Mystik des Marsilio Ficino* (Berlin, 1929).

least two ideas of central interest to him.[28] First, he would have been interested to discover a Platonic version of "chastity," a ready-made "sage and serious doctrine of virginity." Second, he would have been impressed by the neat parallel between the *Tempe Restored* pattern of characters and the Ficinian parts of the soul:

Minerva	Mens
Alice	Reason
Comus (Circe)	Idolum (passion)

In some such way as this may Milton have hit upon the Ficinian doctrine of the Mens to serve as "The Allegory" of his *Mask.* The idea would certainly have had advantages: it preserved the simple fabric of Alice's *Tempe Restored;* it was recognizably learned; it flattered both Alice and Penelope; and it out-Platonized Henrietta herself. But there were difficulties. One was Minerva, the other was the two brothers.

Milton would have wanted to find another mythological figure for the *Mens* in order to avoid repeating *Tempe Restored;* but whom? The action of the *Mask* should show Alice, the soul, lost and wandering away from home toward the body in the dark of the physical world (the forest image, as in Book I of *The Faerie Queene,* was standard). She should then be confronted by Comus (the passions) and repel him by reason (brought to her by Lawes); but reason should only drive Comus away, leaving her still lost. Then her sister should come and find her and lead her home. How to get her sister into the woods? Make her a tutelary deity, a wood nymph? Fletcher used a river god for this kind of thing in *The Faithful Shepherdess.* Penelope could be a river goddess. Two rivers at Ludlow, the Teme and the Corve; neither well enough known. Severn has a good myth, but sixteen miles away; better use it anyway. Giles Fletcher tells the story: Sabra, drowned in the river and changed into a goddess.[29] Call her Sabrina. She can stand for the Mens,

[28] The passage on chastity I have already quoted. The passage on the parts of the soul is as follows: *Haec ratio est, quam inter mentem* (*animae caput*) *et idolum* (*animae pedem*) *mediam collocamus* (*Opera,* p. 290). Elsewhere on the same page Ficino cites Plato's *Republic,* X, as showing that Virtue, not a daemon or Fortune, is the true guide of one's life. What Virtue means he explains by saying that when reason cleaves to the *Mens,* then it rises toward God, but when it worships the Idolum, then it wanders here and there in pursuit of objects of sense.

[29] Milton's principal sources for the Sabrina legend are summarized by Merritt Hughes in *Complete Poems,* p. 109. Milton refers to the story of Sabra twice elsewhere in his own writings, in "At a Vacation Exercise" and in the *History of Britain.*

as that part of the soul which remembers its home with God and leads the soul there.

In some such way as this Milton might have substituted the figure of Sabrina for that of Minerva in *Tempe Restored,* giving his theological allegory some needed local color. There still remained the difficulty of the Brothers, which may be diagrammed as follows:

Sabrina	Mens
Alice	Reason
Brothers	?
Comus	Passion

One possible solution was to identify the Brothers with still another faculty of the soul, the *Spiritus* which Ficino, the Hermeticists,[30] and other Platonists often described as filling that embarrassing hiatus between the soul and the body. If Milton thought of this possibility, he must have rejected it. What he may have done at this juncture was to return to Platonic texts for more ideas.

It might very well have occurred to him, for example, to consult Plato's own dialogue on temperance, called the *Charmides.*[31] If he had read Ficino's commentary on that dialogue (as some readers of the *Mask* have thought likely),[32] he would have found there [33] a repetition of the *Mens*-Reason-Passion doctrine, and he would have noticed a number of

[30] See W. A. Scott, *Hermetica* (Oxford, 1924), Excerpt IV.59.53. For another seventeenth-century application see M-S Rostvig, "Andrew Marvell's 'The Garden', a Hermetic View," *English Studies* [Amsterdam], XL (1959), 65–76.

[31] Renaissance lists of Plato's dialogues customarily give the subject of each dialogue. For example, the subject of the *Ion* is given as "On the Iliad," and this doubtless explains why Ficino's commentary on that dialogue was so heavily plundered by George Chapman. The only dialogue on the subject of temperance is the *Charmides.*

[32] Since my own article was written, Professor Arthos has published an essay suggesting that Ficino's commentary on the *Charmides* is "the source and explanation of Milton's meaning" in *A Mask.* My own conclusions were reached independently and differ a good deal from those of Professor Arthos, but I should certainly agree that Milton is likely to have studied the *Charmides* commentary with some care. See John Arthos, "Milton, Ficino, and the *Charmides,*" *Studies in the Renaissance,* VI (1959), 261–74.

[33] In the Commentary on the *Charmides* Ficino refers to the conquest of passion by reason as temperance, and says that it is a necessary preliminary clearing of the clouds in order that the *Mens* may perceive the light of the divine sun more clearly: *Quo fit ut temperantia opus sit in primis: per quam expulsa perturbationum caligine mens facta cernior, divini solis lumine abunde circunfundatur: unde sapientiam primo recuperet: deinde prudentiam adipiscatur.* Ficino, *Platonis Opera* (Lyons, 1590), p. 767, col. 2B.

other passages which may have suggested lines for his own work; but Ficino would not have solved Milton's problem about the brothers. If, however, Milton had then turned to the other major Latin commentary on the *Charmides,* that of Poliziano,[34] he would have there found an ideal solution, a solution which would have commended itself to him not only because of its consistency with the Ficinian doctrine of the *Mens,* but also because of its being stated in terms of the very Circe-moly myth which he had already planned to adopt for Lawes's part in the masque. What Poliziano's idea amounts to is a distinction between two stages in the process by which the soul conquers the passions: the soul exercises not only pure, uninstructed reason, but also philosophical knowledge.

Poliziano's remarks, couched in language which would have appealed to Milton's intellectual snobbery, are worth summarizing in some detail. The ultimate object of human life, says Poliziano, is sapience, or the knowledge of God. The desire for this knowledge, that is, the love of wisdom, is what is meant by the term philosophy.[35] But the pursuit of wisdom is too esoteric for the rude masses to engage in. The soul must have rejected sensation before it can acquire philosophical insight:

> Only when a man has cast out of his soul all desires . . . may he then receive into his purged soul the true seed [of philosophical instruction].[36]

That instruction, according to Poliziano, is given by means of symbols; thus the *prisci theologi,* from Orpheus and Homer to Plato, always shrouded their teachings in myths and fables, to protect the sacred Truth from the irreverent barbarism of the unworthy. As an illustration of this principle of concealing truths in myths, Poliziano cites Homer's story of Circe and Ulysses and explains that the allegorical meaning of moly in that story is "divine philosophy."

In Poliziano's distinction between the uninstructed and the instructed reason Milton would have found the missing piece to make the allegory

[34] Poliziano's work takes the form of a Latin letter addressed to Lorenzo de' Medici, and was designed as a "Preface" to Poliziano's translation of the dialogue. Poliziano never completed the translation, but it is printed, along with the "Preface," in his *Opera* (Lyons, 1546), II, 293–99. On Poliziano's interesting life there is nothing adequate in English, but see W. P. Greswell, *Memoirs of Angelus Politianus* (Manchester, 1805), pp. 1–151. Poliziano's part in the Platonizing of mythology is best described in Chastel, *Ficin et l'art,* pp. 141 ff.

[35] The standard Renaissance definition of philosophy. See, for example, "Philosophy is nothing else but the love of wisdom," in Francesco Vieri, *Libro in quo calumniis detractorum Philosophia defenditur* (Rome, 1586), fol. a2ʳ; translation mine.

[36] *Opera,* pp. 297–98; translation mine.

of his masque complete: he would have found a theological equivalent for the Egerton brothers:

Sabrina	Mens
Alice	Reason
Brothers	Philosophy
Comus	Passion

In the action of the Mask this doctrine is worked out as follows: The Lady represents uninstructed reason (she thinks, for example, that the woods are "kind and hospitable," l. 181); she is able, by reason alone, to refuse Comus' temptations, but is not able to drive him off. Hence she must be rescued from Comus by philosophical knowledge, a magic herb brought in by her brothers. Because Milton does not want his readers to confuse this herb with the moly of Homer, which was normally identified as reason, he selects a new and more Christian name for the herb; he calls it "haemony" and specifically says that haemony transcends moly. Haemony, then, represents "divine philosophy," [37] and the brothers receive it from their daemon (the Attendant Spirit), just as Socrates had received it from his.

It is because the brothers are to be thought of as bringing philosophy to the assistance of their sister that they themselves engage beforehand in philosophical discussions. Since there are two brothers, Milton makes the further distinction between two kinds of philosophical wisdom. The Elder Brother, the more Platonic of the two, represents the idealist's faith in the superiority and inviolability of the soul. The Younger Brother, the more Stoic of the two, represents the patience which the idealist must always exercise. At the end of the *Mask* the Attendant Spirit compliments their faith and patience (l. 971). Meanwhile, lest we miss the point of their discussion, the Younger Brother refers to his elder's advice as "divine philosophy" and describes it, in Platonic terms, as being as "musical as is Apollo's lute." [38]

[37] See especially John M. Steadman, "Milton's Haemony: Etymology and Allegory," *PMLA,* LXXVII (1962), 200–207. For the Christian meanings of haemony, see E. S. LeComte, "New Light on the 'Haemony' Passage in *Comus,*" *PQ,* XXI (1942), 283–98. J. A. Himes, *Miltonic Enigmas* (Gettysburg, Pa., 1921), pp. 11–19, identifies haemony as the cross. Others have argued that haemony must represent some power such as divine Grace, a power superior to that of the Attendant Spirit, since the Spirit says that the haemony has protected him and that he received it from a shepherd. It should be observed, however, that the Spirit is there speaking in his disguise as Thyrsis, and that the "shepherd lad" may represent Milton himself, as several readers have observed.

[38] The sense in which philosophy may be described as musical is also Ficinian and is described by D. P. Walker, *Spiritual and Demonic Magic from Ficino to Campanella* (London, 1958), pp. 3–29.

When the boys later rush in to rescue their sister from Comus, we are supposed to remember that the magic herb which they wave at the magician represents "divine philosophy." The reason why Comus escapes is not that the boys forget their instructions (that is only the narrative excuse). Comus has to escape because reason and philosophy can only defeat the body; they must not destroy it. So Comus escapes, but in leaving he waves his wand and paralyzes the Lady completely in her chair. This is Milton's narrative equivalent for saying that the soul which has banished physical temptation has lost its emanation toward the flesh, has stopped its downward motion. In order to begin its ascent to God (to rise from its seat) the soul must be raised by the Mens, which is represented in the Mask by the figure of Sabrina, as we have already seen.

Whether or not Milton arrived at his subject by the possible route which I have sketched out here, the action of the *Mask* certainly corresponds with remarkable fidelity to the Platonic account of the soul's history. In the first scene, of 658 lines, Reason is shown wandering in the dark wood of physical existence, where the principal danger is that she may succumb to one of the two kinds of Passion (according to Plato), the appetitive or the irascible. This is what the Younger Brother means in referring to "the direful grasp/ Of savage hunger or of Savage heat" (ll. 357–58). As it turns out, the Lady is subjected to both kinds of passion: Comus both tempts her and threatens her.

In the second scene, of only 300 lines, the heroine is shown immobilized in an "enchanted chair" in Comus' palace. The "marble venom'd seat" on which Comus forces the lady to sit may be interpreted as the seat of forgetfulness [39] in which the soul sits during its sojourn in the body. The action of this scene we have already analyzed.

In the last scene, only 65 lines long, we see the reunion of the children with their parents, and the allegory gives precedence to the singing and dancing involving the participation of the spectators. But the subject of the return of the soul to heaven is not abandoned; it is simply transferred from the children to the Attendant Spirit, who describes in symbolic language the remainder of the journey to heaven as he himself will experience it.

What I have suggested here is that the allegorical subject of Milton's *Mask* is an account of the nature of virtue according to Platonic theology. The fourfold action of the Lady's story reflects the four-step concep-

[39] As suggested by John Arthos, *On "A Mask Presented at Ludlow Castle"* (Ann Arbor, Mich., 1954), p. 46.

tion of virtue which Milton himself invented by combining Ficino's distinction between reason and the Mens with Poliziano's distinction between reason and philosophy. The subject, like the fable of the *Mask,* is thus entirely Milton's own invention, and the Attendant Spirit is right when he observes that it

> never yet was heard in Tale or Song
> From old or modern Bard, in Hall or Bow'r
> (ll. 44–45)

But if the whole of the subject is Miltonic, its two halves are certainly Platonic, and Milton went to some pains to identify and support this Platonism in other details of the *Mask,* as we shall now see.

III

One important Platonic detail is the matter of the light imagery. This matter is spoken of most specifically in the Elder Brother's explanation of the self-sufficiency of the soul. The picture of the soul given in that speech is the Platonic picture of the soul as the center of its sinful earth, by analogy with the sun's being the center of the universe in Plotinus. The notion that the soul is a ray or spark of the divine sun was to become the standard figure with Cambridge Platonists in the "candle of the Lord" image. There is, moreover, a good deal of allusion to the doctrine discussed in Ficino, and the Hermeticists, that the Sun represents God, whereas the Moon, as a mere reflection of the Sun (made in its image) represents man;[40] the force of this association is felt in Comus' remarks in ll. 93–144, and the Lady's wandering around in the moonlit world is also part of it. The light imagery is pervasive, of course, elsewhere in the poem as well. For example, one could argue that Milton's reason for showing the action of the poem as taking place in the dark was that in the Renaissance table of correspondences between the four elements and the four times of day the element of water, in whose realm the action occurs, corresponds with the night part of the daily cycle: one could also argue that Milton's treatment of light imagery is essentially Christian, with backgrounds in James i.17, Dante, and elsewhere. Both of these explanations are doubtless correct, but in the masque they melt connotatively into the syncretism of Christian

[40] A typical Platonic discussion of the sun-moon figure is Ficino's *De sole et lumine;* see also his *Epistolae,* fols. lxii^r, xlviii^r, and clxxxvii^v. Miss Tuve gives a partial exposition of the Platonic significance of the light imagery of the *Mask* in *Five Poems,* pp. 146–51.

Platonism. It was inevitable in a Platonic allegory that the relation between God and the physical world should be expressed in terms of light imagery, with God, as the sun, at the center of the universe, and all physical things at the outer extremities, in varying degrees of darkness. Critics who wish to read the Ludlow *Mask* as an allegory of nature and grace have sometimes been disturbed by the fact that the darkness of the realm of nature at the beginning of the masque does not give way to the light of grace at the end. The explanation, I believe, lies in the fact that the masque is not primarily about nature and grace, but about the soul's achievement of Platonic *castitas.* The fact that it is still dark at the end of the poem merely indicates that the whole action of the achievement of virtue takes place in the realm of natural providence, that is, while the soul is still in the body.

Another point in the poem which deserves further amplification is the character of Sabrina. In the action of the poem, as we have seen, the final stage in the achievement of virtue is represented by Sabrina's restoring of motion to the paralyzed girl. In both Christian and Platonic doctrine, as in common sense, one of the distinctive attributes of life is voluntary motion (i.e., uncaused motion). The standard view is expressed in the *Dream of Scipio,* where Cicero says that the eternality of God is shown by the fact that he is the "first mover" of the world. Similarly the soul must be immortal since it is the mover of the body: "whatsoever is moved of itself," says Cicero, "is eternal." [41] In showing the mind as causing the motion of the body, Milton was dramatizing the basic relation between soul and body as it was understood by the Platonists.[42]

In selecting the figure of Sabrina as the narrative equivalent of the *Mens,* Milton's primary motive was probably the fact that a local deity of Shropshire was an appropriate figure for that faculty of the soul which has as its primary function to remember the soul's proper home and to assist the soul in returning to it. There are also, however, other appropriate associations between Sabrina and the *Mens.* The distinctive characteristics of the *Mens* part of the soul are its immateriality, its

[41] Cicero, *Paradoxa Stoicorum, Scipio hys Dreame,* tr. Thomas Newton (London, 1569), fols. vi^r–vii^r.

[42] *Atque Avicenna sequutus Platonicos, et Hippocratem, probat animum ex ipsa sui natura adeo materiam omnem exuperare, ut cum primum in seipsum fuerit restitutus, possit elementa mundi mira quadam virtute movere; atque habere in corpora quaevis imperium. . . .* Ficino, Commentary on the *Charmides* (*Platonis Opera,* p. 767, col. 2E–F).

immortality, and its memory. Like the *Mens,* Sabrina is both immaterial and immortal. Her immateriality she herself indicates:

> Thus I set my Printless feet
> O'er the Cowslip's Velvet head,
> That bends not as I tread.
> (ll. 897–99)

Her immortality is pointed out by the Attendant Spirit, who explains that Sabrina has achieved chastity at an earlier stage of her existence, at which time, having demonstrated herself as "sincerely" chaste by plunging into a river, she was given over to the daughters of Nereus

> to imbathe
> In nectar'd lavers strew'd with Asphodel,
> And through the porch and inlet of each sense
> Dropt in Ambrosial Oils till she reviv'd
> And underwent a quick immortal change,
> Made Goddess of the River.
> (ll. 837–42)

Sabrina's "quick immortal change" is an apotheosis both mythological and Platonic; the Christian "nectar and ambrosia," in Platonic mythology, mean respectively the knowledge and enjoyment of God.[43] Sabrina asks the Lady to turn her eyes toward her. Sabrina knows how to turn the soul toward God primarily because she remembers having done it before; the soul is able to turn toward God because it retains a memory of God from having gone through the process of achieving chastity in a previous incarnation. The nature of that process is described by the Elder Brother as follows:

> So dear to Heav'n is Saintly chastity
> That when a soul is found sincerely so,
> A thousand liveried Angels lackey her,[44]
> Driving far off each thing of sin and guilt,
> And in clear dream and solemn vision
> Tell her of things that no gross ear can hear,
> Till oft converse with heav'nly habitants

[43] *John Colet and Marsilio Ficino,* p. 89.

[44] Cf. the interesting parallel in Ficino's Commentary on the *Charmides: Tanta vero est excellentia temperantiae, ut et eam omnes in operibus suis observent elegantes, et ipsius virtute non solum corpus sub luna quodlibet, verum etiam caelum ipsum universumque servetur."* (*Platonis Opera,* p. 767, col. 1H.)

Begin to cast a beam on th'outward shape,
The unpolluted temple of the mind,
And turns it by degrees to the soul's essence,
Till all be made immortal . . .

(ll. 453–63)

This account is, among other things, an account of the Lady's own career: the Attendant Spirit ("a liveried Angel") drives off Comus ("thing of sin and guilt"), whereupon Sabrina, "the heavenly habitant," tells the Lady "of things that no gross ear can hear," applying the salve of memory to rid the soul of its attachment to the flesh and so to return it by degrees to its own essence "Till all be made immortal."

In reminding the soul of its home with God, the *Mens* acts as an agent of God, but it is an agency working through the process of natural providence; thus Sabrina is shown as an agent (goddess) of Neptune. If, in Sabrina, God is stooping to assist the human soul, that stooping is done through the normal machinery of natural providence, as is seen in the fact that the soul by nature includes the *Mens,* or spark of divine memory, among its parts. Thus, when the Younger Brother asks, "What hidden strength / Unless the strength of Heav'n, if you mean that" (ll. 417–18), the Elder Brother replies, "I mean that too" (that is, the assistance of divine providence, or grace), "but yet a hidden strength" (that is, a provision of natural providence), "which if Heav'n gave it, may be term'd her own" (ll. 418–19). Thus Sabrina, though Heaven gave her to the Lady, may be termed the Lady's own, as may all the natural powers of the soul. Sabrina does not represent the supernatural power of Grace, but a natural power; as goddess of the river she is an agent of Neptune, or a power provided by natural providence, with the permission and instrumentality of divine providence. The achievement of the virtue which Milton is talking about is the soul's achievement, not God's. Milton's emphasis is, like that of Ficino, humanistic rather than Augustinian.

In the mythology of the *Mask* the figure representing divine providence is Jove. This identification, too, is Platonic.[45] Though Jove often represents the World Soul in the Platonists, he is used as variously as his own spotted career suggests. In Ficino's own works Jove represents many different abstractions, one of which is that of divine providence.

[45] Ficino takes the identification from Plotinus, *Enneads,* IV.iv. 9–10; see Ficino's *Commentary on Symposium,* pp. 127–28, 180. See also Ficino, *Epistolae,* fol. iv^{v}: *Nam mundi totius animum saepenumero iovem platonici nuncupant.*

This providence is communicated to man through the services of Mercury, that is the angels.[46] Divine providence is distinguished by the Platonists from natural providence much as Christian theologians distinguished between the orders of nature and grace.[47] In Ficino divine providence is normally represented by Jove and natural providence by Prometheus.[48]

In the Ludlow *Mask* Milton adopts the distinction between divine and natural providence, and he uses Jove, as Ficino does, to represent divine providence. But the Prometheus myth did not suit his purposes for natural providence, so he used a different myth for that, a myth suggested by another Platonist, Petrus Calanna.[49] In Calanna's version, natural providence is represented by Neptune, whose authority in myth always is subordinate to and corresponds with the authority of Jove. In making everything in his masque take place in the realm of Neptune, Milton refers not only to England's insularity, but also to the philosophical relationship between the realm of natural providence (Neptune) and that of divine providence (Jupiter). Since natural providence cannot conflict with divine providence, everything that happens in Neptune's realm happens under Jove's jurisdiction as well. The correspondence between the two realms is emphasized in the masque in several ways. The Attendant Spirit, for example, says in the epilogue that his

[46] *Epistolae,* fol. clxxii^{r-v}.

[47] For the Christian background see Professor Woodhouse's articles cited in note 6 above. Among many statements of the basic Christian triad of nature-grace-glory, one of the nearest to Milton is that of Richard Baxter in *A Christian Directory* (quoted by B. Rajan in "'Simple, Sensuous and Passionate,'" *RES,* XXI [1945], 290). Baxter, a Presbyterian divine, was educated in part at Ludlow Castle, which he had left in 1633, only one year before Milton's *Mask* was produced there. Platonic theologians also recognized the Christian triad and asserted its correspondence to Plotinus's triad of World Soul–Angelic Mind–One. Francesco Vieri even classifies Plato's dialogues in three groups, according to the three realms, nature, grace, and glory. See *Compendio della Dottrina di Platone* (Florence, 1577), fol. b6^{v}.

[48] *Epistolae,* fols. iii^{r} and xli^{v}. Some Platonists identified the realms of divine and natural providence as respectively the upper and lower halves of the World Soul. In any case the essential distinction between the two realms is that the realm of natural providence involves corporeal substance, whereas the other does not. The higher realm is governed by divine law; the lower, by natural law.

[49] *Nunc vero quia Sacerdotium est nostrum Philosophandi genus, ad Neptunum recurrimus, providentiae naturalis Symbolum, et generationis typum. Est quoque Neptunus, ut nostri sub aenigmate effigunt, aquarum numen, ergo a naturali providentia est, et Neptuno aequarum Praeside* . . . [corresponding to Athena, who represents divine providence, or sapience, because sprung from the mind of God]. Petrus Calanna, *Philosophia seniorum . . . de mundo animarum et corporum* (Panormi, 1599), p. 103 [Bodleian copy].

route back to heaven lies by way of the ocean, and he is able to summon the river goddess, Sabrina. Moreover, the Attendant Spirit and Comus are paralleled in many details;[50] the Attendant Spirit does not himself attack Comus when he sees the girl in his clutches nor later with the haemony. Comus, as one agent of natural providence, argues quite rightly that his functions are natural, that is, they are possible within the realm of natural providence: but a soul's rejection of him is equally "natural."[51] The alternative which is put before the Lady is not a choice between natural and unnatural, but between two equally natural courses. The other victims of Comus have all chosen the fleshly alternative, but the Lady chooses the course which preserves more fully her freedom, her capacity ultimately to throw off the chains of the body and return to God. Her choice is made with the sanction of divine providence, but also, because she is still in the flesh, with the sanction of natural providence.

Still another point about the action of the *Mask* which needs to be understood in terms of Platonic theology is the position of Lawes. In the Trinity Manuscript[52] the Attendant Spirit is referred to as a "daemon" or "guardian daemon." The background of the daemon concept, though available in Plutarch and many other writers, is ultimately Platonic.[53] When he rejected the notion of Mercury, the merely mythological figure, for the more complicated figure of a daemon, Milton was not merely moving in a direction away from mythology and toward Christianity (as the notion of the Attendant Spirit or Guardian Angel might suggest); he was moving specifically in the direction of Platonic theology. Ficino emphasizes the protective as well as the directive powers of God and explains that God's influence upon human affairs is accomplished by mean of daemons, which

[50] Some of these are quite obvious, as for example the fact that they exert opposite influence toward salvation and damnation on the Lady. Other details are more ironic. For example, Comus tells the Lady that "it were a journey like the path to Heav'n" (l. 303) to serve as her guide.

[51] William G. Madsen presents a different view in "The Idea of Nature in Milton's Poetry," *Three Studies in the Renaissance* (New Haven, Conn., 1958), pp. 185–218.

[52] See facsimile edition of W. A. Wright (Cambridge, 1899). In this respect the Bridgewater MS, edited by Lady Alix Egerton (see note 8 above), follows the Trinity MS.

[53] I think that the Attendant Spirit represents the active element (air), whereas Sabrina is a daemon of the passive element, water. A similar contrast is drawn between Ariel and Caliban in *The Tempest*, as spirits of air and earth respectively. This active-passive distinction is reflected in Cleopatra's "I am all air and fire" (i.e., active) as opposed to water and earth (passive).

mix agreeably and eagerly in the governing of lower things, but especially of human affairs, and from this friendly service they all seem good: but some Platonists and Christian theologians claim that there are also bad daemons. . . . The good daemons, our protectors, Dionysius the Areopagite usually calls by the name angels, the governors of the lower world, and this differs little from the interpretation of Plato.[54]

This is the background of the Attendant Spirit in Milton's *Mask:* we should think of him in the poem not so much as an angel from St. Peter's heaven, but as a Platonic airy spirit.

A final mark of attention to Platonism in the writing of the *Mask* is evident in the revisions which Milton made for the 1637 edition of the work.[55] Whatever desire he may have had that the meaning of his allegory be understood at the first performance must have been greatly intensified when it became apparent that the work was going to be printed. He did not feel sanguine enough about its success to acknowledge his authorship in this version,[56] but he did make a number of textual changes. Most of these changes, as Professor Tillyard has pointed out, are additions tending to emphasize the presence in the work of a philosophical or theological allegory—"List mortals if your ears be true," "she fables not," "sage and serious doctrine of virginity," etc. But there is one addition which deserves to be explained at some length. This is the addition of lines 1004–11, that part of the speech of the Attendant Spirit in which he speaks of the story of Cupid and Psyche:

> Celestial *Cupid* her fam'd son advanc't,
> Holds his dear *Psyche* sweet entranc't
> After her wand'ring labors long,
> Till free consent the gods among
> Make her his eternal Bride,
> And from her fair unspotted side
> Two blissful twins are to be born
> Youth and Joy: so *Jove* hath sworn.

[54] *Commentary on the Symposium,* p. 185. On daemons see also Ficino, *Epistolae,* fol. cxlviii^r, ff. Michael Lloyd, "Comus and Plutarch's Daemons," *N&Q,* VII (1960), 426, points out one of many other possible sources of Milton's theory of daemons.

[55] See especially E. M. W. Tillyard, *Studies in Milton* (London, 1951), pp. 82–99. All of the major additions to the original text (ll. 737–55, 780–806, 999–1011) add to the philosophical weight of the work. See studies of textual variants by C. S. Lewis in *RES,* VIII (1932), 170–76; John S. Diekhoff in *PMLA,* LII (1937), 705–27; John Shawcross in *PBSA,* LIV (1960), 38–56 and 293–94; and D. H. Stevens in *MP,* XXIV (1927), 315–20.

[56] For a discussion of the "stigma of print" motive in Milton's anonymity in the 1637 edition, see the article by J. W. Saunders cited in note 17 above.

What this passage suggests is that this story is not merely about the soul's triumph over fleshly desire in this world, but is to be understood in the context of the soul's whole history, including its journey to heaven. The myth of Cupid and Psyche had been understood as a Platonic myth of the soul ever since its first major appearance in western literature, in the *Golden Ass* of Apuleius. Even more important, one may suppose that the reason for Milton's adding this reference to the myth in his 1637 version of the *Mask* is that the Cupid and Psyche story had been made the central topic of a Platonic drama produced at Court in the same year as the Ludlow *Mask* (1634), and published about the time Milton was preparing his own copy for the printer (1636). This was Thomas Heywood's *Love's Mistress, or The Queen's Mask.*[57] The Platonic allegorical meaning of the Cupid-Psyche story in Heywood's work is pointed out as the story proceeds, by Apuleius himself, in conversation with the ignorant Philistine Midas, who wears his asses' ears for the occasion. When Milton faced the prospect of issuing his *Mask* in print, he was not driven to the Townshend expedient of composing a prose explanation of the allegory, but he may very well have felt it perhaps useful to add to his other supplementary hints about allegorical meaning the suggestion that the journey to heaven described by the Attendant Spirit might be understood in Platonic as well as in merely Christian terms.

IV

Such are the principle points, both major and minor, at which Platonic theology seems to me to affect the subject of Milton's *Mask*. The *Mask* certainly has a subject; " 'tis not vain or fabulous,/ (Though so esteem'd by shallow ignorance)" (ll. 514–15). The Attendant Spirit seems to identify that subject in his last six lines:

> Mortals that would follow me,
> Love virtue, she alone is free,
> She can teach ye how to climb
> Higher than the Sphery chime;
> Or if Virtue feeble were,
> Heav'n itself would stoop to her.
> (ll. 1018–23)

To most of the Ludlow audience this speech probably meant that the subject of the *Mask* was the simple theological subject of the golden key

[57] The edition of Heywood which I have used is that of R. H. Shepherd (London, 1874), V, 81–160.

to salvation: the right road to heaven is Virtue, since by Virtue you get as far as you can and by Virtue you earn God's grace to help you the rest of the way. But the action of the *Mask* suggests that what is meant by Virtue is a great deal more complicated than the Christian notion of conformity to the will of God. Virtue, according to the action of the *Mask,* is a four-step process which I think Milton hoped that the learned would recognize as Platonic.

Why then, one may ask, did he not give it a Platonic title, such as *Masque of the Mens, Masque of Chastity,* or *Masque of Sabrina*? I shall conclude by giving two possible answers to this question. One is that he may have felt that it was truer to Platonic esotericism to leave the subject unnamed; there is a suggestion of such a motive in the fact that he suppressed the clearly Platonic name for Lawes's part, "Daemon," which appears in the Trinity Manuscript, and approved for publication only the more general "Attendant Spirit." Perhaps he could not think of a title which did not tell too much or too little about the subject of the work.

Perhaps he had different reasons at different times for not providing a more illuminating title. When the *Mask* was first produced, perhaps he was piqued with the whole project; perhaps he never gave up his preference for the Faith-Hope-Chastity subject; perhaps he was unhappy because the necessity of providing parts for the Brothers had forced him to abandon the simple unity of Ficino's *Mens* concept and introduce the complication of the theory from Poliziano.

Perhaps later, when he saw that whatever he himself thought about the defects of the work, the world admired it, perhaps then he felt that the real distinctions of the work, its conformity to the requirements set by the Egerton household, its superior learning, its superior poetry, its longer speeches, its picture of court life as bestial, its religious rather than erotic Platonism—all these qualities which made it so different from the other masques of the time—were best summed up in the fact that the *Mask* had, after all, not been given at Whitehall, like the rest, but *Presented at Ludlow Castle.*

A Mask Presented at Ludlow Castle: The Masque as a Masque

C. L. Barber

Two questions have confronted me in reading Milton's Ludlow *Mask.* How does Milton succeed—and I feel he does succeed—in making a happy work which centers, seemingly, on the denial of impulse, when typically in the Renaissance such works involve, in some fashion or other, release from restraint? Second, what is the form of the piece? how does it relate to Renaissance comedy and allied traditions? The answer to the question about its form, with which I shall begin, will I hope provide means for understanding how it orders and satisfies feeling.

I. The Form of the Masque as a Noble Entertainment

The *work* of criticism, as against the pleasure, is in good part the altering of expectations to suit the thing in hand. My experience with *A Mask Presented at Ludlow Castle* has been a case in point: it has involved giving up expectations of drama for expectations appropriate to the masque. Invited to consider Milton's masque as comedy, I report back after six months that Milton's masque is a masque! This shift in expectation has permitted me, I think, to get past difficulties which were fundamentally the same as those which Johnson expressed with his usual candor. "A work more truly poetical is rarely found," he said, but went on to object that it is not dramatic:

> The discourse of the Spirit is too long—an objection that may be made to almost all of the following speeches; they have not the sprightliness of a

Reprinted by permission of the publisher from Joseph H. Summers, ed., *The Lyric and Dramatic Milton* (New York: Columbia University Press, 1965), pp. 35–63.

dialogue animated by reciprocal contention, but seem rather declamations deliberately composed, and formally repeated, on a moral question. The auditor therefore listens to a lecture, without passion, without anxiety.

. . . At last the Brothers enter, with too much tranquility; and when they have feared lest their sister should be in danger, and hoped she is not in danger, the Elder makes a speech in praise of chastity, and the Younger finds how fine it is to be a philosopher.

Then descends the Spirit in the form of a shepherd, and the Brother, instead of being in haste to ask his help, praises his singing, and inquires his business in that place. It is remarkable, that at this interview the Brother is taken with a short fit of rhyming. The Spirit relates that the Lady is in the power of Comus; the brother moralises again; and the Spirit makes a long narration, of no use because it is false, and therefore unsuitable for a good being.[1]

I decided to quote Johnson when it struck me that his mocking summary of the plot is just like the fun people make of operas when they do not understand how opera works, or are sick of it. All they have to do is recite the plot. "The Brother, instead of being in haste to ask [the shepherd's] help, praises his singing. . . . It is remarkable, that at this interview the Brother is taken with a short fit of rhyming." It is indeed remarkable—the rhyme has a formal, musical function to which Johnson is turning a deaf ear:

> *2 Bro.* O brother, 'tis my father's shepherd sure.
> *El. Bro.* Thyrsis? Whose artful strains have oft delaid
> The huddling brook to hear his madrigal,
> And sweeten'd every muskrose of the dale,
> How cam'st thou here good swain? hath any ram
> Slip't from the fold, or young kid lost his dam? [2]

Mr. Hardy, in the Brooks and Hardy study, finds this moment of recognition "one of exquisite dramatic irony," and goes after the Elder Brother, who he says "greets his father's hired man with easy condescension," while ironically "the Spirit plays his assumed role dutifully." [3] Throughout his elaborate treatment, Mr. Hardy is intent on finding dramatic irony between or behind the lines. His assumption is that, to

[1] *Lives of the English Poets* (Everyman's Library; New York, n.d.), pp. 98–99.

[2] Quotations are from *Milton's Poems 1645* (Type-facsimile; Oxford, 1924). I have corrected obvious misprints, such as the omission of the possessive in the first line here, which reads "my father Shepherd"; and I have omitted the capitalized first letters of such words as "shepherd."

[3] *Poems of Mr. John Milton: The 1645 Edition with Essays in Analysis,* by Cleanth Brooks and John Edward Hardy (New York, 1951), p. 209.

save the piece from being silly or flat in the way that Johnson thought it, we must find character, drama, irony. There *is* irony and drama in it, certainly. But these are not what makes it work as a whole, as I see it; it works as a whole as a masque. So in the greeting of the Elder Brother to Thyrsis, it seems to me that Mr. Hardy sees a kind of action that isn't there, ignoring the action that is taking place. What is taking place is the creation and relishing of a pastoral setting, by means of a poetry of heightened formal lyricism. The Brother's question serves to set moving in the direction of the lost Lady the conventional pastoral metaphor of the strayed sheep; Thyrsis develops it by antithesis:

> I came not here on such a trivial toy
> As a stray'd ewe . . .
> But O my virgin Lady, where is she?

Dr. Johnson's high praise of the masque's poetry "as a series of lines" combines strangely with his complaint that almost all the speeches are too long—" 'Tis a very excellent piece of work, madam lady: would 'twere done!"

To consider how the masque form operates, let me begin by laying out what is almost self-evident. As drama is shaped by its changing environment, the theater, so the masque form was shaped by its extinct environment, the noble entertainment. The masque, indeed, is only one specialized form of a whole species of entertainment literature or pastime. The basic function of it all was to contribute meaning and beauty to noble persons, noble places, noble occasions. A masque was *presented,* not performed. Its basic method was to extend actuality by fiction, fictions developed out of the circumstances of the occasion and pointing back to realities. At its best, the make-believe was not merely added; it served to find or express meaning which was already essentially present, or ideally might be, should be, present. When Elizabeth visited a noble household, a distressed nymph from Ovid might rive an oak and implore the aid of Diana—in actuality Elizabeth was quite a fierce Diana in governing her ladies in waiting. The idealization tended to become flattery; the elaboration merely decorative. But the masquing could also be revelatory, exemplary, and persuasive, inviting nobility to realize an ideal in miming it.

The action common to almost all entertainments is greeting or encountering, with explanation which describes the occasion of the meeting so as to redefine the place and persons in terms of pastoral mythology and local lore. Visits or embassages were such fine opportunities that the formal court masque developed as a way of arranging for a visit where no actual visit was involved. The masquers tell of their origins and of their journey to the magnetic royal presence, present themselves in dance, are greeted in dance by undisguised lords or ladies, make their obeisance, and depart. In the Jacobean court, Inigo Jones's settings made visible the fabulous places from which and through which the visitors came. The masque became a way of environing a court ball, or "revel," with the pleasures of light opera and ballet. Jonson brought in the antimasque at court, drawing on the tradition at country entertainments of presenting pastimes of the common folk and on the satirical burlesque of the popular stage. The antimasquers are visitors too, or intruders, common and grotesque; they were usually played by professional entertainers who were proof against the obloquy of such miming, and skilled for it; the noble participants mimed beauty, virtue, deity, and the like, which is easy if one has the clothes. Their real skill, and it was a skill, was in dancing.

So majesty visited itself to realize majesty. The court masque was only possible so long as there was majesty to realize, or, in the great households, nobility. If James as a person was scarcely majestic, Jonson and Jones could make him so. Indeed the Stuart elaboration of the masque can be regarded as a compensation: Elizabeth would not have needed it all, and certainly would not have paid for it all! Under James, as Miss Welsford's fine book shows,[4] the masque was an important if precarious means of upholding the sense of a collective life consummated in magnificence at court—even while outside its charmed circle powerful elements in society were finding it irrelevant, or worse.

During the uneasy Caroline calm, Milton was, fortunately, enough a man of the age to enjoy the virtues of aristocratic courtesy and the courteous art of the masque. But, of course, he also felt responsible to a wider frame. In *Arcades* he wrote "part of an entertainment presented to the Countess Dowager of Darby at Harefield."

> Look, nymphs, and shepherds, look,
> What sudden blaze of majesty
> Is that which we from hence descry
> Too divine to be mistook:
>   This this is she
> To whom our vows and wishes bend,
> Heer our solemn search hath end.

[4] Enid Welsford, *The Court Masque: A Study in the Relationship between Poetry and the Revels* (Cambridge, 1927), especially Part Three.

The Presenter, the Genius of the Wood, explains that the masquers have come from "famous Arcady" and arrived at a still better place: "Such a rural queen/ All Arcadia hath not seen." This simple redefinition of Harefield and its household is perfectly conventional and perfectly done: Milton does not withhold himself from compliment.

But the speech of the Genius contains lines which describe a setting beyond Arcady:

> in deep of night when drowsines
> Hath lockt up mortal sense, then listen I
> To the celestial Sirens' harmony,
> That sit upon the nine enfolded sphears,
> And sing to those that hold the vital shears,
> And turn the adamantine spindle round,
> On which the fate of gods and men is wound.

Milton's mind flies up beyond festive song to a permanent music, sublimely Orphic.

> Such sweet compulsion doth in musick ly,
> To lull the daughters of necessity,
> And keep unsteady nature to her law,
> And the low world in measur'd motion draw
> After the heavenly tune, which none can hear
> Of human mould with grosse unpurged ear.

What can be the relevance of such music at a great household's entertainment? At a religious concert or in church, "at a solemn music," sacred music imitates divine, as Milton's poem about such an occasion beautifully says, marking as it does so the sad jar of sin that comes between. Here in *Arcades* all he can do with the music of the spheres is use it in compliment. If we *could* hear it, the Genius says,

> such musick worthiest were to blaze
> The peerless height of her immortal praise,
> Whose lustre leads us, and for her most fit,
> If my inferior hand or voice could hit
> Inimitable sounds . . .

If we pause over this transition, we can feel the difficulty involved in the masque form as a vehicle for Milton's full sensibility. For would such music really be appropriate "to blaze/ The peerless height of [the] immortal praise" of the Dowager Countess of Derby, however sublimed? The word "immortal," when we pause over the use of it in compliment, wavers unsteadily under the weight of the previous immense conception.

II. Milton's Strategy in Using the Masque Form

At Ludlow, Milton did, astonishingly enough, convert the masque to his high purposes. His second masque leaves out all but a decent measure of compliment, converting the approach to the presence, normally a climax of adulation, into a family reunion, with children honoring parents. There was an element of this already at Harefield, where members of the Duchess' family were the masquers. There was doubtless at Harefield an account of their journey to her presence: "Here our solemn search hath end." Milton either did not write that part or did not preserve it—there is nothing in the finale to indicate what sort of difficulties the journey involved. At Ludlow the journey becomes central. One side of our interest is centered in the trial of the Lady in her passage through a Spenserian dark wood. The leading masquer becomes a dramatic protagonist, and the spokesman for the antimasque becomes an antagonist, a vile enchanter who, so far as his attributes are concerned, might have stepped out from the pages of *The Faerie Queene.*

It is often assumed that, in making a drama centering on the Lady, Milton leaves the masque form behind. But this drama develops by the masque's kind of unfolding of the situation in which the drama takes place. And this situation is not simple fiction, as in drama, but rather transformation or translation of the actual, in keeping with the masque form and occasion. Milton was familiar with dramatic works which present a self-contained action shaped by traditions of the noble entertainment, notably *A Midsummer Night's Dream* and *The Tempest,* probably also Fletcher's relatively trivial teen-age pastoral romp, *The Faithful Shepherdess.* Shakespeare's habits as a professional dramatist, and his natural concern to add to the repertory of his company, led him to produce entertainments which could be reused as public stage plays. Milton, working with Henry Lawes at his elbow, for Lawes's patron, had no such further theatrical purpose. When Lawes in 1637 published *A Maske Presented at Ludlow Castle, 1634: On Michaelmasse Night, before the Right Honorable John Earle of Bridgewater,* etc., the title and the dedication invite the reader to share in retrospect the occasion of its presentation. So, in reading, we must reanimate not only the work's fictions but also the literal circumstances which those fictions extended.

To look at what was regularly being done with the masque's resources for transforming or redefining the situation at an entertainment makes one realize what an emphatic thing Milton did with it. In *Coelum Britannicum,* performed on Shrove Tuesday of the same year as Milton's masque, Thomas Carew and Inigo Jones undertook to transform Charles and his chaste court into the stars of heaven, replacing the lewd constellations with which the sky had been cluttered by Jove's lusts! [5] The Egerton brothers played the part of lesser stars, torchbearers to the masquers. The animal heads used at Ludlow for Comus' rout may well have been the same which served at court for a dance of bestial constellations, on their way to oblivion. *Coelum Britannicum* was clearly a very successful occasion. The thing worked by combining a light touch about the mythology with truly effective spectacle, song, and dance—a combination very like that which brings off our better musical comedies. To be subjected to Inigo Jones's settings must have been rather like the 3-D experience of Cinerama: for Carew's masque, lights on a great globe of the heavens progressively went out, later to come on again in a blaze, "expressing the stellifying of our British Heroes." In the interval, a huge mountain rose; clouds caromed, with singers on them. Another of Jones's great resources, not used in this particular masque, was the sudden opening up of vista beyond vista. His goal was not simply to present a scene but to alter the situation of the observer by manipulating perspective, as baroque painters sought to do when, for example, they painted domes to make the observer seem to look straight up a column of air in which angels were descending, some high, others almost on top of him.

What Milton did in his Ludlow masque was to use the masque's altering and extending of situation with his own kind of seriousness. The form sanctioned reaching out to far and high things, "stellifying." As Professor William R. Parker points out,[6] Milton and posterity benefited

[5] *The Poems of Thomas Carew, with His Masque "Coelum Britannicum,"* ed. Rhodes Dunlap (Oxford, 1949), p. 183. The masque was presented by the king to the queen in return for a Twelfth Night performance of *The Faithful Shepherdess.* Dunlap quotes from a letter of Garrard to Stafford: "There are two Masques in Hand, . . . High Expences . . . Oh that they would once give over these Things, or lay them aside for a Time, and bend all their Endeavours to make the King Rich! For it gives me no Satisfaction, who am but a looker on, to see a rich Commonwealth, a rich People, and the Crown poor. God direct them to remedy this quickly" (p. 273). Sir Henry Herbert, however, recorded his satisfaction that "the Q. was pleased to tell mee before the king, 'Pour les habits, elle n'avoit jamais rien vue de si brave' " (*ibid.*).

[6] In his discussion of the Ludlow occasion in his forthcoming biography of John Milton, which he kindly lent me in manuscript.

from the fact that at Ludlow physical scenery was necessarily minimal; this was to be a masque where poetry, rather than Inigo Jones, would present the descents from above and open out the vistas. Milton did not use directly Christian iconography in redefining the entertainment situation as a Christian situation. To have done so would have been discourteous, indecorous in a social sense. In the masque form there was no distinction between social decorum and artistic decorum. Mr. Martz's essay brings out how, in the 1645 volume as a whole, Milton's concern with decorum is social, the conscious development of roles or attitudes of the poet in society. A masque was an occasion for "antique fables" and "fairy toys," classical mythology and native folklore; Milton accordingly puts these in the foreground. He provides the masque's characteristic pleasures of animating familiar reading and fusing creatures from it with shadowy presences of the local countryside. But beyond these pleasures, he provides Christian reference by pursuing in a masque the serious concern of Renaissance humanists to re-understand ancient myth in Christian terms. As an artist and entertainer, he begins with tangibles and opens out meaning through them. The environment of Ludlow Castle is extended in this way to reveal or express a Christian situation. By a daring coup, he uses for his purpose the custom of noble persons masquerading in ideal, exemplary roles: the fifteen-year-old daughter of the house will mime the virtue proper to her stage of life, Chastity; her brothers, the defense of chastity, the role Milton found so enthralling when as a boy he read romances. As the children "present" these parts, their own identities are to be extended, drawn out, educated. If their spiritual situation is understood, Milton's masque says, they are what they masquerade—even if they did not know it before Milton's project for them.

The finding of valid, Christian spiritual realities in classical myth was a great Renaissance enterprise; the high excitement of it is expressed by Thyrsis as he sets out to enlarge the Brothers' awareness of their situation:

> Ile tell ye, 'tis not vain, or fabulous
> (Though so esteem'd by shallow ignorance)
> What the sage poets taught by th' heav'nly Muse,
> Storied of old in high immortal vers
> Of dire Chimeras and inchanted iles,
> And rifted rocks whose entrance leads to hell,
> For such there be, but unbelief is blind.
> Within the navil of this hideous wood
> Immur'd in cypress shades a sorcerer dwels.

To understand Milton's masque, we must be aware of the kind of moral and spiritual meaning which Christian humanism had been finding in classical myth for more than a century. Spenser's mythopoeia was in the foreground for Milton and his audience; but Spenser was part of a wide and complex tradition. Miss Tuve has beautifully exhibited the meanings which variations on the Circe myth were carrying; [7] she and Professor Woodhouse make clear how positive a virtue Milton was celebrating in presenting Chastity as an obligation of the natural order which could find sublime fulfillment in the order of Grace.[8]

But my concern here is to consider how, by the masque form, Milton brings such meanings into view. Dr. Johnson exhibited just the inappropriate assumption when he objected strongly against "the prologue spoken in the wild wood by the attendant Spirit" because it is addressed to the audience: "a mode of communication so contrary to the nature of dramatic representation, that no precedent could support it." [9] This astonishing lapse, which forgets so many instances in Shakespeare, results not only from Johnson's ignoring the masque form but also from the assumptions that go with a stage seen beyond a proscenium arch. The audience, he insists, cannot be in the wild wood! A similar assumption which relates to the whole problem of interpretation appears in a recent extremely suggestive article by Professor Sears Jayne, in which he proposes that Milton's machinery be understood in terms of Ficino's Neoplatonism. Mr. Jayne sets out by saying, "The *Mask* begins with a speech of the Attendant Spirit in which he explains the setting, the world in which the action of the masque is to take place." [10] He then argues that Jove refers not to God but to the Neoplatonic World Soul, and develops Ficino's systematic conception of the individual soul's descent and return, a structure of thought which proves to have fascinating parallels or potential parallels in Milton's masque. What concerns me is not judgment among such possible meanings but the status they have in the work, the way the masque reaches toward them. The Prologue does not once for all "explain the setting, the world"; it only begins a process of opening up which continues, dynamic and fluctuat-

[7] Rosemond Tuve, *Images and Themes in Five Poems by Milton* (Cambridge, 1957), pp. 112–61.

[8] A. S. P. Woodhouse, "The Argument of Milton's *Comus*," *University of Toronto Quarterly*, XI (1941–42), 46–71, and "*Comus* Once More," *University of Toronto Quarterly*, XIX (1949–50), 218–23.

[9] *Lives*, p. 98.

[10] Sears Jayne, "The Subject of Milton's Ludlow *Mask*," *PMLA*, LXXIV (1959), 535.

ing, until the last lines of the Epilogue. In the Prologue's first five lines we are made aware that where we are is "this dim spot,/ Which men call earth," that far above it are "regions milde of calm and serene ayr," and beyond these, "the starry threshold of Joves court." What are we to understand by Jove? At one moment less, at another more, as the reach of the poetry moves through one suggestion to another. We will be unaware of important meanings if we are not conscious of the systematic grids of Renaissance thinkers. But the masque keeps moving in and out of them. A slight hint that Milton was consciously concerned to keep clear of too explicit Christian reference appears in one of his minor revisions. In the Cambridge draft, the Lady, speaking of Chastity, said

> I see ye visibly; and while I see ye,
> This dusky hollow is a Paradise,
> And heaven gates o'er my head.

This seems to have been rejected as too explicit, short-circuiting a tension. In the way it advances through other symbols *toward* the Christian, the masque is, surprisingly, not unlike *The Waste Land.* The circumstances are vastly different; but both poets are concerned to move through "secular" materials to mystery and spiritual discovery.

Speeches seem too long when nothing seems to be happening. Since in many of the speeches what is happening is the *creation* of the situation, if we attend to that, instead of looking for the forwarding of event, there is high excitement and delight. As an example, consider the lines in which Comus tells the Lady that he has seen her brothers, lines where the act of imaginative creation is emphasized by the whole thing's being a downright lie:

> Two such I saw, what time the labour'd oxe
> In his loose traces from the furrow came,
> And the swink't hedger at his supper sate;
> I saw them under a green mantling vine
> That crawls along the side of yon small hill,
> Plucking ripe clusters from the tender shoots,
> Their port was more than human, as they stood;
> I took it for a faëry vision
> Of some gay creatures of the element
> That in the colours of the rainbow live
> And play i'th plighted clouds. I was awe-strook,
> And as I past, I worshipt; if those you seek
> It were a journey like the path to Heav'n,
> To help you find them.

Comus' fabrication opens an exquisite vista, exactly in the manner of the masque. It is his supreme moment as a tempter, because a sight of her brothers is just what the Lady, prisoned from them in darkness, most desires. The "faëry vision" of "gay creatures" who can "play i'th plighted clouds" embodies the delight of perfect imaginative freedom, as in Shakespeare's Ariel. It is as though Comus gave the Lady a subliminal dose of his potion—and then he hypocritically steps into a posture of religious awe! Her response is to accept him as a guide.

III. Discovering the Resources of Chastity

To present a trial of chastity, the masque's way of moving by successive extensions of situation and awareness serves Milton perfectly. For preserving chastity involves keeping a relation with what is not present: the chaste person is internally related to what is to be loved, even in its absence. The experience of being cut off is wonderfully rendered by the poetry which creates the initial setting in the dark wood. The Lady's lines convey the disorientation that darkness can bring about, the thronging fantasies, and the soul's reaching out for objects of sight or sound through which to recover a relation to community. Her brothers, when they enter, express the same experience. "In double night of darkness and of shades," the Elder Brother longs for the sight of "som gentle taper":

> Though a rush candle from the wicker hole
> Of som clay habitation, visit us
> With thy long levell'd rule of streaming light.

In this situation, the young people's first resources are internal. The Lady reflects that she has with her still "a strong siding champion Conscience," and welcomes to her inward eye Faith, Hope, and "thou unblemish't form of Chastity"—"I see ye visibly, and now beleave."

The Elder Brother argues the power of Virtue with the Younger Brother in the "declamations" which irritated Dr. Johnson (and many a reader since):

> Vertue could see to do what vertue would
> By her own radiant light . . .

It is difficult not to hear Juliet's "Lovers can see to do their amorous rites/ By their own beauties"—and difficult to sympathize with the Elder Brother once we hear the echo. Certainly the least satisfactory part of the masque is this presentation, through the Elder Brother, of the resources which "divine philosophy" can provide for the defense of chastity. His speeches do tend to become dogmatic argument: in insisting on the autonomy of the individual will and spirit, he verges on a kind of hubris, so that we sympathize with the Younger Brother's practical concern about external dangers. To try to save the lines by making the presentation of the Elder Brother heavily ironic, as Mr. Hardy does, surely does not square with the fact that he expresses convictions Milton himself held. We are intended, I think, to feel a youthful absolutism, not unlike Milton's own as a boy reading romances. It seems to me that the response called for is not ironic rejection but tutelary approval blended with the sad amusement of experience watching innocence—the response of Thyrsis to the Elder Brother's fighting words about Comus:

> Alas good ventrous youth,
> I love thy courage yet, and bold emprise,
> But here thy sword can do thee little stead.

The Elder Brother's tone is less priggish if we keep his lines in context, feeling them as a reaching out for resources against the tensions of uncertain isolation. Frequently, dogmatism turns into something like invocation, the realization of imaginative realities:

> Do ye beleeve me yet, or shall I call
> Antiquity from the old schools of Greece
> To testifie the arms of Chastity?
> Hence had the huntress Dian her dred bow
> Fair silver-shafted queen for ever chaste.

Milton's marvelous power to slow down a line and dwell on its object brings Diana home as a presence, "Fair silver-shafted queen for ever chaste."

The outreaching gesture around which the first scene pivots is the invocation of Echo; Milton uses dramatically a standard feature of entertainments. The Lady's song "moves the vocal air/ To testifie his hidd'n residence"—it brings that physical resource into play. Nothing in the masque is more beautiful than the epiphany of the Lady's quality conveyed by the song and the descriptions of it. Comus acknowledges that

> such a sacred and home-felt delight,
> Such sober certainty of waking bliss,
> I never heard till now.

The nymph Echo does not answer the Lady; instead it is Comus who comes forward. But Thyrsis, high on "the hilly crofts/ That brow this bottom glade," also hears the song. And the Lady has the strength of assuming that her need *has* an Echo. One of the stunning things about the moment when she sings her song is that at such a moment she should sing such a song; she shows she is a Lady by presuming that she is in a world inhabited by "courteous" Presences:

> my severed company
> Compell'd me to awake the courteous Echo
> To give me answer from her mossie couch.

The act of singing is an exercise of the Lady's integrity; she is internally related, beyond the darkness, to what she looks to and realizes in the song. In the song is exquisite maidenliness—"sweetest nymph, that liv'st unseen/ Within thy airy shell"—along with a rich capacity for sensuous enjoyment and sympathy with passion: the Lady envisages Echo

> in the violet embroider'd vale
> Where the love-lorn nightingale
> Nightly to thee her sad song mourneth well.
> Canst thou not tell me of a gentle pair
> That likest thy Narcissus are?
> O if you have
> Hid them in some flowry cave,
> Tell me but where.

The contribution to Milton's sensibility of Renaissance aristocratic poetic traditions appropriate to the masque appears in the contrast between the Lady's song and the more ungracious moments of the Elder Brother's exposition. The Lady's song does not condemn amorous feeling in lines of moral firmness, addressed perhaps to "thou unblemish't form of Chastity"; instead, its stanza so interwoven and complete holds a vision of delicate eros. The Lady's shy capacity for love, attached at this moment to her brothers, is expressed in Echo's living unseen within her airy shell and yet perhaps hiding the brothers "in some flowry cave." The result is dramatic rather than didactic composition; for the Lady's vulnerability as well as her innocence is given to the air by the song. Its strains

> float upon the wings
> Of silence, through the empty-vaulted night,
> At every fall smoothing the raven doune
> Of darknes till it smil'd,

Milton presents chastity not as a negative virtue but as an intact disposition to love.

The preservation of chastity accordingly depends, his masque shows, not only on inner resources, crucial as these are, but on a world beyond the isolated individual and appropriate to the Lady's reserved ardor: there must be an actual echo. Comus provides a false echo, at first beautifully camouflaged, as we have seen, to fit the Lady's sensibility, later manifestly false in the enticements of his palace. Her security is partly in the strength of her will and the freedom of her mind. But more deeply it rests on the fact of there being other, worthy objects of love as alternatives to Comus' release. The ultimate object of love, the masque repeatedly hints, is heavenly—as in the song's final lines about Echo "translated to the skies," to "give resounding grace to all heav'ns harmonies." But on this side of heaven there is Thyrsis, at once a "glistring guardian" sent by "the Supreme good" and, in human terms, "my father's shepherd."

Here we should notice again what Milton does *not* do with the Christian supernatural. The role of the Attendant Spirit suggests at first affinities with those comedies where the action is overseen by a benevolent, omniscient figure who stage-manages it all: the Duke in *Measure for Measure,* Prospero in *The Tempest,* Reilly in *The Cocktail Party.* In such plays, the presiding figure tends to suggest Providence, and a special kind of humor arises from the contrast of his knowledge, which we share, with the ignorance in which the rest of the persons flounder about in the human condition. The perspective provided initially by Milton's Spirit serves in a somewhat similar fashion to give a background reassurance, furnishing perimeters within which the trial will take place. But it is striking that, once the action is started, the Spirit does *not* preside: he neither foretells what will happen nor speaks from behind his disguise to assure us that all will be well, as does such a figure as the Duke in *Measure for Measure.* The nearest he comes to this is in the narration telling of haemony to which Johnson objected "because it is false"! But here too there is no direct relation made to heaven or Jove's court: haemony is made the highest fruit of pastoral learning, the knowledge of simples. In the immediate context, this would include understanding of "dire chimeras," how they are and how they are not real. More simply, the herb serves as the embodiment of the resource which the presence of Thyrsis has given to the brothers, and so completes the episode. Should we take it as Reason, or as Grace? There are associations with both, it looks *toward* both. That for the brothers it does not entirely work fits with their incompleteness, and also with the further resource which the masque's progress will discover in Sabrina.

That the Attendant Spirit can become Thyrsis reflects the contribution of pastoral and the masque to Milton's art, an art here as elsewhere ultimately religious. The secular traditions provide mediating presences and objects between the human and the divine. One ground of this fortunate mingling of world and spirit was the aristocratic assumption of hierarchy, to which the masque was committed by its very nature as a genre devoted to compliment. A favorite pastime of the masque was "teaching difference," with moral superiority regularly linked—often factitiously enough—to social superiority. Frequently in court masques the antimasque was abruptly stopped by the arrival of some noble presence radiating awe, who would dismiss the antics from the hall with moral and aristocratic contempt. In *Pleasure Reconciled to Virtue,* Atlas dismisses in this fashion Ben Jonson's Comus, a simple god of gluttony, Shrove Tuesday style, with bottle-shaped followers.[11] Milton uses such a break, with rich complication, when his Comus, at the approach of the Lady, abruptly ends the dance of his followers (described as "a wild, rude and wanton antic" in the Cambridge manuscript).

The essence of this encounter of masquer with antimasque, translated by Milton's poetic and dramatic elaboration into a spiritual confrontation, is distilled in the recapitulation of the event which Thyrsis communicates to the Brothers in the second episode of the first scene. This second episode is beautifully designed: it repeats the movement the Lady has been through from isolation in darkness to an encounter opening out the situation toward a world of pastoral generosity; but the succor offered the Brothers is real, not Comus' "glozing courtesy." We re-experience the threat of intemperance from the perspective of the high lawns, in language which cues an active response. "Night by night/ He and his monstrous rout are heard to howl."

> And O poor hapless nightingale, thought I
> How sweet thou singst, how near the deadly snare!

What Milton made of the masque's movement, of the choreographic commonplace of a noble presence suddenly arresting the motion of the antimasque, is concentrated for me in a single remarkable line of Thyrsis' narrative, "Till an unusual stop of sudden silence." He tells how, his labors done, he sat down

[11] *Ben Jonson,* ed. C. H. Herford, Percy and Evelyn Simpson (Oxford, 1941), VII, 482.

> To meditate my rural minstrelsie,
> Till fancy had her fill, but ere a close
> The wonted roar was up amidst the woods,
> And fill'd the air with barbarous dissonance,
> At which I ceas't, and listen'd them a while,
> Till an unusual stop of sudden silence . . .
> At last a soft and solemn breathing sound
> Rose like a steam of rich distill'd perfumes,
> And stole upon the air, that even Silence
> Was took e're she was ware . . .

Of course the power or magic of such a line is implemented by cadence, consonants, vowels: "*T*ill" with "*st*op" and "*sudd*en"; the undulations, between the stops, of "an unusual" and, after them, of "silence." Without the form and pressure of the poetry, the choreography would not carry; but the poetry is expressing or implying choreography, a moment in a dance. One can imagine (though of course one does not need to) that a hand goes up at "stop," a single dancer erect in warning above massed, subsiding figures.

IV. The Masque as a Defense and Resource

We are now in a position to consider how Milton's use of the masque form permitted him to order and satisfy feeling in an entertainment presenting Chastity. In electing to make a Masque of Chastity and put Revel in the role of villain, Milton undertook a particularly difficult task. Nobody but Milton would have tried it! His sense of life prevented his using wholeheartedly one of the great resources of entertainment literature, the release sanctioned by seasonal or periodic holiday. On a tide of such mirth, Shakespeare could move out into magic woods with an implicit confidence in a return, after the holiday moment, with humanity intact. It comes as a shock to hear the Lady speak of country pleasures as "ill manag'd merriment." But what she has actually heard is Comus' rout, who "night by night . . . are heard to howl." Milton has deliberately presented a figure of Revel who under the guise of refreshment tempts to dissolution from which there is no coming back. The whole historical development of English life, regret it though we may, was giving ground for Milton's new vantage toward the pleasures of Merry England. The old agrarian housekeeping society, based on the land and its seasons, was giving way to a dominant culture based on urban conditions, where a leisure class would try to find, and others to furnish, holiday pleasures everyday:

when night
Darkens the streets, then wander forth the sons
Of Belial, flown with insolence and wine.

The first response which the attitudes of our own time suggest is that Milton's project of celebrating Chastity is impossible. For we not only have no cult of chastity, we have a cult of defloration. Crazy Jane, "Learned in bodily lowliness," tells the Bishop that "nothing can be sole or whole/ That has not first been rent." Much contemporary fiction is devoted to a mystique that spiritual exploration requires accepting one kind or another of rape by the world—or it laments the failure of this mystique. When we look at Milton in our psychological perspectives, we cannot help feeling that he was vulnerable, and that in his idealization of chastity we have, clearly, a mechanism of defense. And yet, along with this sense of the artist and his subject, most of us find his masque wonderfully beautiful and satisfying.

One necessary way to understanding the poem's success is to consider what a positive conception chastity was in Milton's thought and in that of his time, as Mr. Woodhouse, Miss Tuve, and others have done. Through the ideal of chastity, Milton could reach to vital resources of his culture and religion. If Milton was vulnerable sexually, we should recognize that sexual vulnerability is just what his masque presents. If it is a defense, it is simultaneously a resource, a gathering of resources from a civilization which did not assume sexual invulnerability as an ideal. Milton fully recognized that unintegrated passion might destroy his particular complex sensibility, with its astonishing range of relation to psychic objects through which he achieved his sense of himself and of his relation to society and deity.

In *A Mask Presented at Ludlow Castle* he presents the possibility of destructive release, and meets it by another sort of release, the release of imagination carried by rhythm out and up to other objects of love. This alternative release is in its way physical, and so can work to counter that which Comus offers. For poetry and song *are* physical, the whole body engaged in the rhythms of articulation, envisagement centered in physical utterance. It is notable that the images which suggest a benign sexual release refer to song: "Silence/ Was took ere she was ware." In so far as the masque fails, it fails by a failure of rhythm. Where instead of poetry we get mere vehemence, mere assertion, and where our imagination is allowed to rest on the merely literal or merely intellectual contest, the defense of chastity lacks the final cogency of pleasure.

I feel a different sort of failure of rhythm in the speeches of Comus:

much of his part seems too shallow rhythmically for the impact it should have, too stilted, as though Milton's auditory imagination could not risk getting more deeply involved. Milton certainly had a genuine artistic problem here; his whole design would not admit of Comus' capturing our imagination fully. His solution, so far as he does solve the difficulty, is to allow his god to revel, to begin each speech strongly, often beautifully, with appeals to the traditional sanctions, youth, feast, and nature's vital dance. Then he spoils it. Professor Joseph Summers, commenting on this difficulty I feel about Comus' part, writes that "I had always assumed that Milton *meant* us to have difficulty there—that the problem is not that Milton's auditory imagination could not risk getting more deeply involved but that he was trying to imitate precisely the failure of Comus' imagination—the mechanical movement and vulgar assumptions that his speech betrays." One can grant, as I do, that Milton's purpose required him to limit Comus in this way, yet a limitation still remains—a necessary limitation, but to be regretted nevertheless, as we regret Merry England. Autolycus can sing heart-whole of a liberty Milton's masque cannot include, a liberty which did not threaten Perdita's exquisite, passionate chastity.

Agreeing with Professor Summers, I find myself clear about *dis*agreeing with the many critics who have read Comus' part with uninhibited delight, as though he were a more cultivated Autolycus. To take him without reserve, as though the release of the masque centered in his part, throws the whole out of balance. For if Comus persuades to a full release, there is nothing to resist him with but will, morality, principles.

The furthest reach of feeling, going out to the objects whose superior attraction defeats Comus, is in the Epilogue, where in the final version the imagination is carried beyond young Adonis and the Assyrian queen to celestial Cupid and "his dear Psyche, sweet entranced." The end of Chastity is love fulfilled, "Two blissful twins . . . Youth and Joy." Closer to the Lady's actual condition, and crucial in her rescue, is the figure of Sabrina, perhaps the most remarkable inspiration or revelation of the whole masque. Sabrina is, of course, exactly the sort of local genius looked for in noble entertainments; but Milton's astonishing mythopoetic power created almost all her particular qualities, qualities that are exactly, deeply right. The Lady is in a state of shock, following the attempted seduction. She cannot move, cannot go out to anything. What sort of figure can release her? Some presence identified with her father's power, the boundary of Wales. Some presence moist and cool—if the danger of seduction is melting heat, the danger of chastity is fevered desiccation. She cannot come out to her brothers, they cannot seize Comus' wand, because they are not men, and anyway they are brothers. A knight might take over from Comus, or, alternatively, a Vocation to the high mystery of virginity wedded to Christ. But a knight, or a Vocation, would take the Lady beyond the stage of life where she *is*. So the Sabrina who is invoked is a virgin who, threatened once, as the Lady has been, "still retains/ Her maiden gentleness." In the story of Sabrina's coming back to life, and the poetry and song which create her, we encounter, along with suggestions of the healing and renewing powers of water, the innocent cherishing of femininity by femininity, waiting and yet not waiting for another destiny, which is the proper resource of the Lady's stage of life:

> Sabrina fair
>   Listen where thou art sitting
> Under the glassie, cool, translucent wave,
>   In twisted braids of lillies knitting
> The loose train of thy amber-dropping hair.

Such is the power of the masque, in Milton's hands, to reach out and find, transformed, what, if embraced, is already there.

The Bridgewater *Comus*: Text of *A Maske*

A MASKE

Represented before the right
ble
ho : the Earle of Bridgewater
Lord president of Wales and the
ble
right ho : the Countesse of
Bridgewater./
At Ludlow Castle the
29th of September 1634
The chiefe persons in the representacion were:/
The Lord Brackley
The Lady Alice } Egerton./
Mr. Thomas }
Author Jo: Milton./

This is the title page of the Bridgewater Manuscript (referred to hereafter as Br.).

The title page of *Comus* in the 1645 edition of *Poems of Mr. John Milton* (referred to as 1645) reads as follows:

A
Mask
Of the same
Author
Presented
At Ludlow-Castle,
1634.
Before
The Earl of Bridgewater
Then President of Wales.
Anno Dom. 1645.

Following the title page in 1645 are a dedication and dedicatory epistle by Lawes, reprinted from his 1637 edition, "To the Right Honourable, John Lord Vicount Brackly, Son and Heir apparent to the Earl of *Bridgewater*, &c." After the dedicatory epistle, the famous letter from Sir Henry Wootton, thanking Milton for the poem and praising it, is inserted.

After Wootton's letter, 1645 lists:

The Persons.

The attendant Spirit afterwards in the habit of *Thyrsis.*
Comus with his crew.
The Lady.
1. Brother.
2. Brother.
Sabrina the Nymph.
The cheif persons which presented, were
The Lord *Bracly,*
Mr. *Thomas Egerton* his Brother,
The Lady *Alice Egerton.*

The text of the poem printed here is Harris Fletcher's transcription of the Bridgewater Manuscript, which is reprinted by his permission and by permission of the University of Illinois Press from Mr. Fletcher's edition of *John Milton's Complete Poetical Works, Reproduced in Photographic Facsimile* (Bibliography, item 6). Where Br. is not clearly legible, Fletcher sometimes gives an alternative reading. I give only his preferred reading. There are a few canceled readings in Br. I have not included them. After consultation with Mr. Fletcher, I have corrected the few errors that I have noticed in his transcription. No doubt I have made others. The close student of the text will use Fletcher's facsimile.

The notes to the poem point out the more significant differences between Br. and the 1645 edition: omissions, accretions, variants. Variations in spelling, capitalization, and punctuation, which are innumerable, are not noted. For notes on such variant readings in the several texts of *Comus* see the Columbia *Milton* (Bibliography, item 15), Vol. I, Pt. II, pp. 474–577. Todd (Bibliography, item 19) also lists variant readings in Br. (VI, pp. 426–33) and I have depended on both Columbia and Todd in the notes. For a description of Br. see Stevens

(Bibliography, item 102), and for a discussion of the relationships among the several texts of *Comus,* see Appendix, "The Text of *Comus,* 1634 to 1645," below, pp. 251–75.

The notes to the poem are numbered by the line numbers of Br., but line-number references to 1645 are given for lines not present in Br.

A Maske./

The first sceane discovers a wild wood, then a guardian spiritt or demon descendes or enters./ [1]

ffrom the heavens nowe J flye
and those happy Climes that lye
Where daye never shutts his eye
up in the broad field of the skye./
5 there J suck the liquid ayre
all amidst the gardens fayre
of Hesperus and his daughters three
that singe about the goulden tree./
there eternall summer dwells
10 and west wyndes with muskye winge
about the Cederne allyes flinge
Nard and Casias balmie smells
Iris there with humid bowe
waters the odorous bankes that blowe
15 fflowers of more mingled hew
then her purfld scarfe can shew
yellow, watchett, greene & blew
and drenches oft wth Manna dew
Beds of Hyacinth and Roses
20 where many a Cherub soft reposes./

Before the starrie threshold of Joves Courte
my Mansion is, where those immortall shapes
of bright a[]reall spiritts live inspheard
in regions mylde of Calme and Cerene ayre
25 above the smoake and stirr of this dim spott
w[ch] men call earth, and w[ch] low-thoughted Care
Confinde and pestered in this pinfold heere
strive to keepe vp a fraile & fevourish beeinge

[1] The stage directions preceding line 1 read as follows in 1645:
The first Scene discovers a wilde Wood.
The attendant Spirit descends or enters.
In the Trinity MS. and in the 1637, 1645, and other editions of *Comus,* the poem begins with what is l. 21 in Br. In those versions the first 20 lines are part of the epilogue. See note to l. 896.

[23] An illegible letter in a[]reall is probably *e.*

[26] The second w[ch] is presumably a scribal error. Other versions read *with.*

vnmindfull of the Crowne that vertue gives
30 after this mortall change to her true servants
amongst the enthroned gods, in sainted seats
yet some there be that with due steppes aspire
to laye their just hands on that goulden keye
that opes the pallace of Æternitie:
35 To such my errand is, and but for such
J would not soile theese pure ambrosiall weedes
wth the ranke vapours of this sin-worne moulde
but to my taske; Neptune besides the swaye
of everie salte flood, and each ebbinge streame
40 tooke in by lott, twixt high and neather Jove
imperiall rule of all the Sea girt Jsles
that like to rich and various gems in laye
the vnadorned bosom of the deepe
wch he to grace his tributarie Gods
45 by Course committs to severall goverment
and gives them leave to weare their saphire Crownes
and weild their little tridents; but this Jsle
the greatest and the best of all the Maine
he quarters to his blew haired dieties,
50 and all this tract that fronts the fallinge sunn
a noble Peere of mickle trust and power
has in his Chardge, wth tempred awe to guyde
an ould and haughty nacion, proude in armes
where his faire ofspringe nurst in princely lore
55 are cominge to attend their fathers state
and newe entrusted scepter, but their waye
lies through the perplext paths of this dreare wood,
the noddinge horror of whose shadie browes
threats the forlorne and wandringe passinger
60 and heere their tender age might suffer perill
but that by quick commaund from soveraigne Jove
J was dispatcht, for their defence and guard
and listen why, for J will tell you now
what never yet was heard in tale or songe
65 from old or moderne bard in hall or bowre

[32] **with.** 1645: ***by.***

Bacchus that first from out the purple grapes
crusht the sweete poyson of mis-vsed wyne
after the Tuscane manners transformed
coastinge the Tyrrhene shore, as the winds listed
70 on Circes Jsland fell (whoe knows not Circe
the daughter of the Sunn, whoes charmed Cup
whoe ever tasted lost his vpright shape
and downeward fell into a grovelinge Swyne.)
This nimphe that gazed vpon his clustringe locks
75 wth Jvye berries wreath'd, and his blith youth
had by him, ere he parted thence a sonne
much like his father, but his mother more,
w[ch] erefore she brought vp and Comus nam'd,
whoe ripe and frolick of his full growne age
80 roavinge the Celtick and Jberian fields
at last betakes him to this ominous wood,
and in thick shelter of black shades imbowr'd
excells his mother at her mightie arte,
offringe to everie weary traveller
85 his orient liquor in a Christall glasse
to quench the drouth of Phebus, w[ch] as they taste
(for most doe tast through fond intemperate thirst)
soone as the potion workes their humane Countenance
th'expresse resemblance of the Gods, is chang'd
90 into some brutish forme of Wolfe, or Beare,
or ounce, or Tiger, Hogg, or bearded goate,
all other parts remayninge as they were
and they soe perfect is their miserie
not once perceive their fowle disfigurement
95 but boast themselves more comly then before,
and all their freinds, and native home forgett
to rowle wth pleasure in a sensuall stie
Therefore when any favour'd of high Jove
chaunces to pass through this advent'rous glade,
100 swift as the sparcle of a glanncinge starre
J shoote from heaven, to give him salfe convoy

[66] **grapes.** 1645: *Grape.*
[68] **manners.** 1645: *mariners.*
[78] **w[ch].** 1645: *whom.* **erefore.** 1645: *therefore.* In Br. the *th,* if present, is hidden by a blot.

as nowe J doe: but first J must put off
these my skye webs, spun out of Jris wooffe,
and take the weeds and liknesse of a Swayne
105 that to the service of this house belongs
whoe wth his softe pipe, and smooth dittied songe
well knows to still the wild winds when they roare,
and hush the wavinge woods, nor of less faith
and in this office of his mountaine watch
110 likeliest and neerest to the present ayde,
of this occasion, but J heare the tread
of hatefull stepps, J must be viewles nowe./

Exit

Comus enters wth a charminge rod in one hand & a glass of liquor in the other wth him a route of monsters like men & women but headed like wilde beasts their apperell glist'ringe, they come in makinge a riotous and vnruely noise wth torches in their hands./

Co: The starr that bids the shepheard fold
now the top of Heaven doeth hold,
115 and the gilded Carr of daye
his glowinge axle doeth allaye
in the steepe Atlantique streame
and the slope sun his vpward beame
shoots against the Northerne Pole
120 pacinge toward the other goale
of his Chamber in the East
meane-while welcome, Joye & feast,
midnight shoute, and revelry
tipsie daunce and Jollitie,
125 braide your locks wth rosie twine
droppinge odours, droppinge wine
Rigor now is gone to bed.
and advice wth scrupulous head,

[103] **webs.** 1645: *robes.*

[112] **Exit.** Not in 1645. There are also verbal differences in the stage direction introducing Comus. 1645 reads as follows:

Comus enters with a Charming Rod in one hand, his Glass in the other, with him a rout of Monsters headed like sundry sorts of wilde Beasts, but otherwise like Men and Women, their Apparel glistring, they com in making a riotous and unruly noise, with Torches in their hands.

[119] **Northerne.** 1645: *dusky.*

strict age, and sovre severitie
130 wth their grave sawes in slumber lye
Wee that are of purer fire
imitate the starrie quire
whoe in their nightly watchfull sphears
leade in swift round the months & years,
135 the sounds and seas with all their finnie drove
nowe to the moone in waveringe morrice move,
and on the tawny sands and shelves
trip the pert fairies, and the dapper Ealves
by dimpled brooke, and fountaine brim
140 the wood nimphs decte with daisies trim
their merry wakes & pastimes keepe
what hath night to doe with sleepe
Night has better sweets to prove
Venus now wakes, and wakens love,
145 Come let vs our rights begyn
tis only day light that make sin
wch these dun shades will neere report
haile goddess of nocturnall sport
Darke-vayld Cotitto, whome the secret flame
150 of mid night torches burne misterious dame
that neere art call'd but when the dragon woombe
of stigian Darknes, spetts her thickest gloome,
and makes one blot of all the aire,
staye thy cloudie Ebon chaire
155 wherein thou rid'st with Hecatt' and befriend
us thy vow'd preists till vtmost end
of all thy dues be done, & none left out
ere the blabbinge Easterne scoute
the nice morne on the Jndian steepe
160 from her Cabin'd loopehole peepe,
and to the tell tale sun descrie
our Conceal'd solempnitie,
come knitt hands & beate the ground
in a light fantastick round./

The measure in a wild, rude, & wanton Antick./

Co: Breake of, breake of, J feele the different pace
of some chast footinge, neere about this ground

143 **has.** 1645: ***hath.***
164 ***The measure in a wild, rude, & wanton Antick.*** 1645: *The Measure.*

run to your shrouds wth in these brakes & trees/
they all scattre
our number may affright; some virgin sure
(for soe J can distinguish by myne arte)
170 benighted in these woods, now to my Charms
and to my wilie traynes, J shall ere longe
be well stockt with as fayre a heard as graz'd
aboute my mother Circe, thus J hurle
my dazlinge spells into the spungie aire
175 of powre to cheate the eye with bleare illusion
and give it false presentments, least the place,
and my quainte habitts breede astonishment
and put the damsell to suspitious flight,
wch must not be; for thats against my course,
180 J vnder fayre pretence of freindly ends
and well plac't words of gloweinge Curtesie
bayted with reasons not vnplausible
winde me into the easie harted man,
and hug him into snares. when once her eye
185 hath met the vertue of this magick dust
J shall appear some harmles villager
whome thrifte keeps vp about his Countrie geare
but heere she comes, J fayrly step aside
and hearken if J may her businesse heere
The lady enters
190 *La* This waye the noise was, if my eare be true
my best guyde nowe, methought it was the sound
of riott and ill-manag'd merriment
such as the iocond flute or gamesome pipe
stirrs vp amonge the loose vnlettered hindes
195 when for their teeminge flocks and granges full
in wanton daunce they praise the bounteus Pan
and thanke the Gods amisse, J should be loath
to meete the rudenes, and swill'd insolence
of such late wassailers; yet o where els
200 shall J informe my vnacquainted feete
in the blinde mazes of this tangled wood,

[167] ***they all scattre.*** Not in 1645.
[181] **gloweinge.** 1645: *glozing.*
[190] **my.** 1645: *mine.*

my brothers when they sawe me wearied out
with this longe waye, resolvinge heere to lodge
vnder the spreadinge favour of these pines,
205 stept as they s'ed, to the next thickett side
to bringe me berries, or such coolinge fruite
as the kynde hospitable woods provide
but where they are, and whye they come not back
is now the labour of my thoughts, tis likeliest
210 they had ingaged their wandringe stepps too farr
and envious darknesse ere they could retorne
had stolne them from me./

207 The following lines not in Br. come after 207 in 1645, where they are ll. 188–90:

They left me then, when the gray-hooded Eev'n
Like a sad Votarist in Palmers weed
Rose from the hindmost wheels of *Phoebus* wain.

208 **come.** 1645: *came.*

212 **stolne.** 1645: *stole.* The following lines not in Br. come after l. 212 in 1645, where they are ll. 195–225. (See discussion of omissions from Br. in "A Maske at Ludlow," above, pp. 6–7.)

els O theevish Night
Why shouldst thou, but for som fellonious end,
In thy dark lantern thus close up the Stars,
That nature hung in Heav'n, and fill'd their Lamps
With everlasting oil, to give due light
To the misled and lonely Travailer?
This is the place, as well as I may guess,
Whence eev'n now the tumult of loud Mirth
Was rife, and perfet in my list'ning ear,
Yet nought but single darknes do I find.
What might this be? A thousand fantasies
Begin to throng into my memory
Of calling shapes, and beckning shadows dire,
And airy tongues, that syllable mens names
On Sands, and Shoars, and desert Wildernesses.
These thoughts may startle well, but not astound
The vertuous mind, that ever walks attended
By a strong siding champion Conscience.
O welcom pure ey'd Faith, white-handed Hope,
Thou hovering Angel girt with golden wings,
And thou unblemish't form of Chastity,
I see ye visibly, and now beleeve
That he, the Supreme good, t'whom all things ill
Are but as slavish officers of vengeance,
Would send a glistring Guardian if need were
To keep my life and honour unassail'd.
Was I deceiv'd, or did a sable cloud
Turn forth her silver lining on the night?

J cannot hollowe to my brothers, but
such noise as J can make to be heard fardest
215 J'le venture, for my new enliv'n'd speritts,
prompt me, and they perhaps are not farr hence,

Songe /

Sweete Echo, sweetest nymphe that liv'st vnseene
within thy ayrie shell
by slowe Meanders margent greene
220 and in the violett imbroderd vale
where the love-lorne nightingale
nightly to thee her sad song mourneth well,

Canst thou not tell me of a gentle payre
that likest thy Narcissus are
225 O if thou have
hid them in some flowrie Cave
tell me but where.
Sweete Queene of parlie, daughter to the spheare
soe mayst thou be translated to the skyes
230 And hould a Counterpointe to all heav'ns harmonies

Comus looks in & speakes

Co Can any mortall mixture of Earths mould
breath such divine enchauntinge ravishment
sure somethinge holye lodges in that brest
and with these raptures moves the vocall ayre
235 to testifie his hidden residence
how sweetely did they floate vpon the wings
of silence, through the empty vaulted night,
at every fall smoothinge the raven downe
of darkness till she smil'd, J have oft heard
240 my mother Circe with the Sirens three
amidst the flowrie-kyrtled Niades
cullinge their potent herbs and balefull druggs

I did not err, there does a sable cloud
Turn forth her silver lining on the night
And casts a gleam over this tufted Grove.

[216] **hence.** 1645: *off.*
[228] **daughter to.** 1645: *Daughter of.*
[230] **And hould a Counterpointe.** 1645: *And give resounding grace.*
[231] ***Comus looks in & speakes.*** Not in 1645.
[239] **she.** 1645: *it.*

whoe when they sung, would take the prisond soule
and lap it in Elisium, Scilla wept
and chid her barkinge waves into attention
and fell Caribdis murmurd soft applause
yet they in pleasinge slumber lulld the sence
and in sweete madnes rob'd it of it selfe,
but such a sacred and homefelt delight
250 such sober certentie of wakinge bliss
J never heard till now, Jle speake to her
and she shalbe my Qweene; Haile forreigne wonder
whome certaine these rough shades did never breede
vnless the goddess that in rurall shrine
255 dwel'st heere with Pan or Silvan, by blest song
forbiddinge every bleake vnkindly fogg
to touch the prosperinge growth of this tall wood
La: Nay gentle Shepheard, ill is lost that praise
that is addrest to vnattendinge eares
260 not any boast of skill, but extreame shifte
how to regayne my severd Companye
Compeld me to awake the Curteus Echo
to give me answer from her mossy Couch
Co: What Chaunce good lady hath bereft you thus?
265 *La:* dym darknesse and this leavye laborinth
Co: Could that devide you from neere vsheringe guydes?
La: they left me weary on a grassie terfe
Co: by falsehood, or discurtesie, or why?
La: to seeke in the valley some coole freindly springe
270 *Co:* and lefte your fayer side, all vnguarded ladye?
La: they were but twaine & purpose quick returne,
Co: perhaps forestallinge night prevented them
La: how easie my misfortune is to hit!
Co: imports their losse, beside the present neede?
275 *La:* noe lesse then if J should my brothers loose
Co: were they of manly prime, or youthfull bloome?
La: as smooth as Hebes their vnrazor'd lipps.
Co: Two such J sawe, what tyme the labour'd oxe
in his loose traces from the furrowe came
280 and the swink't—hedger at his supper sate,

[243] **when.** 1645: *as.*
[257] **prosperinge.** 1645: *prosperous.*

J sawe em vnder a greene mantlinge vyne
that crawles alonge the side of yon smale hill
pluckinge ripe clusters from the tender shoots,
their porte was more then humane as they stood,
285 J tooke it for a faerie vision
of some gaye creatures of the Element
that in the cooleness of the raynebow live
and playe i'th plighted clouds; J was awe-strooke
and as J past J worship't: if those you seeke
290 it were a Jorney like the path to heav'n
helpe you finde them; *La:* gentle villager
what readiest waye would bringe me to that place?
Co: due west it rises from this shrubbie pointe,
La: to finde out that good shepheard J suppose
295 in such a scant allowance of starr light
would overtaske the best land pilots arte
wthout the sure guesse of well practiz'd feete;
Co: J knowe each lane, and every Alley greene,
dingle, or bushie dell, of this wide wood,
300 and everie boskie bourne from side to side
my daylie walks and antient neighbourhood
and if your straye attendance, be yet lodg'd
or shroud wthin these lymitts, J shall know
ere morrowe wake, or the lowe rooster larke
305 from her thatcht palat rowse, if otherwise
J can conduct you ladie, to a lowe,
but loyall cottage, where you may be safe
till furder quest; *La:* Shepheard J take thy word
and trust thy honest offer'd Curtesie
310 wch ofte is sooner found in lowly sheds
with smoakie rafters, then in tap'strie halls
and Courts of princes, where it first was nam'd
and yet is most pretended, in a place
lesse warrented then this, or lesse secure
315 J cannott be, that J should feare to change it

[287] **cooleness.** 1645: *colours.*
[291] *To,* omitted at the beginning of this line in Br., is present in 1645. This is the first line on the page in Br. and *to* is the catchword on the previous page.
[299] **wide.** 1645: *wild.* See Appendix, pp. 267–68.
[304] **rooster.** 1645: *roosted.*

Eye my blest providence, and square my tryall
to my proportion'd streingth; shepheard leade on.

The two brothers

El: bro. Vnmuffle yee fainte starrs, and thou faier moone
that wonst to love the travailers benizon
320 stoope thy pale visadge through an amber cloude
and disinherit Chaos, that raignes heere
in double night of darkness, and of shades
or if your influence be quite damm'd vp
wth black vsurpinge mists, some gentle taper
325 though a rushe candle, from the wicker hole
of some claye habitacion visite vs
wth thy long levell'd rule of streaming light
and thou shalt be our starr of Arcady
or Tirian Cynosure: *2 bro.* Or if our eyes
330 be barr'd that happines might wee but heare
the folded flocks pen'd in their watled cotes
or sound of pastorall reede with oaten stopps
or whistle from the lodge, or village Cock
count the night watches to his featherie dames
335 t'would be some solace yet, some little cheeringe
in this lone dungeon of inumerous bows,
but O that haples virgin our lost sister
where may she wander nowe? whether betake her
from the chill dewe, amongst rude burrs & thistles
340 perhaps some could banke is her boulster nowe
or gainst the rugged barke of some broade Elme
leanes her vnpillow'd head fraught wth sad teares
or els in wild amazement and affright,

[316] Eye my. 1645: *Eye me.*
[336] lone. 1645: *close.*
[342] teares. 1645: *fears.*
[343] or els. 1645: *What if.* The following lines not in Br. come after l. 343 in 1645, where they are ll. 357–65:

Or while we speak within the direfull grasp
Of Savage hunger, or of Savage heat?
Eld. Bro. Peace Brother, be not over-exquisite
To cast the fashion of uncertain evils;
For grant they be so, while they rest unknown,
What need a man forestall his date of grief,
And run to meet what he would most avoid?
Or if they be but false alarms of Fear,
How bitter is such self-delusion?

soe fares as did forsaken Proserpine
345 when the bigg rowling flakes of pitchie clouds
and darkness wound her in: *El. bro.* peace brother peace
J doe not thinke my sister soe to seeke
or soe vnprincipl'd in vertues booke,
and the sweete peace that goodness bosoms ever
350 as that the single want of light and noise
(not beinge in danger, as J hope she is not)
could stirr the constant mood of her calme thoughts
and put them into misbecomminge plight
vertue could see to doe what vertue would
355 by her owne radiant light, though sun & moone
were in the flatt sea sunke, and wisdoms selfe
of seeks to sweete retired solitude
where, wth her best nurse contemplacion
she plumes her feathers, and letts grow her wings
360 that in the various bustle of resorte,
were all to ruffl'd and sometimes impayr'd
he that has light within his owne cleere brest
may sit i'th Center, and enioye bright daye
but he that hides a darke sowle, & foule thoughts
365 walks in black vapours, though the noone tyde brand
blaze in the summer solstice. *2 bro:* tis most true
that musinge meditacion most affects
the pensive secrecie of desert Cell
farr from the cheerefull haunte of men or heards,
370 and sitts as safe as in a senate house
for whoe would robb an hermitt of his weeds,
his few bookes, or his beads, or maple dishe
or doe his graye haiers any violence?
but bewtie like the fayre hesperian tree
375 laden with bloominge gould, had neede the guard
of dragon watch with vninchaunted eye
to save her blossoms, and defend her fruite,
from the rashe hand of bold Jncontinence,

[344-46] Not in 1645.
[351] **hope.** 1645: *trust.*
[357] **of.** 1645: *oft.*
[365-66] These lines read as follows in 1645, where they are ll. 384–85:
Benighted walks under the mid-day Sun;
Himself is his own dungeon.
[369] **or.** 1645: *and.*

you may as well spreade out the vnsum'd heapes
380 of misers treasures by an outlawes den,
and tell me it is safe, as bid me hope
dainger will winke at opportunitie
and she a single helpeles mayden passe
vniniur'd in this wide surroundinge wast
385 of night or lonelinesse, it recks me not
J feare the dread events that dog them both
lest some ill greetinge touch attempt the person
of our vn owned sister. *El bro.* J doe not brother
inferr as if J thought my sisters state
390 secure, wth out all doubt or question, no;
J could be willinge though now i'th darke to trie
a tough encounter, with the shaggiest ruffian
that lurks by hedge or lane, ofthis dead circuit
to have her by my side, though J were suer
395 she might be free from perill where she is,
but where an equall poise of hope, & feare
does arbitrate th'event, my nature is
that J encline to hope, rather then feare,
and gladly banish squint suspition,
400 my sister is not soe defencelesse left
as you immagine brother, she has a hidden strength
wch you remember not, *2 bro.* what hidden strength?
vnless the strength of heav'n, if you meane that?
el:bro J meane that too: but yet a hidden strength
405 wch if heaven gave it, may be tearm'd herowne,
tis Chastitie, my brother Chastitie
she that has that is clad in compleate steele,
and like a quiver'd nimphe with arrowes keene,
may trace huge forrests, and vnharbour'd heaths
410 infamous hills, and sandie perrilous wildes,
where through the sacred rayes of Chastitie

379 **vnsum'd.** 1645: *unsun'd.*
380 **treasures.** 1645: *treasure.*
382 **at.** 1645: *on.*
383 **she.** 1645: *let.*
384 **wide.** 1645: *wilde.*
390 **question, no.** 1645: *controversie.*
391-95 Not in 1645.
396 **but.** 1645: *Yet.*
401 **brother.** Not in 1645. In Br. the line has an extra foot.

noe salvage, feirce, bandite, or mountaneere
will dare to soile her virgin puritie,
yea even where, very desolacion dwells
415 by grots, & Caverns shag'd wth horrid shades
and yawninge denns, where glaringe monsters house
she may pass on wth vnblensh't maiestie
be it not done in pride or in presumption
naye more noe evill thinge that walks by night
420 in fogg or fire, by lake or moorish ffen,
blew meagar hag, or stubborne vnlayed ghost
that breaks his magick chaines at Curfew tyme
noe goblinge, or swarte fayrie of the mine
has hurtefull power ore true virginitie,
425 doe you beleeve me yet, or shall J call
antiquitie from the ould schooles of Greece
to testifie the armes of Chastitie,
hence had the huntress Dian her dread bow
faire silver shafter Queene, for ever chast
430 wherewith she tam'd the brinded Lyonesse
and spotted mountaine Pard, but sett at nought
the frivolous bolt of Cupid, Gods and men
feard her sterne frowne, & shewas Queene o'th'woods
what was that snakie headed Gorgon sheild,
435 the wise Minerva wore, vnconquer'd virgin
wherewith she freezed her foes to congeald stone?
but rigid lookes of chast awsteritie
and noble grace that dasht brute violence
with sudden adoracion, and blanke awe
440 soe deere to heav'n is sainctly Chastitie
that when a sowle is found cinceerely soe
a thousand liveried Angells, lackey her
drivinge farr of, each thing of sin, & guilte
and in cleer dreame and solemne vision,
445 tell her of things that noe grosse eare can heare
till oft converse with hevenly habitants

[414] **even.** 1645: *there.*
[416] Not in 1645.
[419] **naye more.** 1645: *som say.*
[424] **has.** 1645: *hath.*
[425] **you.** 1645: *ye.*
[429] **shafter.** 1645: *shafted.*
[435] **the.** 1645: *That.*

begins to cast a beame on th'outward shape
the vnpolluted temple of the mynde
and turnes it by degrees to the soules essence
450 till all be made immortall, but when lust
by vnchast lookes, loose gesturs, and foule talke
and most by lewde lascivious act of sin
letts in defilement to the inward partes,
the soule growes clotted by contagion,
455 imbodies, and imbruts till she quite loose
the divine propertie of her first beeinge,
such are those thick, & gloomie shadowes dampe
oft seene in Charnell vaults, and sepulchers,
hoveringe and sittinge by a new made grave
460 as loath to leave the bodye that it loved
and linc'kt it selfe by carnall sensualitie
to a degenerate, and degraded state./
2 bro: How charminge is divine philosophie
not harshe and crabbed as dull fooles suppose
465 but musicall as is Appolloes lute
and perpetuall feast of Nectard sweets
where noe crude surfeit raignes, *El:bro:* list, list, J heare
some farr of hollowe breake the silent ayre
2 bro: me thought soe too what should it be, *El:b:* for certaine
470 either some one like vs night founderd heere
or els some neyghbour woodman, or at worst,
some roavinge robber callinge to his fellowes;
2 bro heav'n keepe my sister: agen, agen, & neere
best drawe, & stand vpon our guard, *El: bro.* Jle hallowe
475 if he be freindly he comes well, if not
defence is a good Cause, and heav'n be for vs

he hallows and is answered, the guardian dæmon comes in habited like a shepheard./

El.bro. That hallowe J should knowe, what are you speake,
come not too neere, you fall on Jron stakes els

[447] **begins.** 1645: *begin.*
[452] **and.** 1645: *But.* **lewde lascivious.** 1645: *leud and lavish.*
[459] **hoveringe.** 1645: *Lingering.*
[476] Stage direction following the line reads as follows in 1645: *The attendant Spirit habited like a Shepherd.*

Dæ: what voice is that? my young Lord? speake agen.
480 *2 bro:* O brother tis my fathers shepheard sure
el:b: Thirsis? whose art full straynes have oft delayed
the hudlinge brooke to heere his madrigall
and sweetned every muskerose of the dale,
how camst heere good shepheard, hath any ram
485 slipt from the fould, or young kyd lost his dam
or straglinge weather the pent flock forsooke
how couldst thou finde this darke sequesterd nooke?
De: O my Lov'd masters heire, and his next Joye
J came not heere on such a triviall toye
490 as a strayed Ewe, or to pursue the stealth
of pilferinge wolfe; not all the fleecie wealth
that doeth enrich these downes is worth a thought
to this my errand and the Care it brought./
but O my virgin lady where is she
495 howe chaunce she is not in your Companie?
El:bro: To tell thee sadly shepheard, w[th]out blame
or our neglect wee lost her as wee came,
De: Ay me vnhappie then my feares are true./
El:bro: what feares, good Thirsis prithee briefly shewe
500 *De:* Jle tell you, tis not vayne, or fabulous,
(though soe esteem'd by shallowe ignorance)
what the sage poets, taught by th' heav'nly muse
storied of old in high immortall verse
of dire Chimeras, and enchaunted Jsles
505 and rifted rocks, whose entrance leads to hell
for such there be, but vnbeliefe is blinde,
within the navill of this hidious wood
immured in Cipress shades a sorserer dwells
of Bacchus and of Circe borne, greate Comus
510 deepe skild in all his mothers witcheries
and heere to everie thirstie wanderer
by slye enticement gives his banefull Cup
with many murmurs mixt, whose pleasinge poyson

[479] *Dæ.* 1645: ***Spir.*** Stage directions in Br. consistently refer to Thyrsis as "Daemon," in 1645 as "Attendant Spirit."
[480] **fathers.** 1645: *father.*
[484] **shepheard.** 1645: *Swain.* 1645 inserts *thou* after *cam'st.*
[500] **you.** 1645: *ye.*

the visage quite transformes of him that drinkes
515 and the inglorious likeness of a beast
fixes insteed, vnmouldinge reasons mintage
charactred in the face, This have J learnt
tendinge my flocks, hard by i'th hillie Crofts
that browe this bottome glade, whence night by night
520 he and his monstrous route are heard to howle
like stabled wolves, or tigers at their preye
doeinge abhorred rites to Heccate
in their obscured haunts of inmost bowers,
yet have they many baites and guylefull spells
525 to invegle, and invite the vnwarie sence
of them that passe vnweetinge by the waye,
this eveninge late, by then the chewinge flocks
had tane their supper on the savorie herbe
of knot grasse dew-besprent and were in fold,
530 J sate me downe to watch vpon a banke
with Jvie Cannopied and interwove
with flauntinge hony sucle, and began
wrapt in a pleasinge fitt of melencholy
to meditate my rurall minstrelsie
535 till fansie had her fill, but ere a close
the wonted roare was vp amidst the woods
and filld the aire with barbarous dissonance
at wch J ceast, and listned them a while
till an vnvsuall stop of suddaine silence
540 gave respite to the drowsie frighted steeds
that drawe the litter of close-curtain'd sleepe
at last a sweete, and solemne breathinge sound
rose like the softe steame of distill'd perfumes
and stole vpon the aire, that even silence
545 was tooke ere she was ware, & wisht she might
denye her nature and be never more
still to be soe displac't, J was all eare
and tooke in th streines that might create a sowle
vnder the ribbs of death. but O ere long

542–43 These lines, much revised in the Trinity MS., read as follows in 1645, where they are 555–56:

At last a soft and solemn breathing sound
Rose like a steam of rich distill'd Perfumes.

550 two well J might perceive, it was the voice
of my most honor'd lady, your deere sister
amaz'd J stood, harrow'd with greife, & feare,
and O poore hapless nightingale thought J
how sweete thou singst, how neere the deadly snare,
555 then downe the lawnes J ran wth headlonge hast
through paths and turnings, often trod by daye,
till guyded by myne eare, J found the place
where that damn'd wizard hid in slye disguise
(for soe by certaine signes J knowe) had met
560 alreadie eare my best speede could prevent
the aideless innocent ladie his wisht prey
whoe gently askt if he had seene such two,
supposinge him some neighbour-villager,
longer J durst not stay, but soone J guest
565 yee were the two she meant, wth that J sprung
into swift flight, till J had found you heere
but furder know J not; *2:bro* O night & shades
how are you ioyn'd with hell in triple knott
against the vnarmed weaknes of one virgin
570 alone, and helpeless, Js this the confidence?
you gave me brother? *el:bro:* yes & keepe it still
leane on it salfly, not a period
shalbe vnsaid for me, against the threats
of malice, or of Sorcerie, or that powre
575 wch erringe men call chaunce this J hould firme
virtue may be assail'd but never hurte
surpris'd by vniust force, but not enthrall'd,
yea even that wch mischiefe meant most harme
shall in the happie triall prove most glorie,
580 but evill on it selfe shall back recoyle
and mixe noe more with goodnesse, when at last
gather'd like scum, and setl'd to it selfe
it shalbe in eternall restless change
selfe fed, and selfe consum'd, if this fayle
585 the pillard firmament is rottennesse
and earth's base built on stubble. but come lets on:
against the opposinge will, and arme of heav'n

550 **two.** 1645: *too.* **might.** 1645: *did.*
568 **you.** 1645: *ye.*

may never this iust sword be lifted vp,
but for that damn'd magitian, let him be girt
590 with all the grisley legions that troope
vnder the sootie flagg of Acheron,
Harpies, & Hydraes, or all the monstrous buggs
twixt Africa, and Jnde, J'le finde him out
and force him to restore his purchase back
595 or drag him by the Curles, and cleave his scalpe
downe to the hipps, *Dem:* Alas good ventrous youth
J love the Courage yet, and bold emprise,
but heere thy sword can doe thee little stead
farr other armes, and other weopons must
600 be those that quell the might of hellish Charmes,
he with his bare wand can vnthred thy ioynts
and crumble all thy sinewes, *El:bro:* why prithee shepheard
how durst thou then approach soe neere,
as to make this relacion; *Dem:* Care, & vtmost shifts
605 how to secure the lady from surprisall
brought to my mynd a certaine shepheard lad
of smale regard to see to, yet well skill'd
in every verteus plant, and healinge herbe
that spreades her verdant leafe to th'morninge ray,
610 he lov'd me well, and oft would begg me singe,
wch when J did, he on the tender grasse
would sit, and hearken even to extasie
and in requitall open his letherne scrip,
and shew me simples of a thousand names
615 tellinge their strange, and vigorous faculties,
amongst the rest a smale vnsightly roote
but of divine effect, he cull'd me out
the leafe was darkish, and had prickles on it,

592 **buggs.** 1645: *forms.*
595-96 **and cleave his scalpe/ downe to the hipps.** 1645: *to a foul death,/ Curs'd as his life.*
597 **the.** 1645: *thy.*
603 *thy self* inserted after *then* in 1645.
618 The following lines come after l. 618 in 1645, where they are ll. 632–37:
But in another Countrey, as he said,
Bore a bright golden flowre, but not in this soyl:
Unknown, and like esteem'd, and the dull swayn
Treads on it daily with his clouted shoon,
And yet more med'cinal is it then that Moly
That *Hermes* once to wise *Ulysses* gave.

he call'd it Hemony, and gave it me,
620 and bad me keepe it as of soveraigne vse
gainst all enchauntments, mildew blast, or dampe,
or gastlie furies apparition,
J purst it vp, but little reckoninge made
till now that this extremitie compell'd,
625 but now J finde it true, for by this meanes
J knew the foule Enchaunter, though disguis'd
entered the very lymetwiggs of his spells
and yet came off, if you have this about you
(as J will give you when wee goe) you may
630 boldly assaulte the Negromancers hall,
where if he be, with dauntlesse hardy-hood
and brandisht blade rushe on him, breake his glasse
and shed the lussious liquor on the ground,
but cease his wand, though he and his curst crew
635 fierce signe of battaile make, and menace high
or like the sonns of Vulcan vomitt smoake
yet will they soone retire, if he but shrinke.
El:bro Thirsis leade on apace, J followe thee
and some good Angell beare a shield before vs.

The Sceane changes to a stately pallace set out wth all manner of delitiousness, tables spred with all dainties Comus appears wth his rabble, and the lady set in an inchaunted chayre, to whome he offers his glasse w[ch] she puts by, and goes about to rise./

640 *Co:* Nay ladye sit, if J but wave this wand
your nerves are all chain'd vp in alablaster
and you a statue; or as Daphne was
roote bound, that fled Apollo. *La:* foole doe not boast
thou canst not touch the freedome of my mynde
645 with all thy charmes, although this corporall rind
thou hast immanacl'd, while heav'n sees good,
Co: Whye are you vext ladie, why doe you frowne
heere dwell noe frownes, nor anger, from these gates
sorrowe flies farr, see heere be all the pleasures
650 that fansie can begett on youthfull thoughts
when the fresh blood grows lively, and returnes

[638] J. 1645: *Ile.*
[639] In the stage direction following l. 639, 1645 inserts *soft Musick* after *deliciousness.*

briske as the Aprill budds in primrose season.
and first behould this cordiall Julep, heere
that flames, and dances in his christall bounds,
655 with spiritts of baulme, and fragrant sirrops mixt;
Not that Nepenthes w[ch] the wife of Thone
in Egipt gave to Jove-borne Hellena
is of such power to stirre vp Joye as this
to life, soe freindly, or soe coole too thirst,
660 poore ladie thou hast neede of some refreshinge
that hast been tired aldaye without repast,
a timely rest hast wanted. heere fayre Virgin
this will restore all soone; *La:* t'will not false traytor
twill not restore the trueth and honestie
665 that thou hast banisht from thy tongue wth lies,
was this the Cottage, and the safe aboade
thou touldst me of? what grim aspects are these?
these ougley headed Monsters? Mercie guard me,
hence with thy brewd enchauntments, fowle deceaver
670 were it a draffe for Juno, when she banquetts
J would not taste thy treasonous offer, none
but such as are good men; can give good things,
and that w[ch] is not good, is not delitious
to a well govern'd and wise appetite;
675 *Co:* O foolishnes of men, that lend their eares

[659] The following lines come after l. 659 in 1645, where they are ll. 679–87:

Why should you be so cruel to your self,
And to those dainty limms which nature lent
For gentle usage, and soft delicacy?
But you invert the cov'nants of her trust,
And harshly deal like an ill borrower
With that which you receiv'd on other terms
Scorning the unexempt condition
By which all mortal frailty must subsist,
Refreshment after toil, ease after pain.

[660] Not in 1645.

[661] **hast.** 1645: *have.*

[662] **a timely rest hast wanted. heere fayre Virgin.** 1645: *And timely rest have wanted, but fair Virgin.*

[669] The following lines come after l. 669 in 1645, where they are ll. 697–700:

Hast thou betrai'd my credulous innocence
With visor'd falshood, and base forgery,
And wouldst thou seek again to trap me here
With lickerish baits fit to ensnare a brute?

to those budge doctors of the Stoick furr
and fetch their precepts from the Cinick tub
praisinge the leane, and shallow abstinence;
wherefore did nature power her bounties furth
680 with such a full, and vnwithdraweinge hand,
coveringe the earth with odours, fruits and flocks
throngeinge the seas with spawne innumerable
but all to please, and sate the Curious tast,
and set to worke millions of spinninge wormes
685 that in their greene shopps, weave the smate-haired silke
to deck her sonnes, and that noe corner might
be vacant of her plentie, in her owne loynes
she hutch't th'all worshipt oare, and pretious gems
to store her childeren with if all the world
690 should in a pet of temperance, feede on pulse
drinke the cleere streame, and noethinge weare but freeze
th'allgiver would be vnthank't, would be vnprais'd
not halfe his riches knowne, and yet despis'd
and wee should serve him as a grudgeinge Master,
695 as a penurious niggard of his wealth
and live like natures bastards, not her sonns,
who would be quite surcharg'd wth her owne waite
and strangl'd with her vast fertillitie,
th'earth cumberd, and the wing'd ayre dark'd wth plumes
700 the heards would overmultitude their Lords
the sea orefraught would swell, and th'vnsaught diamonds
would soe emblaze with starrs, that they belowe
would growe enur'd to light, and come at last
to gase vpon the sunn with shameles browes.

[678] **shallow.** 1645: *sallow.*
[685] **smate-haired.** 1645: *smooth-hair'd.* Cf. l. 747 and note.
[702–3] 1645 reads as follows (ll. 733–34):

Would so emblaze the forhead of the Deep
And so bestudd with Stars, that they below.

Todd's note on l. 732 explains the copying error in Br.
[704] The following lines come after l. 704 in 1645, where they are ll. 737–55:

List Lady be not coy, and be not cosen'd
With that same vaunted name Virginity,
Beauty is natures coyn, must not be hoorded,
But must be currant, and the good thereof
Consists in mutual and partak'n bliss,
Unsavoury in th'injoyment of it self

705 *la:* J had not thought to have vnlockt my lipps
in this vnhallowed ayre, but that this Jugler
would thinke to charme my Judgement, as my eyes
obtrudinge false rules prank't in reasons garbe.
J hate when vice can boult her arguments
710 and vertue has noe tongue to check her pride.
Jmposter doe not charge most innocent nature
as if she would her children should be riotous
with her abundance, she good Chateresse
means her provision onely to the good,
715 that live accordinge to her sober lawes,
and holy dictate of spare temperance.
Jf every Just man that now pynes with want
had but a moderate and beseeminge share
of that wch leudly-pamper'd luxurie
720 now heap's vpon some fewe, with vast excesse
natures full blessinge, would be well dispenst
in vnsuperflous even proportion,
and she noe whit encomberd with her store:
and then the giver would be better thank't
725 his praise due payed, for swinish gluttonie
neere looks to heav'n, amidst his gorgeous feasts
but wth beesotted base ingratitude
crams, and blaspheames his feeder, *Co:* Come, noe more

If you let slip time, like a neglected rose
It withers on the stalk with languish't head.
Beauty is natures brag, and must be shown
In courts, at feasts, and high solemnities
Where most may wonder at the workmanship;
It is for homely features to keep home,
They had their name thence; course complexions
And cheeks of sorry grain will serve to ply
The sampler, and to teize the huswifes wooll.
What need a vermeil-tinctur'd lip for that
Love-darting eyes, or tresses like the Morn?
There was another meaning in these gifts,
Think what, and be adviz'd, you are but young yet.

[707] **my.** 1645: *mine.*

[726] **feasts.** 1645: *feast.*

[728] **Come, noe more.** 1645: *Shall I go on?* The following lines come after l. 728 in 1645, where they are ll. 780–806:

Or have I said anough? To him that dares
Arm his profane tongue with contemptuous words
Against the Sun-clad power of Chastity,

this is meere morrall babble, and direct
730 against the Canon lawes of our foundacion
J must not suffer this; yet tis but the lees
and setlinge of a mellancholy bloud,
But this will cure all streite, one sip of this
will bath the droopinge spiritts in delight
735 beyond the blisse of dreames. bewise, and tast;

The brothers rushe in with swords drawne, wrest his glasse of liquor out of his hand, and breake it against the ground his rowte make signe of resistance, but are all driven in, the Demon is to come in with the brothers./

De: What have yee left the false Jnchaunter scape?
O yee mistooke, yee should have snatcht his wand,
and bound him fast, without his rod reverst
and backward mutters of disseveringe power
740 wee cannot free the lady that sitts heere

Fain would I somthing say, yet to what end?
Thou hast nor Eare, nor Soul to apprehend
The sublime notion, and high mystery
That must be utter'd to unfold the sage
And serious doctrine of Virginity,
And thou art worthy that thou shouldst not know
More happines then this thy present lot.
Enjoy your deer Wit, and gay Rhetorick
That hath so well been taught her dazling fence,
Thou art not fit to hear thy self convinc't;
Yet should I try, the uncontrouled worth
Of this pure cause would kindle my rap't spirits
To such a flame of sacred vehemence,
That dumb things would be mov'd to sympathize,
And the brute Earth would lend her nerves, and shake,
Till all thy magick structures rear'd so high,
Were shatter'd into heap o're thy false head.
Co. She fables not, I feel that I do fear
Her words set off by som superior power;
And though not mortal, yet a cold shuddring dew
Dips me all o're, as when the wrath of *Jove*
Speaks thunder, and the chains of *Erebus*
To som of *Saturns* crew. I must dissemble,
And try her yet more strongly. Com, no more.

[732] **setlinge.** 1645: *setlings.*
[735] The stage direction after l. 735 reads as follows in 1645: *The Brothers rush in with Swords drawn, wrest his Glass out of his hand, and break it against the ground; his rout make signe of resistance, but all are driven in; The attendant Spirit comes in.*
[736] **yee left.** 1645: *you let.*

in stonie fetters fixt, and motionlesse.
yet staye, be not disturb'd, nowe J bethinke me
some other meanes J haue that may be vsed
wch once of Millebeus old J learnt
745 the soothest shepheard that ere pipt on playnes

There is a gentle Nimphe not farr from hence
that wth moist Curbe, swayes the smoote seaverne streame,
Sabrina is her name, a virgin pure,
whilome she was the daughter of Locrine
750 whoe had the scepter from his father Brute.
she guiltless dam'sell, flyinge the mad pursuite
of her enraged stepdame Gwendolen
commended her faire innocense to the floud,
that stayed her flight with his Crosse floweinge course,
755 the water nimphs that in the bottom played
held vp their peackled wrists, and tooke her in
bearinge her straite to aged Nereus hall
whoe piteous of her woes, reard her lanke head
and gave her to his daughters to imbath
760 in nectar'd lavers, strewd with Asphodill
and through the portch and inlet of each sence
dropt in abrosiall oyles, till she revived
and vnderwent a quick immortal change
made goddess of the River. still she retaines
765 her maiden gentleness, and ofte at Eve
visitts the heards alonge the twilight meadowes
helpinge all vrchin blasts, and ill luck signes
that the shrewd medlinge Elfe delights to make,
for wch the shepheards at their festivalls
770 Carroll her goodnes loud in rustick layes
and throwe sweete garland wreaths into her streame
of pancies, pinkes, and guady daffadils
and, as the ould swayne said, she can vnlock
the claspinge Charme, and thawe the numminge spell
775 if she be right invok'd in warbled songe:

743 **that.** 1645: *which.*
747 **smoote.** 1645: *smooth.*
750 **whoe.** 1645: *that.*
756 **peackled.** 1645: *pearled.*
768 The following line comes after l. 768 in 1645, where it is l. 847:
Which she with pretious viold liquors heals.

for maydenhood she loves, and wilbe swifte
to ayde a Virgin such as was her selfe
(in hard besettinge neede) this will J trie
and add the power of some adiuringe verse./

Songe./

780 Sabrina faire
listen where thou art sittinge
vnder the glassie, coole, transelucent wave
in twisted braides of lillies knitting
the loose traine of thy Amber-droppinge haire;
785 listen for deere honors sake
Goddess of the silver lake
Listen & save./

The verse to singe or not.

listen and appeare to vs
in name of greate Oceanus,
790 by th'earth-shakinge Neptunes mace,
and Tethis grave maiestick pace,
El bro: by hoarie Nereus wrincled looke,
and the Carpathian wizards hooke,
2 bro: by scalie Tritons windinge shell,
795 and ould sooth-sayinge Glaucus spell,
El br: by Lewcotheas lovely hands,
and her sonne that rules the strands,
2 bro: by Thetis tinsel-slipperd feete,
and the songs of sirens sweete,
800 *El br:* by dead Parthenopes deare tombe,
and fayer Ligeas golden Combe,
wherewith she sitts on diamond rocks,
sleekinge her soft alluringe locks,
De: By all the Nimphes of nightly daunce,
805 vpon thy streames with wilie glaunce,
rise, rise, and heave thy rosie head,
from thy Corall paven bed,

787 *The verse to singe or not.* Not in 1645.

788–810 In 1645, the exchange is between Thyrsis (Spir.) and Sabrina. Only in Br. are these lines taken away from Thyrsis (Lawes) and divided between the brothers. See above, pp. 6, 13. Todd speculates that four lines of the invocation of Sabrina, ll. 788–91, were sung as a trio (VI, 431).

804 of. 1645: *that.*

and bridle in thy headlonge wave,
till thou our summons answered have,
810 Listen & save.

Sabrina rises attended by the water nimphes and singes./

By the rushie fringed banke
where growes the willow, and the Osier danke
my slydinge Charriott stayes,
Thick sett with Agate, and the Azur'd sheene
815 Of Turkiss blew, and Emerald greene
that in the Channell strayes,
Whilst from of the waters fleete
thus J rest my printles feete
ore the Couslips head
820 that bends not as J tread
gentle swayne at thy request
J am heere
De: Goddess deere
Wee ymplore thy powerfull hand
825 to vndoe the Charmed band
of true virgin heere distrest
through the force and through the wile
of vnblest inchaunters vile.
Sab: Shepheard tis my office best
830 to helpe ensnared Chastitie;
brightest lady looke on me,
thus J sprincle on this brest
drops that from my fountayne pure
J have kept of pretious Cure,
835 thrice vpon thy fingers tip,
thrice vpon thy rubied lip,
next this marble venom'd seate
smeard with gumms of gluttenous heate
J touch with chast palmes, moist, & could
840 now the spell hath lost his hold

[810] 1645 omits *the* from the stage direction.
[814] **Azur'd.** 1645: *azurn.*
[818] **rest.** 1645: *set.*
[819] 1645: *O're the Cowslips Velvet head.*
[828] **inchaunters.** 1645. *inchanter.*
[832] **this.** 1645: *thy.*

and J must hast, ere morninge howre
to waite in Amphitrites bower

Sabrina descends and
the lady rises out
of he seate.

De: Virgin daughter of Locrine
sprung of ould Anchises lyne,
845 may thy brimmed waves for this
their full tribute never misse
from a thousand pettie rills
that tumble downe the snowie hills
Summer, drouth, or singed aire
850 never scortch thy tresses fayer
nor wett Octobers torrent floud
thy molten Cristall fill with mud
may thy billowes rowle a shoare
the beryll and the goulden Oare
855 may thy loftie head be Crownd
with many a towre, and terrace round
and heere and there thy bankes vpon
with groves of mirhe and Cynamon.

songe ends./

El bro: Come sister while heav'n lends vs grace
860 let vs fly this cursed place
least the Sorcerer vs intice
wth some other newe device,
not a wast or needles sound
till wee come to holier ground
865 *De:* J shalbe your faithfull guide
through this gloomie Covert wide,
and not many furlongs thence
is your fathers residence,
where this night are met in state
870 many a freind to gratulate
his wisht presence, and beside
all the swaynes that neere abide

858 *songe ends.* Not in 1645.

859 **sister.** 1645: *Lady.* See above, p. 6. The speech (ll. 843–60) is assigned to the Guardian Spirit in 1645.

872 **neere.** 1645: *there.*

with Jiggs, and rurall daunce resorte
wee shall catch them at this sporte,
875 and our suddaine Cominge there
will double all their mirth, and cheere,
el br: come let vs hast the starrs are high
but night sitts Monarch, yet in the mid skye

The sceane changes then is presented Ludlow towne and the Presidents Castle, then come in Countrie daunces, and the like &c, towards the end of these sports the demon with the 2 brothers and the ladye come in. the spiritt singes./

Back shepheards, back, enough your playe
880 till next sunshine holy daye
heere be without duck, or nod
other trippings to be trod
of lighter toes, and such court guise
as Mercurie did first devise
885 with the mincinge Driades
on the lawnes, and on the leas

2 songe presents them to their father & mother./

Noble Lord and Lady bright
J have brought yee new delight
heere behould soe goodly growne
890 three fayer branches of your owne
Heav'n hath timely tri'd their youth
their faith their patience, and their truth
and sent them heere through hard assaies
wth a Crowne of death lesse praise
895 to triumphe in victorious Daunce
ore sensuall folly and Jntemperance

[874] **this.** 1645: *their.*
[877] **are.** 1645: *grow.*
[878] Stage direction following l. 878 reads as follows in 1645:
The Scene changes presenting Ludlow *Town and the Presidents Castle, then com in Countrey-Dancers, after them the attendant Spirit, with the two Brothers and the Lady.*
[886] Stage direction following l. 886 reads as follows in 1645: *This second Song presents them to their father and mother.*
[896] Stage direction after l. 896 reads as follows in 1645: *The dances ended, the Spirit Epiloguizes.*

The epilogue reads as follows in 1645, including 20 lines which begin the poem in Br.:

They daunce, the daunces all ended the
Dæmon singes or sayes./

Now my taske is smoothly done
J can flye or J can run
quickly to the earths greene end
900 where the bow'd welkin slow doeth bend,
and from thence can soare as soone
to the Corners of the Moone
Mortalls that would follow me
love vertue, she alone is free

Spir. To the Ocean now I fly,
And those happy climes that ly
Where day never shuts his eye,
Up in the broad fields of the sky:
There I suck the liquid ayr
All amidst the Gardens fair
Of Hesperus, and his daughters three
That sing about the golden tree:
Along the crisped shades and bowres
Revels the spruce and jocond Spring,
The Graces, and the rosie-boosom'd Howres,
Thither all their bounties bring,
That there eternal Summer dwels,
And West winds, with musky wing
About the cedar'n alleys fling
Nard, and *Cassia's* balmy smels.
Iris there with humid bow,
Waters the odorous banks that blow
Flowers of more mingled hew
Then her purfl'd scarf can shew,
And drenches with *Elysian dew*
(List mortals, if your ears be true)
Beds of *Hyacinth,* and roses
Wher young *Adonis* oft reposes,
Waxing well of his deep wound
In slumber soft, and on the ground
Sadly sits th'*Assyrian* Queen;
But farr above in spangled sheen
Celestial *Cupid* her fam'd Son advanc't,
Holds his dear *Psyche* sweet intranc't
After her wandring labours long,
Till free consent the gods among
Make her his eternal Bride,
And from her fair unspotted side
Two blissful twins are to be born,
Youth and Joy; so *Jove* hath sworn.

[897] **Now my taske.** 1645: *But now my task.*
[899] **earths greene.** 1645: *green earths.*

905 she can teach you how to clyme
higher then the sphearie chime
or if vertue feeble were
Heaven it selfe would stoope to her
Finis

908 **Finis.** 1645: *The End.*

The Airs of the Songs by Henry Lawes with His Version of the Words

The text of the five songs from *Comus* is that prepared by Hubert J. Foss for *The Mask of Comus: The Poem, Originally Called "A Mask Presented at Ludlow Castle, 1634, &c.," edited by E. H. Visiak. The Airs of the Five Songs Reprinted from the Composer's Autograph Manuscript, edited by Hubert J. Foss,* with a Foreword by the Earl of Ellesmere. Ornamented by M. R. H. Farrar. Bloomsbury: The Nonesuch Press, 1937. Pp. 37–44.

Foss collated the Lawes autograph with the other manuscript of the Aires, British Museum Add. MSS. 11518, and added missing bars from it, producing a text which "follows, as closely as is consistent with sense, what Lawes himself wrote in autograph." The following notes are Foss's:

1. The words of the songs have been transcribed mainly from the British Museum text, after collation with the Lawes text. Ampersands, capitals, and punctuation have been retained, but not the long *ſ*.
2. The ♮ sign does not occur in Lawes or in the British Museum MS. I have kept the ♯ of the original.
3. There is no uniformity in the MSS. in the placing of the ♯ sign. Lawes puts it, without logical reason, alongside a note, above it, or below it, as he feels inclined. I have not followed this but put all ♯ signs alongside the notes.
4. I have kept all the dot and tie signs, however arbitrary.

I append some textual notes on the songs as they appear in the MSS. and as they are printed here:

'FROM THE HEAVENS NOW I FLY'

Bar 11. No ♯ or tie appears on the first beat in either MS. It is understood.

For the last four bars there is no bass in the Lawes MS. The bass, as printed here, appears in the British Museum MS.

'SWEET ECHO'

Bar 12. The British Museum MS. is not clear here, but Lawes is quite clear.

Bar 8 from end. The Lawes MS. has a strange barring here:

I have ventured to ignore this in favour of the British Museum MS., Burney and Hawkins.

'BACK, SHEPHERDS, BACK'

Dramatically it is important to notice that the Lawes MS. has repeat marks at the end of the first part.

Bar 4 from end. There is no ♮ in either the Lawes or the British Museum MS. It is again understood.

'NOW MY TASK IS SMOOTHLY DONE'

The British Museum MS. has no key signature: it makes queer reading without the B♭.

Lawes has a clear B♭ indicative of F Major on each line.

Bar 4. Lawes does not mark a B♮ here. The British Museum MS. having no B♭ in the key signature is not helpful. I think Lawes meant a flat, but may be wrong.

Bar 13. Lawes has no indication of a ♮ to C in the treble part (beat 4).

Song 1

rom the Heavn's now I fly, and those hap-py Climes that
lie where day nev - er shuts his eye up in the broad Fields
of the Sky There I suck the li - quid Air all a - midst the Gar - den
fair of Hes - pe - rus & his daughters three that Sing a - bout the gold - en Tree:
I - ris there with hu - mid Bow · wa - ters the od' - rous Banks that blow

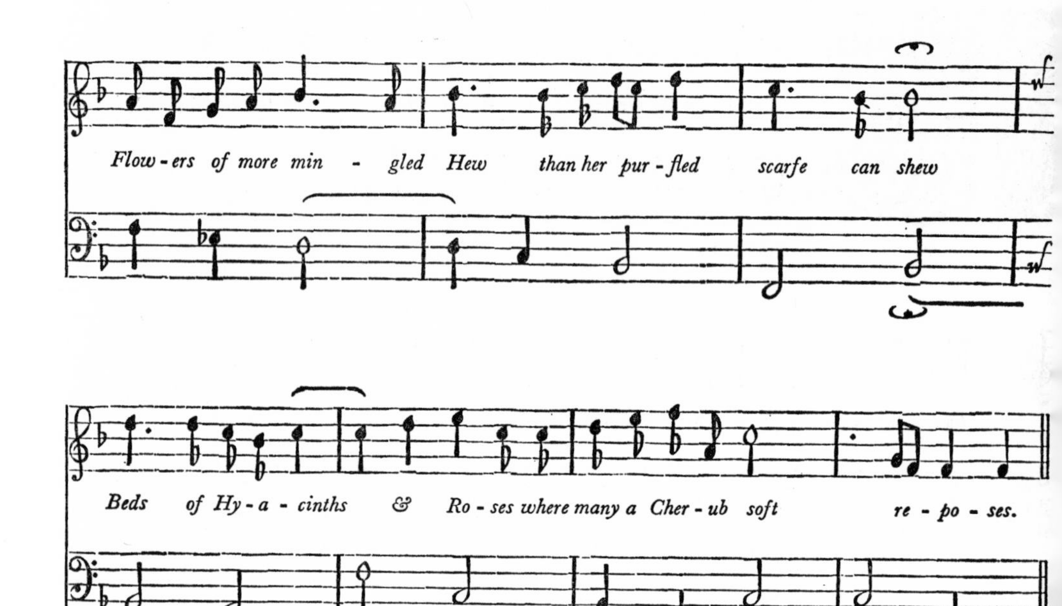
Flow - ers of more min - gled Hew than her pur - fled scarfe can shew
Beds of Hy - a - cinths & Ro - ses where many a Cher - ub soft re - po - ses.

SONG 2

weet Ec - ho, sweet - est Nymph, that liv'st un - seen . .
. . with-in thy Air - y Shell by slow . . . Me-an-der's mar-gent green, & in the vi - o -
- let em-broi-dered Vale . where the Love - lorn Night - in - gale night - ly to
thee her sad . . . song mourn - eth well Can'st thou not tell me
of a gen - tle Pair that lik - est thy Nar-cis - sus are O if thou

have Hid them in some flow - ry Cave, tell me but where sweet . . .
. . . Queen of Par - ley Daugh - ter of the Sphere So maist thou be trans -
- plant - ed to the Skyes And hold a Coun-ter-point to All Heavn's Har - mo - nies.

Song 3

a - bri - - na, Sa - bri - na fair Lis - ten where
thou art sit - ting un - der the glas - sy cool trans-lu-cent wave in twist - ed braids
. . of lil - lys knit - ting the loose Train of thy Am - ber drop - ping Hair;
Lis - ten for dear Hon - ours sake God - dess of the
Sil - ver Lake Lis - ten Lis - ten and . . save.

Song 4

B
ack shep-herds Back e-nough your Play till the next sun-shine Hol-i-day
Here be with-out Duck or Nod o-ther trip-ping to be trod of light-er Toes and
such Court guise as Mer-cu-ry did first de-vise with the minc-ing Dry-a-des o're the
2nd part.
Lawns & o're the Leas No-ble Lord & La-dy bright I have
brought you new De-light Here be-hold so good-ly grown

Song 4 (Continued)

Song 5

ow my Task is smooth - ly done I can fly or I can
run quick - ly to the Earths green end where the bow'd wel - kin slow doth bend
and from thence can soar as soon to the Cor - ners of the moon
Mor - tals that would fol - low me Love vir - tue she a - lone is free
She can teach you how to climb high - er than the Sphe - ry . . .
Clime or if Vir - tue fee - ble were Heav'n its Self would stoop to Her.

Appendix

The Text of *Comus*, 1634 to 1645

John S. Diekhoff

Scholars have sometimes assumed that the version of *Comus* in the Trinity Manuscript[1] is Milton's original draft of the poem. Miss Lockwood, for example, in her study of the corrections in the manuscript, comments upon its extreme neatness—upon the neatness of the lines and upon the even margins; but in spite of this comment, and in spite of

Reprinted by permission of the publisher from *Publications of the Modern Language Association,* LII (1937), 705–28.

[1] There are five important versions of *Comus:* (1) that in the autograph of Milton's minor poems known as the Trinity Manuscript; (2) the Bridgewater Manuscript of *Comus,* long thought to be in the hand of Henry Lawes (but now known not to be—see David Harrison Stevens, "The Bridgewater Manuscript of *Comus,*" *Milton Papers* (Chicago, 1927), pp. 15–16—which is apparently a stage copy—the prompt copy, perhaps, from which Lawes produced the Mask; (3) the anonymous edition of 1637, sponsored by Lawes with the explanation that "Although not openly acknowledged by the Author, yet it is a legitimate offspring, so lovely, and so much desired, that the often copying of it hath tired my pen to give my several friends satisfaction, and brought me to a necessitie of producing it to the publicke view"; (4) the version in *Poems of Mr. John Milton, both English and Latin, composed at several times,* the publication of which Milton authorized in 1645; and (5) the version in the second edition of Milton's minor poems, set from that of 1645, printed in 1673. While the present study requires constant reference to all these versions, the Trinity MS. version is most important to it, and receives most attention, because it is in Milton's hand and represents Milton's own work. With the edition of 1673 I have concerned myself almost not at all, in spite of the fact that it is the last authorized version of Milton's lifetime, because it comes after the period of Milton's blindness.

Readings from the Trinity Manuscript (MS.) are from W. Aldis Wright's edition, *Facsimile of the Manuscript of Milton's Minor Poems Preserved in the Library of Trinity College, Cambridge* (Cambridge, 1899). Those from the Bridgewater Manuscript (Br.) are from the notes to *Comus* in the Columbia University edition of *The Works of John Milton,* Vol. I, pt. II (New York, 1931). Readings from the 1637 edition are from L. S. Livingston's *Comus,* Facsimile Edition with Introduction (New York, 1903). For the 1645 edition I use *Milton's Poems 1645: Type-facsimile* (Oxford, 1924). [When this article was written, Fletcher's facsimile edition was not available.]

her disagreement with Masson's statement that the manuscript is very much revised,[2] it does not occur to her that the manuscript may not be composition at all but transcription.[3]

In his study of the chronology of the minor poems, W. R. Parker raises the question how much of the Trinity manuscript is transcription and how much actual composition when he speaks of some of the material as transcribed and of some as composed in the manuscript.[4] So does Masson in the description of the manuscript in his general introduction to the minor poems, where he describes *On Time* and *Upon the Circumcision* as "in Milton's own hand (apparently a transcript from a former copy)," with the implication that the other poems are not transcriptions, especially since he describes *Comus* as "much corrected throughout: all in Milton's own hand," and *Lycidas* as "with corrections throughout: all in Milton's own hand."

[2] David Masson, ed., *The Poetical Works of John Milton* (London, 1890), I, 109: "Milton erased and changed so much in the act of writing that it is impossible to give an adequate idea of his habits in this respect except by actual reproduction. . . ."

Laura Lockwood, "Milton's Corrections to the Minor Poems," *MLN,* XXV (1910), 201–205. On p. 202: "Although a cursory glance at the pages seems to tell that the poet has altered much, yet when we come to examine them in detail, we find that of the 1813 lines fully three-fourths are without any corrections at all; and, moreover, to this total of firsthand lines, he has added as an afterthought only 53. He has discarded entirely but 56, and has rewritten of whole lines barely 162. The erasures and substitutions are so scattered throughout the pages and are so much more apparent to the eye than the untouched lines, that the judgment at a glance is easily accounted for. So large a number of lines retained just as set down on paper indicates, I think, not that he changed much but that he altered relatively little."

[3] That Miss Lockwood does think of the manuscript as composition is clear from the following sentences:

"What are the poems, if we may judge by the amount of revision shown in the manuscript, which caused him the most labor? *Arcades* was written with much ease, at least with few corrections. *At a Solemn Music* was the result of hours of work and many rewritings; it is entirely rewritten three times, the last ten lines four times, and the first two versions have many changes. *Comus* shows, I believe, more uniform care for the right choice of words than any other poem." (p. 204)

"*Lycidas* came to Milton's imagination, or at least to paper, in a very perfect form. He writes the first fourteen lines, and then tries the flower passage, which was evidently haunting his thought. He sets it down once; crosses it all out and begins over again. . . . After the flower passage is to mind, he takes a fresh sheet and, commencing the poem once more, writes to the end with very little recasting, except at 58–62, which he thrice revises. Save for these two difficult parts, Milton seems to have written *Lycidas* with little premeditation and hence with ease." (p. 205)

[4] W. R. Parker, "Some Problems in the Chronology of Milton's Early Poems," *RES,* XI (July 1935), no. 43.

Grierson, however, in the Preface to his edition of Milton [5] observes that the Trinity manuscript of Milton's minor poems contains not the initial composition, but corrected transcriptions of most of the poems—among them *Comus* and *Lycidas.* His judgment is based upon a comparison of the text of the manuscript with that of the Bridgewater manuscript of *Comus* and with the editions of 1637, 1638 (*Lycidas*), and 1645—a comparison revealing various strata of revision. In the manuscript independent of the differences between the various texts, there is further evidence that the greater part of it is transcription. That *Comus,* the longest and one of the most revised of the poems, is a transcription, I shall try to show.

Miss Lockwood observes the occasional slip that Milton makes of writing a word twice or of omitting a word, giving as instances lines 288 and 483 of *Comus,* among others:

> 288. no lesse then *then* if I should my brothers loose

The second *then* is cancelled.

> 483. either *either* someone like us night founder'd heere

The second *either* is cancelled.
Other instances (among many) are:

> 276. to give me answere *to give me* from her mossy coutch

in which the second occurrence of *to give me* is cancelled, and

> 499. or straggling weather *hath* the pen't flock *flock* forsook?

in which *hath* and the second *flock* are cancelled.[6]

[5] H. J. C. Grierson, ed., *The Poems of John Milton* (London, 1925), I xi–xvii.

[6] The slip of writing a word twice should not be confused with Milton's frequent restoration of a word he has found unsatisfactory and cancelled. When he returns to an earlier choice, Milton restores the cancelled word by underscoring it, or by writing it in the margin and marking the place of insertion by an asterisk, or by writing it again, in which case it is the first, not the second, occurrence of it which is cancelled in the manuscript. E.g., ll. 313, 329, 575:

> 313. & every *bosky bosky* bosky bourne from side, to side

in which *bosky* is written, cancelled, written, cancelled, and then written a third time and left standing,

> 329. eye *eye* me blest providence, & square my tryall

in which *eye* is cancelled and then written in the left margin,

> 575. *who gen* who gently askt if he had seene such tow

in which *who gen* at the beginning of the line is cancelled.

That the presence of this kind of duplication in no way denies the possibility

Occasionally a word is omitted:

> 490. that hallow, I should know, what are *you* speake

as it is first written omits the word *you,* which is inserted between the lines, as is *that* in

> 458. tell her of things *that* no grosse eare can heare.

Sometimes a word is written out of its proper place, cancelled, and put where it belongs:

> 462. and turnes *by* it by degrees to the souls essence

in which *by* before *it* is cancelled, of course. Sometimes a line is miswritten through the influence of a neighboring line, as in

> 590. surpris'd by unjust force, but not enthrall'd *and,*

where *and* is written at the end of the line instead of at the beginning of the next, Milton forgetting for the moment his line division. He cancels *and;* then he changes his mind about it, substituting at the beginning of the next line the word *yea,*

> 591. *Yea* even that wch mischeife ment most harme.

In lines 537–538 we have an instance of another kind of error resulting from the influence of a neighboring line, as well as two further instances of Milton's cancellation and restoration of words:

> 537. yet have *they* they many baits, & *gil* guilefull spells
> 538. to' inveigle & invite th' unwarie *spell* sense.

In 537 *they* is written, cancelled, and written again, *gil* is written, cancelled, and rewritten in the desired spelling *guilefull.* In 538 *spell* is written (surely, since it does not at all fit the context, because of the presence of *spells* at the end of the preceding line). It is cancelled and *sense,* the proper word, is written.

There are also many words in the manuscript from which letters are

---

that Milton is copying is clear when we discover that in *Upon the Circumcision,* which everyone agrees is transcription, the 6th line has *mourne mourne,* with the first cancelled, the 11th *entred enter'd,* with the first cancelled, and the 22nd *wrauth wrath,* with the first cancelled. In the 11th line of the sonnet to Lawes, where we have both drafts and know Milton was copying, he writes *th thir,* and cancels the first *th.* Other similar corrections in passages of *Comus* of which we have two versions in the manuscript and in *At a Solemn Music* will be noted below.

omitted (and then inserted), by no means always in such a way as to allow us to believe that Milton is choosing between alternative spellings, as he may be doing in *guilefull* (537). For example: 314, *neighbour* is written and cancelled, followed by *neighbourhood;* 325, *were* is written for *where,* the *h* inserted between lines by means of a caret; 396, *frite* is changed to *fruite* by the insertion of *u;* 863, *taine* becomes *traine* by insertion of *r.* Sometimes an extra letter creeps into a word and has to be deleted.

All these errors (and these represent many) must be classified as "slips," as mere errors in writing. They exhibit no intention and no changes of intention. In a scribe's writing we should call them copying errors.[7] Even in Milton's hand, I think these particular errors are part of the evidence that the greater portion of the verse in the manuscript is

[7] Indeed we find the same errors in the poems which are in the manuscript in other hands than Milton's:

In Sonnet 14, "On the Religious Memory of Mrs. Catharine Thomason," the amanuensis writes in l. 12

12. And spake the *th* truth of on glorious themes.

The *th* is cancelled, of course, an *a* is inserted in *themes,* and *thee* is inserted after *of* (by means of carets) so that the line reads

12. And spake the truth of thee on glorious theames

following what is in both drafts in Milton's hand except that *on* is substituted for *in,* which is probably an error on the part of the scribe—an error which Wright corrects in his edition of Milton's poems. In the second draft Milton himself copied from the first, l. 8, *Joy,* which he cancels and follows with *joy.* This the scribe properly keeps.

In the scribe's copy of Sonnet 13 ("To Henry Lawes") we find

11. That tun'st *the h* theire happiest . . .

The draft in Milton's hand from which we may assume it is taken reads (see note 6, above)

11. That tun'st *th* thir happiest . . .

with the *th* cancelled. The first draft of the poem, from which Milton himself was copying, and which he was very much changing, reads

11. That tun'st thir happiest lines . . .

The scribe, then, copies an error which Milton himself made in copying, and, of course, makes the correction.

In Sonnet 12, "On the Detraccon . . . ," the copyist writes

7. which after held the sun & moone in *fee* Fee
8. But this is got by casting *peal* pearle to hogs;
sett
10. And still revolt when *tru* Truth would *make* them free:
11. Licence *they* they meane when they cry liberty

The copy in Milton's hand differs from the final version of this only in the spelling *pearl* (8) instead of *pearle.*

not rough draft but a finished copy made from rough drafts on other sheets.[8]

The extreme neatness of most of the manuscript (including almost all of *Comus*) is itself suggestive, especially since we have also some passages by no means so neatly or so precisely written as the rest, in which, because they exist in variant forms, we are able to study specific revisions made in the course of transcription. There are, for example, the three copies of *At a Solemn Music,* the second item in the manuscript. The first copy, a considerable portion of which is no longer legible in the manuscript, is a much reworked, much garbled version in a large bold hand. So is the second, in which there are also many revisions and substitutions, some interlinear, some indicated in the margin. In the main, of course, it is copied from the first draft, which is above it on the page, but there are many changes. Thus in the first draft, the third line ends (the beginning is lost):

> 3. . . . vine power and joint force employ.

The second draft reads

> 3. Mixe your choise chords, & happiest sounds employ,

all of which except the last word is cancelled to make way for the marginal substitution:

> 3. wed your divine sounds, & mixt power (employ).

Home bred woes beguile (l. 8 of the second draft) is a copy of the same phrase in the first draft (where *woes* is an interlinear addition). But in the second, *home bred* is cancelled and replaced by *native,* which is in the margin. In the sixth line of the second draft, *holie spousall* replaces *happie spousall* of the first draft, and then Milton changes his mind again, cancels *holie* and returns to *happie,* which he writes in the margin. And so on. Both the first two drafts are cancelled. Both are written in a heavy, large hand. The third draft is a "clean copy" in which

[8] Except as evidence for the existence of an earlier draft, the revisions noted so far are without much bearing upon Milton's poetic method or upon his development as an artist. I cannot concern myself here, except incidentally, with many of the significant revisions in the manuscript, nor with the significance of those that are mentioned, even though it is from the study of them that this paper grows.

[See: "Milton's Prosody in the Trinity MS.," *PMLA,* LIV (March, 1939), 153–183; "Critical Activity of the Poetic Mind: John Milton," *PMLA,* LV (September 1940), 748–772; "The Trinity MS. and the Dictation of *Paradise Lost,*" *PQ,* XXVIII (January 1949), 44–52.]

except for the omission of a few tentative lines we have a faithful copy, in a small, precise, neat hand, of the second draft in its revised form. There are two corrections and there is one final choice (between alternate readings) which was not made in the second draft:

> 19. as once we did till disproportion'd sin

reads not *did* but *could. Could* is cancelled and *did* is written above it. This is a copying error. In the second draft the text reads *could,* with an asterisk beside it. In the margin is written *did,* similarly marked. But Milton failed to cross out *could* and so made the mistake of copying it and had to make his correction a second time.

> 22. to thire great Lord whose love thire motion *sw* sway'd,

the letters *sw* are written and cancelled before *sway'd.* The second draft reads *swaid.* Milton is correcting his spelling and writes the word fresh from the beginning when he decides to make the change.

Beside l. 14 in the second draft,

> 14. with those just spirits that weare the *blooming palmes

is written **blooming or victorious* (the asterisks are in the text). The clean copy makes the choice and reads *victorious.*[9]

On the whole, the manuscript of *Comus,* though not written in so cramped or so precise a hand as the manuscript of the clean copy of *At a Solemn Music* [10] is much more like in appearance to the clean copy than to the rough drafts. It is neat, the writing is comparatively small, with the words compact instead of sprawled; the lines are straight and the margins even. And there are, as we have observed, strangely few revisions—very few indeed compared to the number in the rougher drafts that we have. There is a passage of sixteen lines, for instance, on the first page of the manuscript of *Comus* where there is not a single correction (29–44). Indeed, only seventeen lines of the sixty-six (including a

[9] Besides the three copies of *At a Solemn Music,* there are other items in the manuscript of which there are two or more versions, the one copied (similarly reworked) from the other: the "Letter to a Friend," for example (containing Sonnet VII), of which there are two copies—the one an expansion of the other—and of which there must have been at least a third copy, the one which was sent. There are two copies of the opening lines of *Lycidas,* three of the sonnet to Henry Lawes (two in Milton's hand), three of the sonnets on the death of Mrs. Thomason (again two in Milton's hand), two of each of the sonnets upon the reception of the Divorce Pamphlets (one of each by a scribe). There are two or three passages of *Comus* of which we have more than one version.

[10] Except for ll. 672–705, which are written on a pasted insert.

passage cancelled as a whole) on the first page have any revision. Of these, two are cancelled to make way for new lines, and a third is simply omitted. There are many passages of equal length about as clean, although some isolated passages contain a good deal of revision.

The text of *Comus* itself as it appears in the manuscript also contains evidence, more interesting than the mere appearance of the page, and perhaps more conclusive, that the manuscript is not a first draft and that many of the revisions were made in the course of transcription.

It is clear that many of the additions and revisions are made to passages earlier considered finished. Although a very large proportion of the revisions are mere substitutions—a word for a word, a phrase for a phrase, a line for a line [11]—involving little or no change of material preceding or following, other insertions—and these are evidence that Milton is returning to material earlier considered finished—do involve changes in the syntax of neighboring lines. Lines 135–136, for example, are an insertion in the margin (arrived at with some difficulty) involving the change of a word in 137. The passage read

> stay thy clowdie ebon chaire
> *till* all thy dues be don & none left out.

The insertion of 135–136 made it read

> 134. stay thy clowdie ebon chaire
> 135. wherin thou ridst wth Hecat & befreind
> 136. us thy vow'd preists till utmost end
> 137. *of* all thy dues bee don & none left out,

of replacing *till*, which is cancelled at the beginning of 137.

Line 422 is a substitution involving a change in syntax in succeeding lines:

> 421. she that has that is clad in compleate steele
> 422. and like a quiverd nymph wth arrows keene
> 423. may trace huge forests, & unharbour'd heaths
> 424. infamous hills & sandie perilous wilds

Here 422 is written in the margin to replace two lines which are deleted:

> 421a. & upon any needfull accident
> 421b. may be it not in pride or in praesumption
> 423. walke through huge forests . . .

[11] Ll. 279, 371, 713; ll. 403, 452, 432; ll. 384–5, 658.

These lines first read

> 421a. & may on any needfull accident
> 421b. be it not don(?) in pride or wilfull tempting

The two lines are cancelled for present 422, the substitution requiring the change of *may trace* to *walke through* in 423. (Cancelled 421b becomes 431.)

At the very beginning of the poem there is a deletion which involves a similar change of syntax in neighboring material and in which we can see Milton actually at work. After line 4, fifteen lines are cancelled. They are a description of the "regions mild of calme & serene aire" from which the Guardian Spirit has come. In the first draft they end:

> I doubt me gentle mortalls these may seem
> strange distances to heare & unknowne climes
> yet thence I come and oft from thence behold . . .

This connects with what follows in the poem except for the single alteration of which we have spoken, made when the passage was cancelled. The next line (5 as the poem now stands), which reads "above the smoake and stirre of this dim spot," stood first "the smoake and stirre of this dim, narrow spot." The only change is the addition of the preposition at the beginning of the line and the cancellation of *narrow* to make room for it in the metrical pattern. The line "yet thence I come and oft from thence behold" Milton's second judgment retains. For the two that preceded it he substitutes: "but soft I was not sent to court your wonder/with distant worlds, & strange removed clim(es)." His last judgment strikes out the whole passage.[12]

[12] Since the cancellation of the fifteen lines involved only the insertion of *above* and the cancellation of *narrow* (5), it is not possible to tell how far Milton had progressed with his composition or transcription when he made the revision. He may have finished the poem. (See note 16.) He may have written to the end of the period at what is now line 11 of the poem. Perhaps he wrote only one line beyond what is now line 8, for there is a cancelled line following it which brings to a full stop the cancelled passage and the intervening lines, which, going on to line 11, would have been a less close-knit sentence unit. It would then originally have been as follows:

> yet thence I come and oft from thence behold
> the smoake & stirre of this dim, narrow spot
> wch men call earth, & with low-thoughted care
> strive to keepe up a fraile & feavourish beeing
> beyond the written date of mortall change.

The last of these lines is cancelled, and the sentence goes on as it now stands, and as it could not have gone on without the cancellation:

After this cancellation, the manuscript proceeds for eighty-three lines with only slight verbal changes—only sixteen lines requiring any correction, and five of them corrections in spelling only. Then, at l. 92 (as the poem has come to us) we find a very curious error indeed, and its correction. In the text of 1645 the passage (Thyrsis is speaking) reads:

> 82. . . . But first I must put off
> 83. These my skie robes spun out of Iris Wooff
> 84. And take the Weeds and Likenes of a Swain
> 85. That to the service of this house belongs,
> 86. Who with his soft Pipe, and smooth-dittied Song,
> 87. Well knows to still the wilde winds when they roar,
> 88. And hush the waving Woods, nor of less faith,
> 89. And in this office of his Mountain watch,
> 90. Likeliest, and neerest to the present ayd
> 91. Of this occasion. But I hear the tread
> 92. Of hatefull steps, I must be viewles now.

In line 92 of this passage, Milton first wrote *virgin* instead of *hatefull. Virgin* he cancels, of course, and *hatefull* is written above it; and we are

---

> confin'd & pester'd in this pinfold heere
> unmindfull of the crowne that vertue gives
> after this mortall change to her true servants
> amoungst the enthron'd gods on sainted seates

(The lines "strive to keepe up . . ." and "confin'd . . ." are interchanged by means of the numbers *1* & *2* before them.) The material of the cancelled line, *beyond the written date of mortal change* is (more amply) supplied by the lines of the final text as is the cancelled adjective *narrow* by the line

> confin'd & pester'd in this pinfold heere.

Milton's transcription, then, if such it were, proceeded with many pauses for revision and even for the composition of new material, at least to the end of the cancelled line *beyond the written date. . . .* At this point, a full pause and a good stopping place, Milton perhaps considered what he had written and threw away what was after all a digression, making the necessary change in l. 5. Reading now the eight lines he intended to retain, he found that he had not sufficiently amplified "the mortal lot" and, cancelling "*beyond the written date . . .* ," he proceeded to the end of the period as it now stands, with no further revisions save the interchange of ll. 7 and 8. Because, when he wrote them, lines at present numbered 4 and 6 were separated by fifteen lines instead of by one, I think it quitely likely that he did not notice the rhyme of *Ayr* and *care* with which they end—and on the basis of his practice elsewhere that he did not think their rhyme sufficient reason for changing them if he noticed it later. The presence of the rhyme, however, is added evidence that l. 6 was written before the cancellation which brought it into close juxtaposition with l. 4. Certainly Milton had gone beyond the lines cancelled, as the single change necessary in the first line retained is enough to prove. Whether he had done so on another sheet or not this passage alone can hardly tell us.

faced with the problem of explaining how Milton could ever have written the word *virgin* as descriptive of Comus. An explanation is on the next page of the manuscript, at ll. 145–150, in which Comus speaks to his rout when the Lady approaches:

> 145. Breake off, breake off, I feele the different pace
> 146. of some chast footing neere about this ground
> 146a. some virgin sure benighted in these woods
> 146b. for so I can distinguish by mine art.[13]

The word *virgin* (l. 92) is a verbal reminiscence, I surmise, of ll. 145–150. Its presence means that when Milton was recording l. 92 he had already composed a passage which comes over fifty lines later in the poem, and we are not watching him in the throes of initial composition. He has written his poem—at any rate parts of it—elsewhere, and is now transcribing it with final revisions and occasional additions and deletions.

Fortunately we have one fairly long passage in which we can see Milton working as a revising copyist. In the margin of the manuscript beside l. 670 we find written: "that wch follows heere is in the pasted leafe begins and first behold this &c." After *begins, poore Ladie* is written and cancelled; *poore ladie* is the beginning of a cancelled line, the eighth line on the "pasted leafe." Evidently at one time Milton meant that to be the first line of the insertion. The Columbia Milton [14] has the following note:

> . . . the inserted leaf, which is smaller, consists of lines 671–704. Lines 671–677 also appear in Manuscript after *thinke what* line 754, where they are deleted.

As a matter of fact, the greater part of the whole passage, save for nine lines which are a marginal insertion even in the pasted leaf, are in the manuscript at 755. In the main text of the manuscript (at 755) we see Milton working upon a very difficult passage, very rough and very much revised. On the inserted leaf and in ll. 662–665 (which are a marginal

[13] In line 145 *feele* is substituted for the first draft *heare.* Ll. 146a and 146b are cancelled and written again two lines later. The final version reads (1645)

> Break off, break off, I feel the different pace
> Of som chast footing neer about this ground,
> Run to your shrouds, within these Brakes and Trees,
> Our number may affright: Som Virgin sure
> (For so I can distinguish by mine Art)
> Benighted in these Woods.

[14] Vol. I, pt. 2, p. 545.

insertion in the manuscript proper) also copied from the passage cancelled after 755, we see him working as a revising copyist.

662. . . . foole doe not boast
663. thou canst not touch the freedome of my mind
664. wth all thy charmes although this corporall rind
665. thou hast immanacl'd, while heavn sees good

When he made the insertion, Milton first wrote (662) *foole though art overproud,* which he cancelled and replaced with *doe not boast.* The sheet from which he is copying reads:

stand back false traitor
thou can'st not touch the freedome of my mynd
wth all thy charmes although this corporall rind
thou hast immanacl'd, while heaven sees good

Save for the change of the half-line 662, the only revisions are that of the spelling of *mynd* (perhaps to provide an eye- as well as ear-rhyme for *rind*) and of *heaven* to *heavn* to mark it as monosyllabic. The insertion ends with the new line: 666, "Co. why are you vext Ladie, why doe you frown"—the last half of which, *why doe you frown,* comes from original 662, "root-bound, that fled Apollo. why doe ye frown," *ye* being changed to *you.* But Milton, copying, wrote not *you* but *yo,* the *u* being an interlinear interpolation.

The insertion on the separate sheet, ll. 672–705,[15] also shows Milton as a revising copyist. Line 672, "and first behold this cordiall julep here," is taken from "thinke what, & look upon this cordiall julep." Then follow the five lines:

673. that flams & dances in his chrystall bounds
674. wth spirits of baulme, & fragrant syrops mixt
675. not that Nepenthes wch the wife of Thone
676. in Aegypt gave to Jove borne Helena
677. is of such power to stirre up joy as this

In them no corrections are made on the separate leaf and there are only differences of spelling from the final form of the manuscript sheet:

[15] It is a fact a little disturbing to the present argument that this sheet resembles in appearance more closely than anything else in *Comus* the clean copy of *At a Solemn Music,* but there are two possible explanations: (1) Milton has already worked the passage out rather completely elsewhere, and hence needs to make fewer changes as he copies than usual. (2) He is cramped for space—here by the fact that his insertion is on a small quarto sheet, in *At a Solemn Music* by the fact that he has already filled a large portion of his sheet with a rough draft.

flames becomes *flams; balme, baulme* (and a comma is added after *baulme*); *Thon* becomes *Thone.* The next line, 678, "to life so freindly or so coole to thirst," is also unchanged from manuscript final draft, but in the manuscript it is written *to life freindly so, or so coole to thirst* and the desired change in word order is indicated by *1* under *so* and 2 under *freindly.* The changed order requires the omission of the comma.

After 678 in the separate leaf is the cancelled line 678a, "poore ladie thou hast need of some refreshing"—which is copied without change from the source (and which was first indicated in the margin of the manuscript proper as the beginning of the insertion). It is cancelled to make way for the new lines inserted in the margin of the leaf—inserted apparently after 1634, since the passage is not in the Bridgewater manuscript. The cancelled line is in Bridgewater. The lines substituted for it in the margin of the insert, appearing for the first time outside the manuscript in 1637, are:

679. why should you be so cruell to yourselfe
680. And to those daintie lims wch nature lent
681. For gentle usage, and soft delicacie,
682. but you invert the cov'nants of her trust,
683. and harshly deale like an ill borrower
684. wth that wch you receav'd on other terms
685. Scorning the unexempt condition
686. by wch all mortall frailtie must subsist
687. refreshment after toil, ease after paine,
688. that have bin tir'd &c.

The last four words in this marginal insertion, *that have bin tir'd,* simply mark the place of insertion; for the line following the cancelled 678a, "poore ladie thou hast need of some refreshing," is taken from the cancelled source passage in the manuscript proper and is in the text on the separate leaf: 688, "that hast bin tir'd all day wthout repast." After it is copied, *hast* is cancelled and *have* substituted (as it is also written in the margin) because with the insertion replacing 678a the antecedent of the subject pronoun *that* is no longer *thou,* but *you.* The same change is made in the next line, which is copied from the main text:

689. & timely rest hast wanted, heere faire virgin
690. this will restore all soone . . .

In this line, in the separate leaf, *hast* is cancelled and *have* substituted, as in 688, and *heere* is cancelled to make way for *but.* Both *hast* and *heere* are copied from the source passage.

Beginning in the middle of 690, there are two and a half lines of new material to replace three and a half from the source passage which are the marginal insertion at 662 (662–665). After this new material, Milton returns to his copying once more:

> 693. was this the cottage & the safe abode
> 694. thou toldst me of? what grim aspects are these
> 695. these ougly-headed monsters? mercie guard me!

Here, except for the omission of a comma after *cottage* and a question mark at the end of 694, and the addition of the punctuation in 695, he copies exactly from the final draft in the source, where 694 and the lines that follow it are much reworked. Line 696, "Hence with thy brewd enchauntments foule deceaver," is written in the margin in the source passage as "hence wth thy hel bru'd liquor lest I," where it is followed by "throw it against ye ground were it a draft &c"—which marks it to come several lines later, since it leads into what becomes 701, "were it a draft for Juno," etc. In the separate insert, the copy, Milton begins "Hence wth thy hel brewd opiate fowle"; then cancels *hel brewd opiate foule.* Then *brud* is written and cancelled, followed by *brewd,* and the line finished out as it stands, 696, "Hence wth thy brewd enchauntments foule deceaver."

The next four lines are present in the source in idea, but by no means in form, and are followed by five lines not copied from, but obviously based upon, the source passage.

> 696. Hence wth thy brewd enchauntments foule deceaver
> 697. hast thou betrayd my credulous innocence
> 698. wth visor'd falshood & base forgeries
> 699. and wouldst thou seeke againe to trap me heere
> 700. wth lickerish baites fit to ensnare a brute?
> 701. were it a draft for Juno when she banquets
> 702. I would not taste thy treasonous offer, none
> 703. but such as are good men can give good things
> 704. and that wch is not good is not delicious
> 705. to a well govern'd, & wise appetite.

These nine lines take, really, only phrases from the original.

We find the following phrases in various places in the original passage:

696. hence with thy hel brew'd liquor	697. Source:
bru'd sorcerie	O my simplicity
treacherous kindness	how have I been betrai'd

698. Source:
darke disguises
soothing lies
soothing flatteries
lies and falsehood
treacherous bruage
false traitor
thou man of lies and fraud

701. Source:
were it a draft for Juno

702. Source:
I hate it
I should reject it
treasonous offer
treacherous kindness

Finally, line (702–)703 is taken over bodily: ". . . none/ but such as are good men can give good things." Lines 704–705 are new.

Of the epilogue of the poem we also have two copies, one containing 34 lines, of which the second is a 48-line expansion. The changes were made, clearly, upon another sheet which we do not have, for the 48-line version contains only 4 corrections (one verbal substitution, two deletions of whole lines, and one insertion of a whole line). It has all the appearance of being a copy. The shorter version has perhaps the normal amount of revision and correction and is not so strikingly neat as the longer. It may perhaps be actual composition—a real epilogue added when the poem was finished—or it may be, like the greater part of the poem, transcription from another, now lost, draft. Whatever its stages, the epilogue, nineteen lines of which become a prologue in the Bridgewater manuscript (and hence were probably so used when the mask was performed), contains in both versions ideas and phrases taken over from the fifteen lines cancelled at the very beginning of the poem (i.e. after l. 4). The left-hand column following contains excerpts from the cancelled beginning, the right excerpts from the epilogue:

amidst th' Hesperian gardens	amidst the gardens faire of
& fruits of golden rind, on whose faire tree	Hesperus golden tree
aeternall roses grow & hyacinth	beds of hyacinth & roses.[16]

[16] Milton used this cancelled beginning in another place as well. The following lines are from the cancelled passage:

4a. amidst th'Hesperian gardens on whose bancks
b. bedew'd wth nectar, & celestial songs
c. & fruits of golden rind, on whose faire tree
d. the scalie-harnest dragon ever keeps
e. his uninchanted eye . . .

Compare these lines with 393–396:

393. but beautie like the faire Hesperian tree
394. laden with blooming gold had need the guard

Milton's method of composition, then, at least during the period in which *Comus* was written and before the change in his technique which his blindness must have required, was to write a more or less hasty draft of "unpremeditated verse" which often required a great deal of revision, and then to copy it, making further revisions. Then, if necessary, he made another, a "clean," copy, as in *At a Solemn Music* and as in lines 349–365 of *Comus,* which are so much revised as to be almost illegible: wherefore Milton copied them on another leaf which he pasted in and which some souvenir-collector has removed. Whether or not Milton wrote his whole poem in rough draft before he began its transcription and revision (as he did in *At a Solemn Music*) we can hardly be certain, although it is unlikely. That the greater part of the manuscript as we have it is transcription (with accompanying revision in varying degrees) we may be sure.

The various strata of revision that Grierson mentions show us that Milton continued to work with his poems (and in the manuscript) even after he had once considered them finished. In the study of this material, the data with which we have to work are various, and they lead us to various conclusions. There are corrections and additions in a hand not Milton's which lead us to one or two emendations of the traditional text of *Comus* and which add to our knowledge of Milton's relationship with his scribe and his printer—knowledge further supplemented by the comparison of the 1637 and 1645 editions, which shows the one to be printed from the other. There are corrections and additions in Milton's

---

395. of dragon watch with uninchanted eye
396. to save her blossoms and defend her fruit.

These lines, which at the beginning were a description of the regions mild from which the Spirit has come and which in the end are a description of the realm to which he is going, are here used not so directly, but as a simile of great effectiveness, and are an interesting example of the reality to Milton first of the realms of myth and second of his own creations. Here indeed we have a passage which, recurring as it does three times, we may say was haunting his memory. We can see Milton, coming to this passage, recalling his cancelled opening lines—referring to them either in his memory or on paper—and recognizing their aptness for the comparison he desires. At the end, in the "Epilogue," he may or may not remember that he has already used them in the text of the poem. I think it more likely that he remembered only that he had cancelled them.

This passage (ll. 393–396), which seems like almost all the rest of the poem to be transcribed, suggests that the transcription progressed piece by piece as the poem was written rather than beginning after the composition was finished, for surely the opening lines were cancelled before these were written. It was in the Trinity Manuscript, the transcribed copy, that that cancellation was made.

hand which we may judge, on the basis of handwriting or of differences of line which suggest the employment of different pens, to have been inserted after the passages in which they occur had once been left as finished. Other changes, also in Milton's hand, we may be sure are late because they are not found in Br. (and therefore were almost certainly not in the mask as it was performed in 1634) but appear in the text of 1637. By them we are led to new probabilities of the relationship between Milton and Lawes and to the certainty that Lawes could not have prepared the text for the 1637 edition of *Comus* without consultation with Milton.

Perhaps the most challenging of these corrections are those in the foreign hand, of which Wright[17] and the Columbia University edition of Milton's works note three in the manuscript of *Comus: thirst* beside l. 167, *wild* beside l. 312, and *pallat* beside l. 318. There are at least three other corrections, I think not heretofore noted, which are certainly not in Milton's hand. The six are as follows:

In the margin beside l. 167, "whome thrift keeps up about his countrie geare," in which the word *thrift* is underlined, the nonsensical word *thirst* is written and underlined in a hand certainly not Milton's. Br. and all the printed texts have *thrift.*

In line 175, "when for thire teeming flocks, & granges full," itself a marginal insertion, the word *when* is crossed out and *that* is written above it. *That* is cancelled, and *when* is underscored. (Underscoring is one of Milton's usual methods of restoring a cancelled word, though he often also writes it in the margin.) The word *when* is written then in a hand very clearly not Milton's (among other things using the old-fashioned, the secretary, *e,* which Milton never uses) above the cancelled *that,* the double cancellation having made the original *when,* restored by underscoring, not easily legible. This *when* may very well be in the same hand that wrote *thirst. When* is in Br. and all the printed texts.

At line 214 on the same manuscript page, "thou flittering angell girt wth golden wings," the word *hov'ring* is written in the margin, apparently in the same hand that wrote *when* (175) and certainly not in Milton's hand. Before *hov'ring* is a sort of triangle instead of the asterisk which usually marks marginal substitutions. A similar triangle stands before *flittering* in the main text of the manuscript. The word *flittering* is not crossed. The passage in which this line occurs is omitted in Br.; 1637 reads *flittering,* the other editions *hovering.*

[17] William Aldis Wright, ed., *The Poetical Works of John Milton* (Cambridge, 1903).

At line 312 *wild* is written in the margin in the same foreign hand. In the text, "dingle, or bushie dell of this wide wood," the word *wide* is underscored and has before it an asterisk made quite differently from Milton's. There is no mark before *wild,* nor is *wide* crossed out. Br. has *wide,* the printed editions *wild.*

At 318 on the same page, the word *pallat* is written in the margin in the same hand. In the text *palate* is underscored, but not otherwise marked. Since the word means *bed,* the correction is a just one. Br. has *palat,* 1637 *palate,* the other editions *pallat.*

At line 353, "perhaps some cold bank is her boulster now," the first five words, *phapps some cold bancke is,* are heavily cancelled and restored by underscoring. Above them, again in the hand we have been observing, again with the secretary *e,* they are written again: *perhaps some cold bank is,* as with *when* (175) no doubt because they are not easily legible under the cancellation. Br. and 1637 spell *banke;* otherwise all the versions follow the simpler, more modern spellings.[18]

Other corrections in the manuscript are also clearly made after the poem was completed, although they are probably in Milton's hand.

In the right margin at line 58, for example, the word *whome* is written, apparently by Milton, but with a different pen from that used in the body of the text at this point. The line reads, "wch therfore she brought up, and Comus nam'd." *Whome* replaces *wch* in the printed editions, but not in Br. It is Milton's usual practice, when he makes such marginal substitutions, to cancel the word to be replaced, to put an asterisk before it, and to put an asterisk before the word to be inserted. Here *wch* is not cancelled and there are no asterisks.

At line 99 the word *dusky* is written in the margin, also in a doubtful hand, to replace *northren* in the body of the text: "shoots against the northren pole." *Northren* is not deleted, but is underscored, and beside each word there is a cross instead of an asterisk. Two lines before, the word *Atlantick* is substituted for *Tartessian* in the usual manner, un-

[18] I have not found any words in this hand or anything like it after this line. But after this point, Milton only once more in *Comus* restores a cancelled word merely by underscoring, without also writing it again—the word *daughters* in 982. "Of Hesperus & his daughters three," in the cancelled version of the epilogue, where it is very lightly crossed and perfectly legible. Before and including l. 353 he does it five times: l. 4a. *on whose banks,* in the first line of a cancelled passage; l. 92. *glasse,* in a stage direction after l. 92; l. 175. *when,* already noted; l. 176. *they praise;* l. 353. *phapps some cold bancke is,* Milton himself, as we have seen, not having written over again the words cancelled in 175 and 353.

questionably in Milton's hand. *Tartessian* is heavily cancelled and the asterisks are present. The printed texts all follow both revisions; Br. has *Atlantique* but *Northerne* instead of *dusky*. We may therefore safely assume that the revisions were made at different times—those in ll. 58 and 99 after Br. was prepared, since it follows the main text and not the marginal substitution.[19]

What has happened, I think, is this: the words *whome* (58) and *dusky* (99) were substititions made for *wch* and *northren* by Milton after Br. was prepared but before a text was prepared for the 1637 edition. After the preparation of Br., and after Milton had made some other revisions, I think the manuscript was turned over to a copyist who was to prepare a copy for the printer. The copyist first looked it through to make sure there were no passages that he could not make out. *When* in 175 and *phapps some cold bancke is* in 353, since they were heavily cancelled, he found difficult to read. Those words he wrote over, above the cancelled words, changing the spellings to *perhaps* and *bank* in 353.[20] In 318 he corrected the spelling of *palate* to *pallat.* In 167, where

[19] There are a considerable number of corrections in the manuscript, certainly in Milton's hand, which find their way into the printed texts but not into Br. (and which hence we may assume to have been made before 1637 but after the performance of *Comus* in 1634). E.g. the following from among many:

243. And give resounding grace to all Heav'ns harmonies

Manuscript first read *And hold a counterpoint,* which is cancelled and replaced by *And give resounding grace.* Br. has *And hold a counterpoint* (as does MS. Additional 11518 in the British Museum). [See Song 2, herein.]

349. In this close dungeon of innumerous boughs

Manuscript has *lone* cancelled and replaced by *sad,* which is cancelled for *close.* Br. has *lone.*

384. walks in black vapours, though the noontyde brand
385. blaze in the summer solstice . . .

is cancelled for

384. benighted walks under ye midday sun
385. himself is his own dungeon . . .

Br. follows the original version.

Some changes were not made in the manuscript at all. Thus 5 lines present in manuscript and Br. after l. 409 are omitted in all the printed editions, and ll. 357–365 of the printed editions are not present at all in either of the manuscripts. In 409, *question, no* (the reading of both manuscripts) becomes *controversie* in print.

[20] The passage is the one of which there was a clean copy made and pasted to another manuscript sheet. This clean copy, which has been lost, was evidently made after Br. was prepared and before 1637 since it includes lines (according to Todd's readings from it) not in Br. nor in manuscript as we have it although

Comus announces his intention to appear to the Lady

> 166. . . . some harmlesse villager
> 167. whome thrift keeps up about his countrie geare,

The copyist is misled by his knowledge of Comus's descent from Bacchus and by the revelry in which Comus has just been indulging to wish to substitute *thirst* for *thrift.* Since the substitution does not appear in any of the printed texts, we may assume that in making his copy he saw his error or that the error was caught in proof later.

In 214, where *hov'ring* is written in the margin to replace *flittering* in the phrase *flittering angell,* we may have a change dictated, or approved, by Milton, but in the light of the substitution of *wild* for *wide* at 312, I think it at least doubtful. It seems more likely that the scribe is meddling with the text on his own authority, saying to himself, as it were, that *flittering* is no proper word, and making the substitution on his own responsibility. I am not prepared to say whether there is harm done or not, but of the substitution of *wild* for *wide* in 312 I am sure that it is harmful.

Comus, in the guise of a harmless villager, is speaking to the Lady, offering to be her guide and boasting of his knowledge of the country:

> 311. Co. I know each lane, & every alley greene
> 312. dingle, or bushie dell of this *wide* wood
> 313. and every bosky bourne from side, to side
> 314. my dayly walks and ancient neighbourhood.

Here, surely the phrase *wild wood* is commonplace, whereas the phrase in the text, *wide wood,* which is also the reading of Br., gives point to

---

present in 1637. The clean copy was apparently in Milton's hand. At least the note directing the reader to it is, which Wright reads as follows: "(r)ead the (pa)per over (a)gainst (i)nstead of . . . downe . . . (per)happs soe (c)old banke is." The copyist's clarification of the text, obviously, must have been made before Milton made the clean copy—the copyist would not bother to correct what had been superseded. Yet we know that Milton's clean copy was made before 1637, and the additions in the strange hand were apparently made after 1634, or at least after Br. was prepared. If, as I think, the copyist was making a text for Lawes to use in 1637, Milton must have worked with his poem (in the Trinity MS.) after the copy was made (at any rate after the manuscript had been prepared for copying) but before it reached print, and then in the printer's copy or in proof (if the changes were not finished before the actual copying) he must have indicated his deletions, additions, and changes. The presence of revisions in the manuscript and the edition of 1637 which are not in Br. makes it more than probable that the text for the edition of 1637 was prepared from the Trinity manuscript.

the passage, since the extent of the wood is clearly more important both to the lady's distress in her separation from her brothers (as the cause of it) and to the boast of Comus than its wildness. In 944–945 Thyrsis promises to be to the Lady a ". . . faithful guide/ Through this gloomy covert wide," and in 403, where the 2nd brother expresses his doubt that a "helpless mayden" may "passe uninjur'd in this wide surrounding wast," *wide surrounding wast* replaces a cancelled phrase, *vast & hideous wild.* Br. follows this version, *wide surrounding wast,* but all the printed texts have *wild surrounding wast.* One cannot help suspecting that the copyist has done it again, this time without indicating the change on the sheet from which he is copying. I am therefore inclined to believe that, as Milton intended the text, *wide* should replace *wild* in 312 and 403, and that quite possibly *flittering* should replace *hovering* in 214. That *thrift* is the proper reading in 167 is obvious.

Hov'ring (l. 214) is the only one of the corrections that we have been studying which is in a passage omitted from Br. and it is the only word of the group which comes first into print in 1645. This may mean that this correction was made after 1637, and hence not at the same time as the others, as I have been assuming. Consequently, whether the others are or not, it may be by Milton's direction. It may only be, however, that it was not copied with the others or that it was corrected in proof, sharing the fate of *thirst* (l. 167) in 1637 but not in 1645. Since the word *flittering,* which it replaces, was not cancelled in the manuscript, it seems to me quite possible that *hov'ring* was not copied. Since other corrections are made between the publication dates of the two editions which would require reference to the manuscript in the preparation of a text for the printer of the 1645 edition, *hovering* might easily appear in the 1645 edition even though it was not copied for the 1637 edition or in it was corrected in proof. If the 1645 edition was set up from a corrected copy of the 1637 edition, the process of correction must have included constant reference to the manuscript—whether it was done by Milton or by some amanuensis. That an amanuensis was employed sometimes, as this study shows, makes it seem likely that Milton did not himself undertake the arduous task of preparing a printer's copy.

That *Comus* in 1645 edition was set from a corrected copy of the 1637 edition seems quite likely. Of the 1638 edition of *Lycidas* (the commemorative volume for King) a copy exists with corrections in Milton's hand. Professor James Holly Hanford has shown me that *Lycidas,* at least, in 1645 was printed from the earlier text. That *Comus* was also so printed in the 1645 edition is suggested by the inclusion of *wild* for *wide* in ll. 312 and 402, since a completely new text would have been more likely to return to the original manuscript reading. So also does a study of the punctuation of *Comus,* for it shows [21] that from the manuscript through the edition of 1637 to that of 1645 there is a fairly consistent progression toward fuller and heavier stopping. While there is a good deal of addition, there is little omission in later versions of marks in the earlier. Where stops occur in both editions, but are not alike, the heavier stop is usually in 1645.

The variations in spelling are the largest obstacle to the proof that the one edition was printed from the other. But since the spelling of neither text is very like Milton's own in the manuscript, I conclude that the spelling is the printer's—especially since Milton had not at this time arrived at the consistent orthography of which we see evidences even in the printed text of the later poems and was consequently probably less concerned with spelling than later. In any case, the printer's *e* font could hardly stand the strain of the Trinity manuscript spelling. The chief difference between the spellings of the 1645 edition and that of 1637 is the omission of *e's.* That of 1637 uses fewer than the manuscript.

The presence of passages other than those which we have mentioned in which the editions of 1637 and 1645 agree and differ from manuscript and Br. is further evidence. Thus in l. 657 Br. and manuscript read . . . *I follow thee.* 1637 and 1645 (and 1673) substitute *Ile* for *I.* In l. 780, where the manuscript reads *anow,* 1637 reads *enough,* 1645 *anough,* and 1673 returns to *anow.* In l. 664, the editions of 1637 and 1645 are alone in the reading *Withall thy charms.* . . . All other versions (earlier and later) space *With all.* . . .[22]

There are many corrections made in the manuscript which do not appear in Br. but are followed in 1637; e.g., *whome* and *dusky* in lines 58 and 99, already discussed. Some corrections are made outside the manuscript and transcribed into it. Thus ll. 679–688 (omitted from Br.) are found in the margin of the "pasted leaf" which remains in the manuscript, evidently a transcription. Lines 356–364 are in neither of

[21] John S. Diekhoff, "The Punctuation of *Comus,*" *PLMA,* LI (1936), 757–768.

[22] That Milton once followed this practice (after his blindness, to be sure) we know, for the 1673 edition was certainly set from that of 1645, as witness the note in the Trinity Manuscript before the scribe's copy of the sonnet "On the detraccon which followed upon my writing certaine treatises"; "These sonnets to follow ye 10, in ye printed booke," an instruction as to the ordering of the new poems with reference to those included in the 1645 edition. Beeching observes that the 1673 edition reproduces certain "pointless eccentricities" of the 1645.

the manuscripts, although apparently they also were in a "pasted leaf," the fair copy of lines 349–365 originally attached to the manuscript but now lost.[23]

Some corrections are made outside the manuscript and are not transcribed into it. These are made even after 1637. In lines 608–609, for example, "to a foule death curs'd as his life" replaces "& cleave his scalpe down to the hipps." The later reading appears in the editions of 1645 and 1673, the earlier in both manuscripts and the edition of 1637. There are no certain instances of corrections made in the manuscript itself after 1637.

We are now ready, perhaps, to reconstruct in imagination (always remembering that we cannot be certain of much) the history of the text of *Comus* from 1634 to 1645. First, Milton wrote his poem—rapidly and imperfectly—as a whole or in part. Then he made a transcript of it, piece by piece, or in its entirety. It is here, in the course of transcription, that Milton made the earliest of the revisions which are available for our study, and it is with this manuscript that he worked when he wished to make further corrections even after the mask had been stamped as finished by public performance.

The copy which Lawes used as a script for his production of the mask and from which (if it is not itself that copy) Br. was taken, directly or indirectly,[24] was made we may assume from Milton's working manuscript, the Trinity, or from a copy of it.

The stage version, represented to us by Br., Stevens has shown [25] to be the result of some degree of collaboration between Lawes and Milton, although he seems to think of Lawes as making changes on his own authority without consultation with Milton. It seems at least as probable, however, that the two men worked together in conference when we examine the most important of the changes that have been attributed to Lawes. This is the much discussed transformation of the epilogue into an opening song for Thyrsis (i.e. Lawes). But we have seen [p. 265 herein] that these lines are based upon a cancelled passage at

[23] A third instance is the second version of the epilogue, clearly written after Br., which consistently follows the first version in the opening song. Apparently this second epilogue was also written outside the manuscript and transcribed into it.

[24] Lady Alix Egerton, ed., *Milton's Comus, being the Bridgewater Manuscript* (London, 1910), p. 31: "If the Bridgewater Manuscript, as is generally accepted, is the stage copy of the Masque, there must have been an intervening one between it and the manuscript in Milton's handwriting at Cambridge. . . ."

[25] David Harrison Stevens, "The Bridgewater Manuscript of *Comus*," in *Milton Papers* (Chicago, 1927), pp. 14–20.

the beginning of the poem. In other words, the idea of using the material of this passage to begin the mask was Milton's, originally, even though he abandoned it.[26] We know, too, that Milton was not satisfied with the epilogue in its first form, the form in which it is reworked as the opening song of the Bridgewater version, because he rewrites it with generous additions before it appears in the 1637 edition.

We can imagine Milton, then, meeting with Lawes in the summer of 1634[27] at Horton, perhaps, or at Milton's father's in London, and working with him on the stage version of *Comus*—cutting considerably some of the less dramatic speeches, dividing others between various characters, rearranging, writing stage directions, and planning the production. The manuscript that resulted from this conference was then turned over to a copyist, who produced the Bridgewater text, from which perhaps Lawes produced the Mask and in which he added other stage directions and (on the title page) the names of three of the actors.

Stevens points out that the stage directions in the Trinity manuscript are changed, in Milton's hand, to correspond (with slight alterations) to those in Br.—not only those which are incorporated in the copyist's hand, but also those added later by Lawes. Whether this was done at the time of the conference in preparation for the performance in 1634 that we have been assuming, or after the performance, perhaps in another conference with Lawes about the text for 1637, must remain a question. Since on the evidence of the two hands in Br. the stage directions themselves were written at two different times, perhaps it is most likely that their transfer to the Trinity manuscript was made on two occa-

[26] Stevens (*Milton Papers,* 15) suggests that the song may have stood first in Milton's original draft of the poem without noting the cancelled lines basic to it. He comments on the passage as follows: "One unique feature of the manuscript has been noted, namely, the use of nineteen lines of the Epilogue as printed in the 1637 text for the opening of the first speech. Henry Lawes in the role in the Attendant Spirit spoke these lines and made them more significant dramatically than they are in the printed versions of the masque. Presumably in Milton's original draft they actually stood first or else they were shifted at the request of Lawes for his own advantage as an actor. Another variant from all other versions is the breaking of the lines preluding the rising of Sabrina into seven speeches. . . . Only the two passages noted above evidence textual handling that cannot as plausibly be credited to Milton."

[27] Lady Alix Egerton, *Milton's Comus,* 29: "How and when Lord and Lady Bridgewater and the three children reached Ludlow I do not know, but their household and private effects left Ashbridge on 2nd July 1634 with a caravan of coaches, waggons, saddle and sumpter horses." Lawes, we may suppose, certainly did not precede the family, and may very well have been in London or within visiting distance of Horton at Harefield (the Countess of Derby's place) or more probably with the Egerton family at Ashbridge.

sions—that those which are in Br. in the copyist's hand were copied back into the Trinity manuscript at the time they were worked out by Lawes and Milton together and that those which were added later to Br., in Lawes's hand, were added still later to the Trinity manuscript.

Whether or not this was done in the course of preparation for the 1637 publication, we know that between 1634 and 1637 Milton has been making other revisions—or else makes them now in preparation for print; e.g. ll. 679–688. Of at least one passage (ll. 350–366) not easily legible, Milton himself apparently made a "fair copy" and makes a note telling his copyist where to find it. Certainly it is clear, since the 1637 edition follows these revisions made in the manuscript after the preparation of Br. (or its direct ancestor), that Lawes could not have prepared the printer's copy for the 1637 edition from the copy he carried with him to Ludlow in 1634.

Once content with his poem, then, Milton turned it over to the copyist who was to prepare the text for the printers. Some of that copyist's activities we have already observed. Since Lawes was the agent in charge of the 1637 anonymous publication, having tired his hand preparing copies of the mask to satisfy requests from his friends (and one copy would be enough to tire it, if we wonder that none in his hand have survived), we may assume that the manuscript prepared by the copyist was entrusted to Lawes and by him conveyed to the printer.

When in 1645 Milton was ready to acknowledge his authorship by including *Comus* among his collected poems, it was necessary again to prepare a text for the printer. Of this text, we have seen, the 1637 edition was the basis. Whether or not Milton himself undertook the task we can hardly determine with any certainty; that whoever did it must have made his corrections by means of constant reference back to the Trinity manuscript, the inclusion of Trinity readings not in the 1637 edition is enough to show.

Bibliography

Studies Referred to but Not Included in This Volume

I. EDITIONS

1. Brooks, Cleanth, and John E. Hardy, eds. *Poems of Mr. John Milton: The 1645 Edition with Essays in Analysis.* New York: Harcourt, Brace, 1951.
2. Chambers, E. K., ed. *Poems and Masques of A. Townshend.* Oxford: Clarendon Press, 1912.
3. Dunlap, Rhodes, ed. *The Poems of Thomas Carew, with His Masque "Coelum Britannicum."* Oxford: Clarendon Press, 1949.
4. Egerton, Lady Alix. *Milton's Comus, being the Bridgewater Manuscript, with Notes and a Short Family Memoir.* London: J. M. Dent, 1910.
5. Fletcher, Harris Francis, ed. *The Complete Poetical Works of John Milton.* Boston: Houghton Mifflin, 1941.
6. ———. *John Milton's Complete Poetical Works, Reproduced in Photographic Facsimile.* 4 vols. Urbana: University of Illinois Press, 1943–48.
7. Greenlaw, Edwin, and others, eds. *The Works of Edmund Spenser.* A variorum edition. 10 vols. Baltimore, Md.: The Johns Hopkins Press, 1932–57.
8. Grierson, H. J. C., ed. *The Poems of John Milton.* 2 vols. London: Chatto & Windus, 1925.
9. Herford, C. H., and Percy and Evelyn Simpson, eds. *Ben Jonson.* 11 vols. Oxford: Clarendon Press, 1925–52.
10. Hughes, Merritt Y., ed. *John Milton: Complete Poems and Major Prose.* New York: Odyssey Press, 1957.
11. ———. *Paradise Regained, the Minor Poems, and Samson Agonistes.* New York: Odyssey Press, 1937.
12. Livingston, L. S., ed. *Comus: Facsimile Edition with Introduction.* New York: Dodd, Mead & Co., 1903.
13. Masson, David, ed. *The Poetical Works of John Milton.* 3 vols. New York and London: Macmillan, 1874. [Revised edition, 1890.]
14. *Milton's Poems, 1645: Type-facsimile.* Oxford: Clarendon Press, 1924.
15. Patterson, Frank Allen, ed. *The Works of John Milton.* 18 vols. in 21. New York: Columbia University Press, 1931–38.
16. St. John, J. A., ed. *The Prose Works of John Milton.* 5 vols. London: Bell & Son, 1848–81.
17. Scott, W. A., ed. *Hermetica.* 4 vols. Oxford: Clarendon Press, 1924–36.
18. Shepherd, R. H., ed. *The Dramatic Works of Thomas Heywood.* London: J. Pearson, 1874.
19. Todd, Henry J., ed. *The Poetical Works of John Milton, with Notes of*

Various Authors. . . . Second Edition. . . . 7 vols. London: J. Johnson, 1809.
20. Verity, A. W., ed. *A Maske.* Cambridge: Cambridge University Press, 1909.
21. ———. *Paradise Lost.* Cambridge: Cambridge University Press, 1910.
22. Visiak, E. H., and Hubert J. Foss, eds. *The Mask of Comus.* London: The Nonesuch Press, 1937.
23. Warton, Thomas, ed. *John Milton: Poems upon several occasions.* London: Dodsley, 1785.
24. Wellock, Gladys D., and Alice Walker, eds. *George Puttenham. The Arte of English Poesie.* Cambridge: Cambridge University Press, 1936.
25. Wright, W. Aldis, ed. *Facsimile of the Manuscript of Milton's Minor Poems Preserved in the Library of Trinity College, Cambridge.* Cambridge: Cambridge University Press, 1899.
26. ———. *The Poetical Works of John Milton.* Cambridge: Cambridge University Press, 1903.

II. BOOKS AND MONOGRAPHS

27. Agar, Herbert. *Milton and Plato.* Princeton, N. J.: Princeton University Press, 1928.
28. Arthos, John. *On "A Mask Presented at Ludlow Castle."* Ann Arbor: University of Michigan Press, 1954.
29. Bush, Douglas. *Mythology and the Renaissance Tradition in English Poetry.* Minneapolis: University of Minnesota Press; London: Oxford University Press, 1932.
30. Chastel, André. *Marsile Ficin e l'art.* Geneva: E. Droz, 1954.
31. de Tolnay, Ch. *Werk und Weltbild des Michelangelo.* Zurich: Rhein-Verlag, 1943.
32. Dress, Walter. *Die Mystik des Marsilio Ficino.* Berlin: W. de Gruyter & Co., 1929.
33. Evans, Willa McClung. *Henry Lawes, Musician and Friend of Poets.* New York: Modern Language Association of America; London: Oxford University Press, 1941.
34. Hanford, James Holly. *John Milton, Englishman.* New York: Crown, 1949; London: Victor Gollancz, 1950.
35. Harrison, J. S. *Platonism in English Poetry.* New York: Columbia University Press, 1903.
36. Himes, John A. *Miltonic Enigmas.* Gettysburg, Penn. (privately published), 1921.
37. Jayne, Sears. *John Colet and Marsilio Ficino.* Oxford: Oxford University Press, 1963.
38. Katz, Joseph. *The Philosophy of Plotinus.* New York: Appleton-Century-Crofts, 1950.
39. Kristeller, P. O. *The Philosophy of Marsilio Ficino.* New York: Columbia University Press, 1944.
40. Lewis, C. S. *The Allegory of Love.* Oxford: Clarendon Press, 1938.
41. Marlan, Philip. *From Platonism to Neoplatonism.* The Hague: M. Nijhoff, 1953.

42. Masson, David. *The Life of John Milton: Narrated in Connexion with the Political, Ecclesiastical, and Literary History of His Time.* 7 vols. Cambridge and London: Macmillan, 1859–94. [Vol. I revised 1881. Index added 1894.]
43. Nicolson, Marjorie. *John Milton: A Reader's Guide to His Poetry.* New York: Farrar, Strauss and Company, 1963.
44. Osgood, C. G. *The Classical Mythology of Milton's English Poems.* New York: Holt, 1900.
45. Panofsky, Erwin. *Studies in Iconology.* New York: Oxford University Press, 1939.
46. Parker, William Riley. *Life of Milton.* 2 vols. Oxford: Clarendon Press (forthcoming).
47. Rajan, B. *Paradise Lost & the Seventeenth Century Reader.* London: Chatto & Windus, 1947.
48. Rice, Eugene F., Jr. *The Renaissance Idea of Wisdom.* Cambridge, Mass.: Harvard University Press, 1958.
49. Robb, Nesca. *Neoplatonism of the Italian Renaissance.* London: Allen & Unwin, 1935.
50. Ross, M. M. *Poetry and Dogma.* New Brunswick, N. J.: Rutgers University Press, 1954.
51. Saillens, Emile. *John Milton: Man, Poet, Polemist.* Oxford: Basil Blackwell, 1964.
52. Samuel, Irene. *Plato and Milton.* Ithaca, N. Y.: Cornell University Press, 1947.
53. Saurat, Denis. *Milton: Man and Thinker.* London: Jonathan Cape; New York: Dial Press, 1925.
54. Schultz, Howard. *Milton and Forbidden Knowledge.* New York: Modern Language Association of America, 1955.
55. Seznec, Jean. *La survivance des dieux antiques.* London: Warburg Institute, 1940.
56. ———. *The Survival of the Pagan Gods.* New York: Pantheon, 1953.
57. Tillyard, E. M. W. *Milton.* London: Chatto & Windus; New York: Dial Press, 1930.
58. Walker, D. P. *Spiritual and Demonic Magic from Ficino to Campanella.* London: Warburg Institute, 1958.
59. Welsford, Enid. *The Court Masque.* Cambridge: Cambridge University Press, 1927.
60. Wind, Edgar, *Pagan Mysteries in the Renaissance.* New Haven, Conn.: Yale University Press, 1958.
61. Woodhouse, A. S. P. *Puritanism and Liberty, Being the Army Debates (1647–49) from the Clarke Manuscripts, with Supplementary Documents.* London: J. M. Dent, 1938.
62. Yates, F. *The French Academies of the Sixteenth Century.* London: Warburg Institute, 1947.

III. SHORTER STUDIES

63. Allen, Don Cameron. "The Rehabilitation of Epicurus," *Studies in Philology,* XLI (1944), 1–15.

64. Arthos, John. "Milton, Ficino, and the *Charmides*," *Studies in the Renaissance,* VI (1959), 261–74.
65. Bagehot, Walter. "John Milton," in *Literary Studies.* 2 vols. London: Longmans, Green, 1879. I, 173–220.
66. Benziger, James. "Organic Unity: Leibniz to Coleridge," *Publications of the Modern Language Association,* LXVI (1951), 24–48.
67. Blenner-Hassett, R. "Geoffrey of Monmouth and Milton's *Comus*," *Modern Language Notes,* LXIV (1949), 315–18.
68. Clarke, C. "A Neglected Episode in *Comus*," *The Wind and the Rain,* VI (1949), 103–7.
69. Diekhoff, John S. "Critical Activity of the Poetic Mind," *Publications of the Modern Language Association,* LV (1940), 748–72.
70. ———. "Milton's Prosody in the Trinity MS," *Publications of the Modern Language Association,* LIV (1939), 153–83.
71. ———. "The Punctuation of *Comus*," *Publications of the Modern Language Association,* LI (1936), 757–68.
72. ———. "The Trinity Manuscript and the Dictation of *Paradise Lost*," *Philological Quarterly,* XXVIII (1949), 44–52.
73. Finney, Gretchen L. "*Comus.* Dramma per Musica," *Studies in Philology,* XXXVII (1940), 482–500.
74. Gombrich, E. H. "Botticelli's Mythologies," *Journal of the Warburg and Courtauld Institutes,* VIII (1945), 7–60.
75. Gordon, D. J. "The Imagery of Ben Jonson's *The Masque of Blackness* and *The Masque of Beautie*," *Journal of the Warburg Institute,* VI (1943), 122–41.
76. Haller, William. "Hail Wedded Love," *English Literary History,* XIII (1946), 87–90.
77. Hanford, James Holly. "That Shepherd, who first taught the chosen Seed," *University of Toronto Quarterly,* VIII (1938–39), 403–19.
78. ———. "The Youth of Milton: An Interpretation of His Early Development," in *Studies in Shakespeare, Milton, and Donne.* New York: Macmillan, 1925. Pp. 89–163.
79. Haun, Eugene. "An Inquiry into the Genre of *Comus*," in *Essays in Honor of Walter Clyde Curry.* Nashville, Tenn.: Vanderbilt University Press, 1954. Pp. 221–39.
80. Hughes, Merritt Y. "Spenser's Acrasia and the Circe of the Renaissance," *Journal of the History of Ideas,* IV (1943), 381–99.
81. Johnson, Samuel. "Life of Milton," in *Lives of the English Poets,* edited by G. B. Hill. 3 vols. Oxford: Clarendon Press, 1905.
82. Le Comte, Edward. "New Light on the Haemony Passage in *Comus*," *Philological Quarterly,* XXI (1942), 283–98.
83. Lewis, C. S. "A Note on *Comus*," *Review of English Studies,* VIII (1932), 170–76.
84. Lloyd, Michael. "Comus and Plutarch's Daemons," *Notes & Queries,* VII (1960), 426.
85. Lockwood, Laura. "Milton's Corrections to the Minor Poems," *Modern Language Notes,* XXV (1910), 201–5.
86. Macklem, M. K. "Love, Nature and Grace in Milton," *Queens Quarterly,* LVI (1949–50), 534–47.

87. Madsen, William G. "The Idea of Nature in Milton's Poetry," in *Three Studies in the Renaissance: Sydney, Jonson, Milton,* by Richard B. Young, W. Todd Furniss, and William G. Madsen. New Haven, Conn.: Yale University Press, 1958. Pp. 181–283.
88. Martz, Louis L. "The Rising Poet, 1645," in *The Lyric and Dramatic Milton,* edited by Joseph H. Summers. New York: Columbia University Press, 1965. Pp. 3–33.
89. Maxwell, J. C. "The Pseudo-Problem of *Comus,*" *Cambridge Journal,* I (1948), 376–80.
90. Muir, Kenneth. "Three Hundred Years of Milton's Poems." *Penguin New Writing,* No. 24, 1945.
91. Parker, W. R. "Some Problems in the Chronology of Milton's Early Poems," *Review of English Studies,* XI (1935), 276–83.
92. Praz, Mario. "Milton and Poussin," in *Seventeenth Century Studies Presented to Sir Herbert Grierson.* Oxford: Clarendon Press, 1938. Pp. 192–210.
93. Rajan, B. " 'Simple, Sensuous and Passionate,' " *Review of English Studies,* XXI (1945), 289–301.
94. Rostvig, M-S. "Andrew Marvell's 'The Garden,' a Hermetic View," *English Studies* [Amsterdam], XL (1959), 65–76.
95. Saunders, J. S. "Milton, Diomede, and Amaryllis," *English Literary History,* XXII (1955), 254–86.
96. Sensabaugh, George F. "Love Ethics in Platonic Court Drama, 1625–1642," *Huntington Library Quarterly,* I (1938), 277–304.
97. ———. "The Milieu of *Comus,*" *Studies in Philology,* XLI (1944), 238–49.
98. ———. "Platonic Love and the Puritan Rebellion," *Studies in Philology,* XXXVII (1940), 457–81.
99. Shawcross, John. "Certain Relationships of the Manuscripts of *Comus,*" *Proceedings of the Bibliographical Society of America,* LIV (1960), 38–56.
100. Steadman, J. M. " 'Haemony' and Christian Moly," *History of Ideas Newsletter,* IV (1958), 59–60.
101. ———. "Milton's Haemony: Etymology and Allegory," *Publications of the Modern Language Association,* LXXVII (1962), 200–207.
102. Stevens, David Harrison. "The Bridgewater Manuscript of *Comus,*" in *Milton Papers.* Chicago: University of Chicago Press, 1927.
103. Whiting, G. W. "Comus, Jonson, and the Critics," in *Milton and This Pendant World.* Austin: University of Texas Press, 1958.
104. Woodhouse, A. S. P. "Milton, Puritanism, and Liberty," *The University of Toronto Quarterly,* IV (1935), 483–513.
105. ———. "Nature and Grace in the *Faerie Queene,*" *English Literary History,* XVI (1949), 194–228.
106. ———. "Notes on Milton's Early Development," *University of Toronto Quarterly,* XIII (1943), 66–101.